AN INTRODUCTION TO

BRAZIL

AN INTRODUCTION TO

BRAZIL

BY CHARLES WAGLEY

COLUMBIA UNIVERSITY PRESS

NEW YORK AND LONDON 1963

Dedicated to the memory of
Bill
CARLOS WILLIAM WAGLEY 1945–60

PREFACE

This is a book about a complex nation written by a social anthropologist. I have been studying Brazil for over twenty years and I have traveled and lived in almost every region of the country. As a social anthropologist, my research in Brazil during these two decades was carried out in what Robert Redfield called "the little community." I have studied relatively untouched tribes, acculturated Indian villages in touch with the Brazilian frontier, small peasant communities in northern Brazil, and small towns. In these "little communities" where people live in face-to-face contact with one another (and with the resident anthropologist), I learned much about Brazilian society and culture. In each of the small communities where I lived and did research (and even in those I read about), I saw the force of Brazilian regional ecology at work. In each of them, I learned something about Brazilian institutions and behavior, such as the system of social classes and race relations, the family and the wider web of kinship, the religion, the local government, the economy, and the educational system. In all of these communities, and in the large cities as well, I found a common denominator of Brazilian thought, behavior, and attitude. One cannot understand a nation without knowing how its institutions are lived out within the confines of a local community.

My experience in local communities, even a series of them in selected regions of the country, did not, however, explain to me the unity of Brazil as a nation or the complexities of its social and economic structure. Many aspects and institutions of a complex nation are not present in the small community. Certain social classes, such as the urban proletariat, the middle class, and the metropolitan elite, may be totally absent. In a rural community the superstructure of state and national politics is merely reflected. National institutions such as education, religion, money and banking, and trade and commerce appear only in partial form. I have long been aware that a local society must be projected against the background of the region or nation in order to understand the wider implications of its local institutions and the place it occupies in the range of variation of the national society. For this reason, among others, I became interested in Brazil as a nation and I read in Brazilian politics, history, economics, education, literature, sociology, and even philosophy. In these disciplines, I am hardly as competent as I am in social anthropology. However, my grass-roots knowledge of Brazilian society and culture provided me with the basis for a sensitive and solid understanding of Brazilian national problems. In this book, I am stepping out of my role as a student of Brazilian local communities and attempting to describe, analyze, and interpret Brazil as a nation. If sometimes I am slightly deficient as a student of history, economics, education, or some other discipline, I hope that specialists in these aspects of Brazilian society will be tolerant of my failings.

Another motive for writing this book is obvious. Until very recently Brazil was one of the least known countries in Latin America, despite the fact that it is the largest and perhaps the most important. In the process of my research, I became enamored of my "scientific laboratory." I wanted to explain this gigantic and magnificent country to my friends, students, and

finally to the general public. People in the United States have
so many misconceptions. "You have lived in Brazil, so of course
you speak Spanish?" was a query that I heard far too many times
during the 1940s and 1950s. In the 1960s Brazil has become
better known to us in the United States as an international
power and ally. Ignorance about Brazil and its significance in
the present and in the future on the international scene has
become almost a danger to our nation. So, I have for many years
wanted to write a book that would help explain Brazil to my fellow North Americans.

My knowledge of Brazil owes much to many Brazilian mentors and friends. Many of the facts, insights, and interpretations
contained in this book derive from lengthy and often spirited
discussions, dialogues, and even arguments with such friends as
Anisio Teixeira, Thales de Azevedo, Herbert Baldus, Eduardo
Galvão, Darcy Ribeiro, Frederico Rangel, Yedda and José Lin-
hares, Hider Correia Lima, Heloïsa Alberto Torres, Josildeth
Gomes Consorte, Luís Castro Faria, Roberto Moreira, Maria
and Paulo Rebouças Brandão, René Ribeiro, Oracy Nogueira, Carlos Delgado de Carvalho, Fernando Tude de Souza,
and so many other close Brazilian friends that the list might
well extend for pages. Friendship in Brazil is a serious relationship; it can extend beyond political frontiers and it includes
much mutual aid. I am also indebted to North American colleagues like Harry W. Hutchinson, Ben Zimmerman, Carlo
Castaldi, Anthony Leeds, and Marvin Harris, who have shared
my research experience and my continued interest in Brazil.
Here, I am especially indebted to Marvin Harris. At one time
this book was planned in a more ambitious form as a collabora-
tive effort. His contributions in theory and fact are scattered
throughout the book; but particularly in Chapter 4 on the Bra-

zilian community, his thinking has been important to me. I also owe much to my students at Columbia University who have patiently listened to my analysis of Brazilian society and culture in courses given during this last decade or more.

Some sections of this book have been published before in different contexts and in different form. Chapter 2 leans heavily on my article "Brazil" in *Most of the World*, edited by Ralph Linton (New York, Columbia University Press, 1949). It is highly modified here in terms of my later thinking and brought up to date in facts and figures. Some parts of Chapter 3 are further developments of my chapter entitled "The Brazilian Revolution: Social Change since 1930," which was published in *Social Change in Latin America Today* (New York, Vintage Books, 1961).

I am grateful to the Brazilian Consulates in New York City and Miami for the photographs which appear on pp. 70, 73, 95, 234, and 273. The photographs on pp. 44, 116, and 169 were taken by Miss Nancy Flowers of the Nancy Palmer Agency in New York City. The other photographs in this work were taken by myself.

I wish to acknowledge the invaluable assistance of Miss Ariane Brunel. She has been more than a research assistant. Her personal experience of living in Brazil and her continued interest in the Brazilian scene enabled her to contribute as a creative critic to the writing of this book. William Bridgwater, Editor-in-Chief of the Columbia University Press, a student of Brazil from a distance, helped me to improve my manuscript. Robert Tilley, Assistant Director of the Columbia University Press, encouraged me in many ways to undertake this book, which covers broader ground than my usual field of specialized interest. Finally, I wish to thank my wife, Cecilia Roxo

Wagley, who has been my companion in research and travel in Brazil over the last twenty years, and who has helped me always in my attempts to understand her native land. None of my mentors, colleagues, collaborators, editors, or friends are of course responsible for the facts, interpretations, or theories set forth in this book.

New York City   CHARLES WAGLEY
May, 1963

CONTENTS

❦1❦ BRAZIL: UNITY AND DIVERSITY

BRAZIL is an immense nation of many contrasts and inner differences, and yet it has achieved a remarkably homogeneous national culture. Covering over 3 million square miles, about half the continental land mass of South America, it contains many physical environments. There are the humid Amazon Lowlands and the arid semidesert of the Northeast, the Eastern Highlands, and the southern pampas—to mention only some of the physical contrasts in this huge country. In 1962 there were over 70 million Brazilians. These people come from the three major racial stocks of the world: the Mongoloid American Indian, the African Negro, and the European Caucasoid. They have adapted to their environment in many ways. The way of life of the isolated rubber gatherer in the Amazon forest differs strikingly from that of the sugar-cane cutter on the plantation of the Northeast Coast; and in contrast to both of these is the way of life of the worker on the coffee farm of São Paulo or Paraná, the homesteaders of Polish, Italian, or German origin in the extreme South, the cowboy on the cattle ranches of the pampas, and the placer miner in the West. Likewise, rural Brazilians live in an entirely different social and material world from that of the cosmopolitan middle and upper classes in Brazil's great cities. There are indeed many *Brasís* (as the plural of Brazil would be written in Portuguese).

Yet there is always one Brazil. This enormous and variegated country has achieved a remarkable political and cultural unity. Brazil is closer to the model of a nation state than most other modern nations. It is this paradox of oneness enclosing many differences that underlies a true understanding of Brazil. The purpose of this book is to study the diversity of Brazilian cultures and to look beyond these differences to the basic unity of the national culture.[1]

Diversity in Brazilian society results from a number of factors: climate, topography, general ecology, industrialization and economic development, ethnic origin, historical accident, and other variables. Perhaps the most obvious of these factors is the physical nature of the country itself, divided as it is into various regions. The differences in way of life between the rubber gatherer in the Amazon Valley and the cowboy on the southern pampas may be traced to regional factors. But not everyone in the Amazon Valley is a rubber gatherer; actually the isolated rubber gatherer differs as much from the dwellers in such Amazon cities as Manaus and Belém as the poor cowboys on the ranches of the pampas do from the inhabitants of the large city

---

[1] This approach to the study of Brazil is hardly original. Several students of Brazilian society have, each in his own way, looked at Brazil from a similar point of view. Pedro Calmon, for instance, calls it a "juxtaposition of historical epochs" (*Espírito da sociedade colonial*, pp. 192–99); as one moves away from the metropolitan centers, social and cultural differences mirror periods of the past. The great Brazilian social historian, Gilberto Freyre, uses the phrase, "a process of balancing antagonisms" to describe the unity and diversity within Brazil (*The Masters and the Slaves*, p. 79). Alceu Amoroso Lima speaks of an "equilibrium of contrasts" ["Psicologia do povo brasileiro," *Revista do Instituto Geográfico e Histórico da Bahia*, No. 60 (1934), 219], Jacques Lambert of a "modern and archaic Brazil" (*Os dois Brasís*) and Manuel Diegues Junior talks of the Brazilian "unity within diversity" and of "the formation of Brazilian unity, or the formation of Brazil itself, amid the diversity of circumstances of the human settlement" (*Regiões culturais do Brasil*, p. 504). The French sociologist, Roger Bastide, who spent several years in Brazil, entitles his book *Brésil: terre des contrastes*.

of Pôrto Alegre. In other words, sociocultural diversity within the natural and cultural regions is as great as it is between them. Diversity must be explained in other ways. One of the most striking and noticeable contrasts in Brazil is that between the urban and the rural population. This dichotomy, however, seems too simple to explain the social and cultural diversity within the various regions. In Brazil people live on isolated farms, on plantations of one kind or another, in small towns which are market places and seats of countylike *municípios*, in small cities, and in great modern capitals and industrial centers. We must know something of the types of communities in which Brazilians live in order to understand many of the variants in the Brazilian way of life.

Furthermore, Brazilian communities are characteristically heterogeneous from both a social and cultural standpoint. Few villages throughout the country are made up of a homogeneous group of peasant farmers. Instead peasants form a segment of a community which also includes government officials, merchants, artisans, and large-scale landowners. Brazilian towns and cities have become increasingly complex in relation to their size. Significant contrasts in occupational and educational status and in the standard of living are found in almost all Brazilian communities. Taken together, these and other indices of prestige and power form the basis of Brazil's sharply defined system of social classes. Membership in a particular class signifies a way of life different in actual and ideal behavior from the way of life of the other classes. The Brazilian class system is therefore just as fundamental as regionalism and community differences in describing Brazil.

The fact of unity in Brazilian national culture is as evident as the fact of diversity. Except for a handful of people of German, Polish, and Italian origin in the South and less than a hundred thousand tribal Indians deep in the interior of the North, all Brazilians speak Portuguese. Differences in accent between one region and another are less noticeable than those between a New England Yankee and a person from our Deep South. Everywhere Brazilian Portuguese contrasts with that of Portugal in the distinctive usage of words, syntax, pronunciation, and slang.

Few other nations have the religious unity of Brazil; 94 percent of all Brazilians profess Catholicism, although their religion is often tempered with African, Amerindian, or spiritualist elements. Catholicism and the Church are closely related to the entire history of Brazil—its colonization, the occupation of its territory, and the establishment of its fundamental institutions. Catholicism has contributed strongly to Brazilian cultural unity.

Although Brazil is a federal republic which grants many rights, theoretically, to the twenty-two states, there is unusual uniformity in formal political and administrative structure throughout the country. From the Amazon to the pampas of Rio Grande do Sul, state and municipal governments conform to the same system, although local conditions may cause differences in the way the system functions. Along with administrative and political uniformity there is uniformity in education, public health, finance, and other public services. In fact, one of the common complaints in Brazil is that local and regional differences and problems are too seldom recognized by state and federal bureaucratic structures. Brazil has all of the formal institutional apparatus of a unified modern state.

National unity, however, does not rest on formal institutions alone. There is a strong and deep feeling among Brazilians of all racial backgrounds and national origins that they form a "people" and a nation. They share common ideals, common tastes, common problems, common heroes, a common past, and a common sense of humor. From one end of Brazil to the other people celebrate the pre-Lenten carnival, and most of them regard it as a uniquely Brazilian festival. Independence Day (September 7) is honored in the great metropolis of São Paulo and in the most insignificant towns of Mato Grosso and Goiás, where many people do not understand fully why they are listening to exalted patriotic speeches. Throughout Brazil, even among the semicivilized Indians on the Araguaia River, little boys and young men play soccer, which is even more of a national sport than baseball is in the United States. And everyone recognized Pelé,[2] the young Negro who at nineteen led Brazil to victory in the world soccer championships of 1958, as a national hero. These, and many other informal institutions, behavior traits, and social values weld Brazil into a unified nation as much as its formal institutions.

The nationwide formal institutions of government, education, religion, and economics form the nexus of the Brazilian Great Tradition—to borrow Robert Redfield's term. That Great Tradition is mainly Portuguese in origin, but it incorporates elements from other nations as well as non-Portuguese Brazilian elements. It rests on literacy and consists of written codes of law, historical records, philosophy, theology, literature, works of art and music, architecture, scientific discoveries, and other traditional aspects of art and learning of the Western world developed in Europe and continued in the New World. Camões, the great Portuguese writer of the sixteenth century, was certainly not Brazilian

[2] His name is Edison Arantes do Nascimento, but all Brazilians know him simply as Pelé.

in any sense, but his epic poetry has been incorporated into the Brazilian Great Tradition. The people of the rural countryside, the small villages and towns, and the urban slums are so often illiterate or semiliterate that they cannot fully participate in the Great Tradition, but it influences their way of life just the same.

That influence appears most prominently in the social values and the ideal patterns of behavior shared by all groups. These are historically derived abstractions, concepts of what is desirable and what is admirable in conduct. They are guiding principles of action. It is true that neither the values nor the patterns are necessarily reflected in the behavior of particular individuals or groups of individuals in a society. People often believe and maintain that they should do one thing while doing quite another. For various reasons—personal, economic, or situational—people very often do not behave in accordance with commonly accepted values or ideal patterns. In fact members of a society may not even be consciously aware of the social values of their society until a philosopher or a social scientist points them out. As a rule, however, men and women are generally aware of the ideal pattern for a specific situation. They know how and when they are normally expected to get married, how they should treat their relatives, and how and when to pray to their gods. Actual behavior often deviates from the ideal patterns, but only within a range that is generally considered acceptable and "normal." [3]

[3] I use "value" in Clyde Kluckhohn's sense. "A value," he wrote, "is a conception, explicit or implicit, distinctive of an individual or characteristic of a group, of the desirable which influences the selection from available modes, means, and ends of action" ("Values and Value Orientations in the Theory of Action," in Talcott Parsons and Edward A. Shils, eds., *Toward a General Theory of Action* (Cambridge, Mass., 1952), p. 395. The term "ideal pattern" is adopted from Ralph Linton: "Ideal patterns . . .

Most Brazilians, despite differences in the social and cultural scene and despite recent dynamic social and economic changes, share a series of traditional ideal patterns. Most of these ultimately come from the Luso-Brazilian tradition rather than from the American Indian and African elements in Brazilian culture, and most of them were shaped for an agrarian society of a semifeudal Brazil and are out of keeping with the dynamic metropolitan centers of modern Brazil. Even in the past many of the traditional patterns were suitable only for the landed gentry and urban upper class. Brazilians reading of the ideal patterns described in this book may complain that such patterns are "old-fashioned," claim that they have entirely disappeared from modern Brazilian culture, and even say that Brazilians never behaved in accordance with them.

In one sense these criticisms are justified. Brazil is changing more rapidly than ever before, and new values and patterns are emerging. But no matter how abstract, how nebulous, how divorced from actuality they may be, these traditional ideal patterns and their underlying values have shown remarkable stability through time and space; they persist, though reinterpreted, despite modifications in the most basic aspects of the social system. This stability makes them important not only in understanding a culture at any given point in time, but also in plotting the potential directions of change. As Evon Vogt has

---

represent the consensus of opinion on the part of the society's members as to how people should behave in particular situations" (*The Cultural Background of Personality*, New York, 1945, p. 52). This term, as I use it, includes also the consensus as to the form an institution should take and how it should function. As stated above, both values and ideal patterns are abstractions. However, value systems underlie and are expressed through the ideal patterns, which are situational and more specific in scope, and thus more useful to the anthropologist.

pointed out, values (in my terms, ideal patterns) have a "selective function" that determines the direction of social change.[4] It was in terms of the "old-fashioned" and traditional ideal patterns that most adult Brazilians of today were educated, and it is in these terms, reinterpreted into the present, that they are educating their children. It is not simply the case that "Plus ça change, plus c'est la même chose"; every generation does not and cannot invent its own set of social values and patterns of behavior.

Let us take an extreme example to illustrate my point. It is commonly agreed that in traditional Brazil what Gilberto Freyre has so aptly called a "gentleman complex"—a great preference for white-collar and gentlemanly occupations and the deprecation of all forms of manual labor—was important in determining behavior in many situations. The gentleman complex stemmed from a series of cultural values dating back to the time of slavery. The ideal patterns of behavior implied by the gentleman complex could never have been realized by the large mass of sharecroppers, rural peasants, and urban lower class, and the exigencies of urban life make many of these patterns an impossibility for the modern middle class. As soon as the underprivileged groups move upward into the middle class through added education and income, they seek white-collar jobs and tend to look down on manual labor. In other words, they share, though vicariously, the gentleman complex. Members of the emerging middle class work exceedingly hard, some-

[4] Evon Vogt, *Modern Homesteaders* (Cambridge, Mass., 1955), pp. 13, 183 ff. Vogt describes a small community of Texans settled in New Mexico but remaining firmly attached to certain values (and, in my terms, ideal patterns), which are blocks to adaptation to changing environmental and economic conditions, and which pose a serious threat to the continued existence of their community.

times holding two to three jobs, but these jobs are always white-collar. Though there is increased interest in technical education in modern Brazil, the Brazilian educational system still emphasizes the literary and gentlemanly pursuits. Perhaps the old and popular Brazilian saying, "Trabalho é para cachorro e negro" (Work is for dogs and Negroes), is no longer pertinent, but the gentleman complex is far from dead in modern Brazil. Traditional attitudes and views of society seem to have been grounded in the code of the landed gentry, and the ultimate kernel was seemingly Portuguese. Brazilian society has been called a "cultural mosaic" of Lusitanian, American Indian, and African elements. African and American Indian traits have indeed survived and have contributed much to Brazilian national culture. But that national culture is not a fusion or a mosaic of Indian, African, and Lusitanian traditions. Rather, African and Amerindian traits were welded into an essentially Luso-Brazilian culture. The only cultural models for the African slave, the Indian, and their mixed descendants were their Portuguese, Catholic, and aristocratic masters. That the majority of these people have not been able to live according to the models set before them has been in the past, and continues to be in the present, a dilemma of Brazilian society.

As the dominant group in colonial days, the Portuguese were able to impose their European culture on many of the aboriginal peoples and on the African slaves. Yet in turn the Indians and the Africans exerted as strong an influence upon their European masters as did the exotic force of the new physical environment. Thus, the Brazilian national culture is not simply a Portuguese way of life transposed to the New World, but a unique development of diverse heritage molded into a distinctive whole. To understand Brazilian culture and the process by which it took form, we need to know something of its sources —of the three peoples who contributed to it.

Of these three peoples, only the Portuguese were in the sixteenth century literate and with their own written history. They are, therefore, the best known. We know of the romance and grandeur of Portuguese expansion across the world in the fifteenth and sixteenth centuries. Before the end of the fifteenth century Madeira, the Azores, and the Cape Verde Islands had been discovered and occupied, and Portuguese navigators had sailed down along the west coast of Africa to reach and round the Cape of Good Hope, opening the way to India. In the sixteenth century they extended their voyages to Southeast Asia, China, and Japan. The discovery of Brazil by Pedro Alvares Cabral, supposedly blown off his course on his way to India in 1500, seemed but an incident in the panorama of Portuguese expansion. In 1494, by the Treaty of Tordesillas, the Portuguese had already established the right to lands east of an imaginary line situated 370 leagues off the Cape Verde Islands, while all those west of the line were to belong to Spain. So, at least legally, the coast of Brazil belonged to Portugal even before it was discovered.

The Portuguese included adventurers, missionaries carrying the Catholic faith to the infidel and seeking the mythical Christian kingdom of Prester John, and, above all, traders. They were not imperialists in the nineteenth-century sense, wishing to establish military and political sovereignty over a conquered people. Rather, they sought commerce—often on their own terms to be sure. Along the coast of Africa, in India, Southeast Asia, and even Japan, they established *feitorias* (trading posts) controlling favored positions from which they traded with local chiefs, potentates, and kings. Not even in Africa did the Portuguese actively occupy and fully control their colonial territories until the nineteenth century. When they penetrated inland they made trading expeditions that often established trading posts, but rarely set up effective control over the local population. At first, this same system of trading posts was extended to Brazil, but there was little for which to trade—*pau brasil* (a dyewood) and a few other tropical products were all that the land had to offer.

Gilberto Freyre has portrayed the Portuguese as an especially adaptable, racially tolerant, and malleable people. He writes of Luso-Tropicalism, a special adaptability of the Portuguese to the tropical climates and to non-European peoples. After centuries of contact with the Moors, they were accustomed to peoples of different customs and with skins of darker hue. Thus, wherever they went—to Africa, Asia, or Brazil—they mixed freely with the natives, creating a hybrid population and establishing a way of life adapted to local conditions yet basically Iberian in institutions.[5] There is much to be said for this view of the sixteenth- and seventeenth-century Portuguese. They were obviously attracted by the charms of native women. In their voyages they transferred numerous plants from one continent to another. Thus, Brazil is today shaded by mango trees brought from India, and one of the main food crops of tropical Africa today is manioc brought from Brazil. There was a similarity of adaptation in Africa, Asia, and the New World. In fact, the physical setting and the city plan of Lourenço Marques in Mozambique and of Luanda in Angola remind one strikingly of Bahia in Brazil.

On the other hand, this view of the Portuguese may be ex-

[5] See Freyre, *Um brasileiro em terras portuguêsas* and *O luso e o trópico*.

aggerated. Portugal was in the sixteenth century a small country with hardly more than a million people. It lacked manpower to carry out its widespread commercial ventures and to man its overseas posts. The men traveled, traded, and explored while the women stayed home. It is neither strange nor specifically Portuguese that these men should have become known for their adaptability and their tolerance of racial differences, especially in the sexual realm. Furthermore, the Portuguese were perhaps the first European country in the African slave trade, just as Brazil was the last country in the Western Hemisphere to abandon that trade. There were Negro slaves in Lisbon by 1450, and slaves were imported to Brazil as late as the middle of the nineteenth century. No matter how benign the treatment of slaves might be under the Luso-Brazilians as compared with other parts of the world, slavery was a bloody business comparable to the mass murder of the European Jews by the Nazis in the twentieth century. The Portuguese of the sixteenth and seventeenth centuries may be said to have been men of their times—neither more nor less tolerant and accommodating, cruel and rapacious than the Spanish, French, English, or Dutch.

Little is to be found in written histories of sixteenth- and seventeenth-century Portugal about the structure of the community or about the family, the rites of marriage, the religious and civil ceremonies, the techniques of artisans, or a hundred other aspects of everyday life which interest the social anthropologist studying the Portuguese contribution to Brazilian culture. There are studies of isolated Portuguese communities in the twentieth century which provide valuable data, but they are mostly important in showing how different culture change has been in the Old World and in the New. It is not difficult, however, to recognize traits and elements of Portuguese origin in Brazilian culture. The June festivals, for example—St. Anthony (June 13), St. John the Baptist (June 24; the night before is Midsummer Night), and Sts. Peter and Paul (June 29)—are equally important in Portugal and in Brazil. So is the widely extended web of kinsmen, the patriarchal family, and the ritual kin system (*compadresco*). These and hundreds of other customs, beliefs, and practices in the modern Brazilian community are obviously of Portuguese origin. But it is difficult today to know how much these customs differed from those of sixteenth- and seventeenth-century Portugal, how they were adapted to their new setting, and what elements of Portuguese culture failed to transfer to Brazil. Brazil inherited the main body of its culture from Portugal, but the cultures of Brazil and of Portugal today are very different indeed.

Perhaps because it was strange and exotic, the Portuguese left amazingly good records of the way of life of the American Indians they met along the coast of Brazil after discovery. Travelers and missionaries of the sixteenth and seventeenth century often left vivid accounts. Furthermore, studies by trained anthropologists of the surviving tribes help us to reconstruct the way of life of these primitive peoples. It was from the Indian that the Portuguese newcomer learned how to live in the New World, how to eat strange new foods and how to cultivate new crops. The Indians were the first laborers for the Portuguese to command, they furnished concubines for the masters, and they were souls to be saved by the missionaries. There are few Indians left in modern Brazil. Less than a hundred thousand tribesmen live in different stages of assimilation throughout the country. The aboriginal population has been decimated by disease, slavery, and force of arms—or assimilated into the total population. But in the process the Indian has left a strong mark on Brazilian national culture.

The aboriginal population of that part of South America

Native tribesmen of the Xingú River headwaters participating in an aboriginal ceremony

which now constitutes Brazil was never a dense one. Previous to the arrival of the European, it is probably safe to say that the area never held more than one to one and a half million people. These American Indians were not a homogeneous people: they were divided into literally hundreds of tribes speaking a variety of aboriginal languages, and they differed from one another strikingly in customs and in level of economic development. None of them were civilized in the sense of the Maya and the Aztec of Central America and Mexico or the Inca of highland South America. Generally speaking, there were in Brazil two ways of life among the primitive tribesmen: that of the Tropical Forest peoples, who were primarily horticulturists and fishermen in the rain forest, and that of the Marginal or Semimarginal peoples, who depended upon hunting and food gathering, with some incipient horticulture in the open plains country and on the semiarid plateaus. They spoke a variety of languages belonging to several distinct families, the most important of which were Tupí-Guaraní, Carib, Arawak, and Gê. Seldom was a tribe a political unit; rarely was there a tribal chieftain. The villages of a tribe were generally united only by a common language, common customs, and kinship deriving from intervillage marriages. This lack of unity among the Brazilian Indians was a major factor in their lack of resistance to the small groups of Europeans who came to Brazil after 1500.

Not all of the Indian groups influenced Brazilian culture in the same measure. The coast of Brazil was inhabited mainly by Tupí-speaking peoples. They played the major role in the initial formation of Brazilian culture, for it was with them that the Portuguese, the French, and the Dutch first came in contact. These coastal Tupí were also the major concern of the missionaries, who adopted Tupí-Guaraní as the intermediary or contact language of their missions—just as they selected Nahuatl in Mexico and Quechua in Peru. Tupí-Guaraní was quickly recorded in European script, and the missionaries, especially the Jesuits, learned to speak *língua geral*, an intertribal jargon based on Tupí-Guaraní languages. It was used in teaching and preaching Christianity, and it was taught to Indians of various tongues. It became the language of the *mamelucos*, the offspring of native mothers and Portuguese fathers, and, in time, the language of the common people, even of the Negro slaves and the European colonists. For a time *língua geral* may have been spoken even more widely than Portuguese. In some localities, especially in the Amazon Basin, it gave way to Portuguese only in the late nineteenth century.

Língua geral contributed a vast vocabulary of terms, chiefly those applying to animals, plants, and places, to Brazilian Portuguese. To select random examples, Itabuna (black rock) is a city in southern Bahia, and Itapetininga (place of the white rock) is a town in São Paulo. *Mandioca* (manioc) and its derivative, *tapioca*, are products native to Brazil with Tupí-Guaraní names. *Caititu* is the Brazilian white-lipped peccary. and *mandubi* is a fresh-water fish. Associated with the use of *língua geral* were many of the concepts expressed through language, such as folk myths and religious beliefs. Indian supernaturals joined the pantheon of the mixed population, while the witches and werewolves of European belief were Indianized and given aboriginal names.

The coastal Tupí were Tropical Forest peoples. They cleared garden sites in the thick semideciduous forest along the coast and in the Amazon-type selva to the north. Each year the men prepared the clearings by hacking away at the trunks with their stone implements and slowly burning the bases of the large trees. The whole site was burned over before planting. Women are said to have done the comparatively light tasks of planting and harvesting, and they were kept busy preparing flour from the manioc tuber. This process involved grating the tuber and squeezing out the juice, which contains prussic acid, before roasting the flour over a griddle. Both men and women worked hard at this primitive agriculture; the Indian male was not merely a "hunter, fisherman, and warrior" disdainful of agriculture, as some writers on Brazil would have us believe.

Indian agriculture was hardly efficient. It is known that tropical soils are not particularly fertile, and the process of burning contributed to the destruction of the thin humus. After a year or so the gardens became so unproductive that they had to be abandoned, and a new site was cleared whenever possible from virgin forest. In time, an Indian village would be compelled to move in order to find suitable garden sites nearby, and thus Indian horticulture was quasi-nomadic. This technique has persisted in large areas of rural Brazil, modified only by iron tools and a few crops imported from Europe.

From the Indian gardens, however, came many plants which have become important crops in Brazil and elsewhere in the tropical world. Aside from the staple manioc, the Indians planted yams (of the genus Diascorea), cotton, gourds, tobacco, maize, pepper, beans (both lima and kidney), squash, pineapple, and sweet potatoes. Several native fruits, such as cashew and papaya, seem to have been semicultivated, or at least transplanted near the villages, while other fruits such as *piqui* (*Caryocar vellosum*), *jaboticaba* (*Myrciaria cauliflora*), and *assaí* (*Euterpe cleraca*) were collected in the wild and are much appreciated by Brazilians today.

The Portuguese learned much from the Indian in adapting to their new environment, but in other ways the European newcomers were hardly impressed by the Indian society they encountered. The material life of the coastal Tupí was rudimentary and crude. Both sexes went completely nude. They slept in cotton hammocks, and many Portuguese adopted the custom. Their houses were long thatched huts, sometimes 250 to 300 feet long and 30 to 50 feet wide, in which as many as thirty families, or more than a hundred people, lived together. The longhouse was not divided into rooms, but each family group had its own definite sector of the house in which the members cooked, kept their belongings, and swung their hammocks. Each house was inhabited by a group of kinsmen, usually related on the maternal side. Each longhouse had a headman, or household chieftain, who gathered about him the young men married to the daughters of the household. These household headmen made up the village council, and the strongest among them was the village chief. This loosely knit and segmented political organization was confusing to the Portuguese, who sought to establish treaties with entire tribes only to find that an agreement reached with one village was not honored by the other.

Tupí religion was loosely organized and lacked a well-defined pantheon and a systematic theology. The origins of natural phenomena and useful arts were ascribed to several mythical culture heroes. One of them, Maira-monan, taught man the technique of agriculture; another, Monan, had created the sky, the earth, the birds, and the animals. Still another, Tupan, who was identified by the missionaries with the Christian God, seems to have been a secondary ancestral figure who controlled lightning and thunder. In addition to the ancestral heroes, there were numerous varieties of forest spirits and demons such as Yurupari, a forest goblin equated by the missionaries with the devil. The Tupí were afraid of the ghosts of the dead, who sometimes appeared, they believed, in animal form. Many of these religious concepts survive in the folklore of rural Brazilians, and some have been incorporated into literature by Brazilian writers.

The religious leaders of the Tupí were medicine men or shamans (*pagés*, as they were called in *lingua geral*). These shamans went into trances—even into cataleptic seizures—while communicating with forest demons and ghosts. It was believed that they while in trance could cure the ill, divine the future, and even travel far to the land of the dead. Such shamans enjoyed tremendous prestige. They might wander from village to village, even into enemy camps, and be welcomed everywhere. In the sixteenth century, perhaps as a reaction to Portuguese domination, there were several revivalistic and messianic movements among Tupí groups, led by shamans who preached a return to the land of the culture heroes and led their people on long treks across Brazil. Some of the later messianic movements in the Northeast may have been rooted, at least in part, in aboriginal shamanism.

The aspect of Indian culture that most horrified the Portuguese, however, was cannibalism. Warfare was a corollary of cannibalism; it was usually waged for revenge and to secure prisoners for a cannibalistic feast. The gory details and rites connected with the execution of the prisoner and the consumption of his body are well described by several eyewitnesses. A prisoner of war would be kept for several months. He was treated well and sometimes given a wife. But finally on an appointed day he would be clubbed to death. Then the feast began. Old women drank the warm blood, and mothers smeared blood over their breasts. The body was quartered and roasted to be eaten by the entire populace and their guests. Certain delicacies such as the fingers and the grease around the heart and liver were reserved for important guests. If the prisoner had been given a wife, she wept for him, but shortly she too joined in the feast. Only the executioner was forbidden to participate; he had to go into seclusion to protect himself and the village from the victim's ghost. Cannibalism was one of the first Indian customs to be prohibited by the Europeans. But, according to Jesuit reports, there were frequent backsliders, even among Indians who had been converted to Catholicism and had traveled to Portugal.

The Portuguese were hardly tolerant of the aboriginal peoples, whom they called *bugres* (buggers), barbarians, and animals. The Indians were enslaved, massacred, driven from their lands, and exploited in a dozen ways. They died off rapidly from smallpox, measles, infections of the respiratory system, and venereal disease. Not even the idealistic efforts of the great General Cândido Rondon, who in the twentieth century organized the Indian Protection Service, could check the rapid disappearance of the Brazilian Indian. Compared to the national population of Brazil, only a handful of tribesmen remain today, and many of them are in miserable condition—starving, diseased, and landless. Yet the Indian remains a romantic symbol, for Brazil has often idealized him in its literature, and Indian culture has left an indelible mark on the national way of life.

It was soon evident that the Indian would not provide the labor supply that Brazil needed, and it was equally certain that the Portuguese colonist had not come to the New World to work with his hands. The need for labor became acute after the middle of the sixteenth century, when sugar cane, introduced from the Azores, became a source of wealth for the colony. Portugal was already in the African slave trade, and sugar provided the motive and the wherewithal. The story of the slave

trade is well known and need not be repeated here except inso-
far as the Brazilian version differed from the norm. Like the
slaves of the West Indies and the southern United States, the
Africans who were shipped to Brazil came mainly from the area
of West Africa lying between the Senegal and Niger rivers.
But many slaves were also brought to Brazil from Angola and
a few from Mozambique, since these areas were controlled by
the Portuguese. Their origins can be established with relative
accuracy through modern studies of language and culture in
Brazil. The number of slaves imported to Brazil is more difficult to ascertain, however, for in 1891 the great Brazilian statesman Rui Barbosa, in order to keep any stigma from being per-
petuated, signed a decree ordering all records of slavery—logs
of the slave ships, custom house records, documents of sale,
ownership papers, and even civil and religious papers—to be
destroyed.

Estimates of the total number of Negroes brought to Brazil
during the entire period from the middle of the sixteenth to
the middle of the nineteenth century vary widely, from as few
as 4 million to as many as 18 million. As T. Lynn Smith states:
"Unless it is granted that they failed almost entirely to reproduce or that they died like flies in the new country, one can
hardly accept even the more conservative estimates as to the
number of slaves that were transported from Africa to Brazil." [6]
It is known that they did not reproduce enough to maintain
their numbers, and, in fact, there was some effort to prevent pro-
creation since it was cheaper to import a slave than to raise one.
Likewise, death took an exceedingly heavy toll. In any case, the
Negro soon became the largest element in the population of
the colony. In 1585 Father José de Anchieta estimated the

[6] T. L. Smith, *Brazil: People and Institutions*, pp. 141–42.

total population of the colony at 57,000, of which only 14,000 were African slaves. But by the end of the eighteenth century all estimates place the Africans in the majority. One estimate made by Alexander von Humboldt in 1825, just before the slave traffic became illegal, sets the total Brazilian population at 4 million, of whom 1.96 million were Negroes, 1.12 million mixed breeds and Indians, and 920,000 whites.[7] Other estimates of the time are in basic agreement. Thus, in sheer numbers, the Negro dominated Brazil until race mixture and increased European immigration in the nineteenth and twentieth century made the whites more numerous.

The cultural contribution of Negroes to Brazilian culture has not been in keeping with their numbers. This is not to underestimate the African elements in modern Brazilian life, for their presence has been strongly felt. But the African slaves were torn from their homeland and their communities, and in the New World they lived in absolute subjection to their European masters. Under such conditions, it is not surprising that many African institutions and culture patterns should have disappeared. Many of the Africans, especially the Yoruba, the Dahomeyans, and the Fanti-Ashanti peoples, came from cultures with a sophisticated political life—kingdoms with ministries, royal courts, armies, and taxation. None of this could be brought to the New World, although for a time in the seventeenth century a group of escaped slaves were able to reconstruct their political organization in the so-called Republic of Palmares in northeastern Brazil. Likewise, although students of African cultures find strong African influences in

[7] Arthur Ramos, "The Negro in Brazil," in Smith and Marchant, eds., *Brazil: Portrait of Half a Continent*, p. 131.

the Negro family in Brazil and elsewhere in the New World, the slave family, when it existed, was largely patterned after that of the Portuguese. And, although the Yoruba language survived for a long time in Brazil, especially in religious cults, Portuguese rapidly became the means of communication of the slaves among themselves and with their overseers and owners. Yet the Africans retained a surprising amount of their heritage and strongly influenced the Portuguese colonist.

The influence of Africa is felt most strongly on those levels of Brazilian culture which are transmitted within the family. For, in the formative period of Brazilian culture, the African was the cook, the nursemaid, the servant, the playmate, the storyteller, and the sexual partner of the European. Thus, African custom was learned early and in the context of the family. The Portuguese slave owners learned from their African slaves folk tales similar to those recorded by Joel Chandler Harris as the Uncle Remus stories in the United States. They learned to eat African foods and European dishes modified in the New World by African cooks. They came to half believe in, or even fully accept, African witchcraft, curing practices, and methods of divination. They learned to sing and dance to African rhythms. And, above all, they retained affection for their Negro *babás* (nursemaids), and were attracted to the often receptive women of color about them. African influence entered Brazilian life in numerous subtle ways, and the plantation system itself conditioned both the African and the European heritage. Today the Brazilian Negroes may retain vestiges of their African heritage, but above all they are Brazilians sharing, whenever economic status and education permit, the basic patterns of the national culture. Brazil is made up of three races and its culture is derived from three continents, but its major institutions, its language, and its basic ideal patterns of behavior are European ones, modified and developed in the New World environment. It was the Portuguese heritage and the common experience in the New World that gave unity to the Brazilian "mosaic."

❦2❦ REGIONS

ALL Brazilians are aware of their country's regional diversity. There are popular stereotypes regarding the personalities and behavior patterns of various regional groups. The *paulista* from the state of São Paulo is an energetic, efficient businessman. The *gaúcho* from Rio Grande do Sul is a crude cowboy. The *carioca*, the inhabitant of Rio de Janeiro, is sly, urbane, talkative, and fun-loving. The *cearense* from the northeastern state of Ceará is a keen commercial man and a wandering exile driven by drought from his beloved homeland like the proverbial Jew. The *mineiro* from Minas Gerais is political and highly traditional, with a dry sense of humor, and the *bahiano* from Bahia is eloquent and superficially brilliant. "Bahiano burro nasce morto" (The stupid Bahian is a still birth), as the saying goes. Although these stereotypes are no truer than their counterparts in other countries, they do have some basis in fact. Regionalism has been an important factor in Brazilian politics, economics, literature, and art.

While all students of Brazil agree as to the importance of regionalism, each of them divides the country somewhat differently.[1] On the basis of a series of criteria such as surface features, climate, racial composition of the population, histori-

[1] Diegues Junior, *Regiões culturais do Brasil*, pp. 3–26, contains a critique of the numerous attempts to subdivide Brazil into cultural regions or culture areas by geographers, sociologists, historians, anthropologists, and even students of literature.

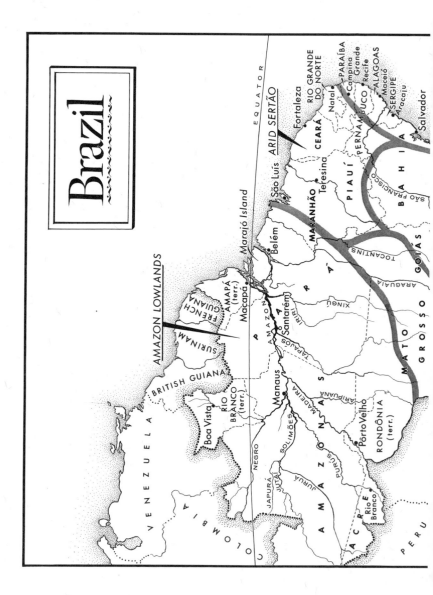

Brazil

AMAZON LOWLANDS

ARID SERTÃO

EQUATOR

Maraj**ó** Island

Belém

São Luís

Fortaleza

CEARÁ

RIO GRANDE
DO NORTE

Natal

PARAÍBA

Campina
Grande

Recife

PERNAMBUCO

ALAGOAS

Maceió

SERGIPE

Aracaju

Salvador

BAHIA

SÃO FRANCISCO

PIAUÍ

Teresina

MARANHÃO

TOCANTINS

GOIÁS

ARAGUAIA

MATO GROSSO

XINGU

Santarém

TAPAJÓS (RÍO)

P A R Á

A M A Z O N S

ARIPUANÁ

MADEIRA

Manaus

Pôrto Velho

RONDÔNIA
(terr.)

PURUS

SOLIMÕES

NEGRO

JURUÁ

JUTAÍ

JAPURÁ

Rio E
Branco

A C R E

PERU

COLOMBIA

VENEZUELA

BRITISH GUIANA

Boa Vista

RIO
BRANCO
(terr.)

SURINAM

FRENCH
GUIANA

AMAPÁ
(terr.)

Macapá

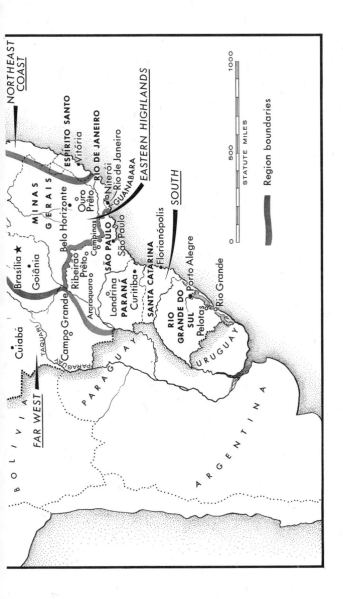

cal past, economics, and modern culture patterns, it seems to me that the regions of Brazil are six in number, namely, the Amazon Lowlands, the arid Northeast *sertão* (backlands), the Northeast Coast, the Eastern Highlands, the Far West, and the South. Each of these contains subregions—especially the South, with its Rio de Janeiro-São Paulo industrial complex, coffee frontier, European mixed-farming area, and *estância* zone in the far South. These six large cultural regions seem to me to reflect the past development of the country and to represent the chief regional variants of Brazilian national culture.

Regionalism is old in Brazilian history and does not arise merely from differences in geographical environment. Soon after 1500, the Portuguese Crown divided Brazil into seventeen *capitanias,* each of which was almost a separate state subordinate to Lisbon. In 1549, Tomé de Sousa was nominated governor of Brazil mainly for purposes of defense, but for over a century each *capitania* functioned for all practical purposes as a separate colony with its own regional economy and way of life. In fact, Maranhão, which in the seventeenth century extended from Ceará to Amazonas, was officially a separate colony linked directly to Lisbon. During the first two centuries of colonial rule, there must have been almost no communication between one region of Brazil and another. The prevailing winds made it easier to sail to Europe than from north to south Brazil, and travel by land was an almost impossible venture. Even early in the twentieth century, the only way to travel between coastal cities was by slow coastwise boats. Railway systems were, and most of them still are, local links between a coastal port such as Recife, Salvador, Rio de Janeiro, or Santos and the immediate hinterland. Not until the advent of the airplane could

Brazilians travel from one part of the country to another with any ease. Not until the construction of Brasília in 1960 did an interregional system of motor roads become a reality. Yet, even today, Brazil's system of national communications is far from satisfactory.

Each major cultural region of Brazil, and some of its subregions, had its heyday, and each is associated with an economic cycle—a boom and a bust. In a sense these regions reflect the economic history of Brazil. The oldest is the Northeast Coast. In the middle of the sixteenth century, sugar cane was planted along a narrow strip of coast extending from Recife in Pernambuco south to Salvador in Bahia. For a hundred years, this region retained what practically amounted to a world monopoly on sugar. Inland from this sugar coast is the Northeast *sertão*. In this region a grazing economy took form in the days of the sugar plantations. It provided the meat to feed the slaves and sugar barons of the Coast. This "other Northeast," as it had been called, never prospered. It came to be characterized by large estates worked by a few *vaqueiros* (cowboys) and subsistence farmers. It is of interest today as perhaps the most important "problem" region of Brazil.

By the middle of the seventeenth century, Brazil's sugar monopoly was broken by the competition of the French, English, and Dutch in the West Indies, who had markets in their home countries. The technical knowledge of sugar production seems to have been imparted to the West Indies by the Jews who fled Brazil with the Dutch in 1654 after being expelled from Olinda (Recife). The sugar plantations of the Northeast Coast entered a slow decline. Today Bahia and Recife (including Olinda), with their colonial churches and monuments built before the founding of any North American city, are witnesses to the opulence of the past. The Northeast Coast sugar industry, with its dependence on the meat and labor of the arid Northeast *sertão*, persists as part of the Brazilian scene.

In the eighteenth century, the spotlight focused on another region of Brazil. Gold was discovered in Minas Gerais, in the Eastern Highlands (east-central mountain region). The gold which poured into Europe for over a century more than doubled the world's supply. The gold boom attracted many Portuguese colonists to Brazil and led to the creation of cities of great beauty, such as Vila Rica (Ouro Prêto, as it was later called). Rio de Janeiro gained importance as the port through which the gold was shipped. By the end of the eighteenth century, the gold boom was over. Mining continued to be important in several forms in the Eastern Highlands, but the lands were increasingly turned over to pasture and small farming.

In the nineteenth century, other regions came to the fore. While the northeastern sugar coast was rich and thriving, São Paulo was a sleepy little settlement which made a living from grazing, subsistence agriculture, and the hunting of Indian slaves. By the middle of the nineteenth century, coffee had been planted in the Paraíba Valley between Rio de Janeiro and São Paulo and, as the century progressed, coffee moved south and west into São Paulo state. The coffee frontier moved on with time, west into São Paulo state and then south into Paraná. It exhausted the land, like cotton in the United States, but it provided the basis for a coffee aristocracy comparable to the sugar aristocracy of the Northeast Coast. It also provided the capital for a later industrial expansion.

The center of Brazilian life turned to the South. Like the arid Northeast, the extreme South developed a cattle industry to feed the coffee *fazendas* of São Paulo. The pampas of Rio

Grande do Sul had been the setting of a grazing economy from very early times, but theirs remained an isolated hide-selling industry until the development of the São Paulo market. Now they began to prosper. In-between São Paulo and the southern region of the great cattle *estâncias* was an area of mountains and araucaria pines. European colonists flocked to this region in the latter part of the nineteenth century. Germans, Italians, and Poles attempted to establish a mixed-farming way of life whereby grains were planted to feed animals and each family farm produced its own meat, cereals, fruits, and vegetables.

The end of the nineteenth century and the beginning of our own century witnessed the dramatic rubber boom in the Amazon Lowlands. Hundreds of thousands of people from the drought-stricken Northeast sought their fortune in the rubber forests of the Amazon. Manaus and Belém grew into large cities. Great steamers moved up the Amazon River to take rubber to the United States and Europe. But by 1913, when the plantations of the Far East came into full production, the Amazon rubber boom was over. Another cultural region of Brazil had had its heyday, and the Opera House of Manaus and the mansions of Belém were left as reminders, like the churches of Bahia.

There were other minor booms in Brazil during the latter part of the nineteenth century and the beginning of the twentieth. For a time, long-fiber cotton brought considerable income to the arid Northeast. Cacao was planted in southern Bahia and is still a highly lucrative enterprise. Each of these products gave rise to subregions within the larger cultural regions. But the next great economic cycle was industrial. Beginning in the 1930s, the area around and between Rio de Janeiro and São Paulo slowly became Brazil's industrial center. São Paulo was its heart, and today it is perhaps the world's fastest-growing industrial area. Industry brought urban development and the growth of universities and scientific institutions. Industrial cities called for modern communications and attracted a cosmopolitan population. Today, this area is "modern Brazil," lacking none of the conveniences of Europe and the United States. But it also holds poverty, isolated peasants, and illiterate urban dwellers—the full contrast characteristic of Brazil.

Last but not least, Brazil is finally moving inland toward the West. Known as a country with but a population crust along the coast, Brazil long neglected the area beyond the Eastern Highlands. The São Paulo *bandeirantes* (flag bearers) penetrated deep into the continent in the seventeenth and eighteenth century, but the aim of their expeditions was gold, precious stones, and slaves. They seldom formed permanent settlements. During the eighteenth century towns grew near mines, such as those of Cuiabá and Goiás in the West, and in the nineteenth century a primitive grazing economy developed in the southern portions of Goiás and Mato Grosso. However, much of the West remained literally unexplored and inhabited only by primitive Indians. It was not until the twentieth century that Brazil began its westward expansion. In the 1930s, President Getúlio Vargas gave great publicity to the slogan "Marcha para Oeste" (March to the West), and the new capital of Goiás state, Goiânia, was built toward the end of the decade. Still, motor roads were few and railroads stopped short of the great heartland of Brazil. The construction of Brasília and the move of the national capital into the deep interior in 1960 caught the imagination of the nation. Roads are being built, airlines crisscross what still largely remains unexplored territory, the last Indian tribes are being brought under control, and

Brazilians are speculating in western lands. The Far West may be the scene of the next Brazilian boom—this time without a bust.

Thus, each of these cultural regions has historical depth and each is associated with a period of Brazilian economic history which gave rise to a particular form of settlement, attracted a different element of the Brazilian population, and, in short, created a regional variant of Brazilian national culture. Let us look in turn at each major cultural region and at some of the subregions.

The Northeast Coast

In 1500, the coast of what are today the states of Rio Grande do Norte, Paraíba, Pernambuco, Alagoas, Sergipe, and Bahia was fringed by a narrow strip of thick tropical forest. In this area, the rainfall is dependable and the underlying soil very rich. By the middle of the sixteenth century, sugar cane had been imported from the Azores, and by the end of that century prosperous cities such as Olinda and Salvador had become the ports of the expanding sugar industry. Salvador became the capital of the colony, and the beauty and splendor of its numerous seventeenth-century churches attest to its greatness at a time when the English were struggling to establish themselves at Jamestown, Virginia. The lucrative sugar industry also attracted invaders, and from 1632 to 1654 the Dutch held Olinda and controlled a wide area of the sugar-producing Northeast Coast. They were driven out by the Portuguese-Brazilians with little help from the mother country, which from 1580 to 1640 had been ruled by a Spanish king. In Brazil, however, the Dutch had learned much about the sugar industry and they carried that knowledge with them to the Antilles. Many of the Dutch financiers and technicians were Sephardic Jews, and when they left Brazil they established a thriving sugar industry in the Dutch, French, and English Caribbean islands. Some of these Jewish refugees from Pernambuco in Brazil came to New Amsterdam (New York) and established the first synagogue in North America.

After the middle of the seventeenth century, the sugar industry of northeastern Brazil slowly declined owing to the competition of the West Indies. It did not disappear, however, and sugar cane continues to be the most important cash crop in the region. Brazilians, who have a sweet tooth and a habit of drinking frequent cups of coffee half-filled with sugar, provide a large domestic market. About three-eighths of the present-day Brazilian sugar cane output (by value) is produced in the Northeast. Protected against foreign producers by tariffs and by a kind of government subsidy against its domestic competitors in São Paulo, the northeastern sugar industry has staged a comeback. Nowadays, the sugar is produced mainly on large corporation-owned plantations whose center is the sugar-processing plant (the *usina*). These are relatively large "factories in the field" (but generally not as large as those of Cuba, Puerto Rico, or São Paulo). They are run by an impersonal management and by salaried workers both in the field and in the factory. They depend upon migrant workers from the dry backlands for seasonal labor during the harvest. There is little that is aristocratic about the modern sugar plantation-factory of the Northeast.

Yet, these factories in the field grew out of the *banguês* and *engenhos* of the past. These words literally refer to the small sugar mills run by water power or by animals, but by extension they also refer to family-owned plantations. Until the end of the nineteenth century, the *engenho* was the principal economic institution of the Northeast. The villages and towns were, as Diegues Junior says, but an extension of the *engenho*, without independence of action; they lived under the influence of the *engenho*.[2] In town, there were commercial houses, town halls, courts, a church, and other appurtenances of civil, religious, and commercial life. But the dominant class of *engenho* owners lived on the plantations as did the slaves and later the wage laborers. Thus, the community was made up of a series of rural *engenhos* dominating a town; at best, the owner class kept a house in town where they occasionally spent a few days.

Each *engenho* was almost a world in itself. It had a *casa grande*, or mansion house, where the family and the domestic slaves lived. It often had a chapel with a resident priest, who was sometimes a member of the family and who might serve also as a teacher of religion, arithmetic, music, Portuguese, and French to the children of the plantation owner. Each *engenho* had its *senzala*, that is, its row of slave houses, which continued little changed after abolition. And, each plantation had its *engenho* properly speaking, that is, the installations for the refining of sugar. In addition, there were the shops of the carpenters, ironsmiths, and other necessary artisans. In areas not planted in cane, cattle was pastured and gardens were planted in manioc and other food crops. The owners of *engenhos* within a community were generally related; there was a very high incidence of cousin marriage. Relations between the owners and the slaves, and later even the free laborers, were intimate. Miscegenation between the owners and the slaves was frequent. It is the development of this pattern of life that

[2] Diegues Junior, *Regiões culturais do Brasil*, pp. 82 ff.

Gilberto Freyre describes in his Brazilian masterpiece, *The Masters and the Slaves* (*Casa grande e senzala*).

With the abolition of slavery in 1888, and the development of the *engenho central* or steam-powered sugar mill at about the same time, the *engenho* began to wane. The family-owned plantations became furnishers of cane to be milled in the new steam-run factories; slowly these factories began to acquire the surrounding farms, as capital from England, France, and Brazil itself flowed into the sugar industry of the Northeast. Then came the giant *usina* and the corporation-run factory in the field. However, the way of life engendered by the *engenho* did not entirely disappear from the Northeast Coast. The *engenho* had created an aristocratic, paternalistic, semifeudal society. It had created a lower class dependent upon the upper class whose members were expected to protect their followers out of a sense of *noblesse oblige*. Even though they moved to the cities, the descendants of the *senhores de engenho* continued to act out their roles as aristocrats and patriarchs. It was from the Northeast sugar coast that the gentleman complex entered Brazilian culture along with other aristocratic traits.

The Northeast sugar coast thus became, in a sense, the Virginia of Brazil. It produced many of Brazil's early statesmen, and in modern times it has produced a large proportion of its writers. There is José Lins do Rêgo, whose novels of the sugar-cane cycle[3] retell in fiction the story of life on an *engenho* and the move of the hero to the city. Jorge Amado has given us the epic figure of *Jubiabá*, the Negro whose life is a composite of the experience of many workers in the region. In our

[3] Lins do Rêgo, *Menino de engenho* and O *moleque Ricardo* among others.

generation, the Brazilian minister of education is most often a man from Bahia or some other northeastern state. The concept of regionalism in literature and art grew out of the writings and thought of Gilberto Freyre, the social historian from Pernambuco. The cities of the Northeast have grown rapidly; each of them has expanding modern districts with apartment houses and beautiful homes as well as extensive slums. Recife in Pernambuco has today almost a million people, and Salvador in Bahia over 600,000, but in these cities one feels the presence of the past—a large docile lower class, a small upper class accustomed to being served, a leisurely pace of existence, and the continuation of much that is traditional in Brazil.

A very large proportion of the slaves imported into Brazil came to the sugar plantations of the Northeast Coast. Salvador and Recife were the great slave marts until the mines of Minas Gerais attracted the slavers to Rio de Janeiro. Today, the Negroid element in the population of the Northeast Coast is stronger than in any other region of Brazil. In Bahia state, for example, the 1950 census showed that 30 percent were white, 51 percent brown, and 19.2 percent black in skin color according to the standards of the census-takers. These figures were averages for the whole state; as in other northeastern states, only a small portion of Bahia lies within the Northeast Coast region. Large areas of these states fall within the arid Northeast *sertão*, where Indian-European mixtures predominate. Hence the percentage of Negro and mulatto elements along the coast must be even higher than these figures indicate. In fact the mulatto has been called the regional type of the Northeast; certainly, a few artistocratic families have preserved their European lineages and appearance, but the vast majority of the people of the region are to some degree racially mixed.

As one might expect, African cultural elements are stronger in this cultural region than in any other part of Brazil. Africa has contributed not only to the way of life of the Negroes and of the mixed population, but also to that of the "white" aristocracy itself. As Gilberto Freyre has described so vividly, the African influences were transmitted from the slaves to their masters through close relationships. A number of African terms have entered the daily vocabulary, and, according to Gilberto Freyre, the soft melodious accents of the Portuguese spoken in this region are a result of Negro influence.[4] Nursery rhymes, stories for children, and the mythical bogeyman characters used by adults to frighten children are a fusion of Iberian and African forms. African culture contributed much to the cuisine of the region. Such dishes as *vatapá*, made with *dendê* oil, peanuts, fish and dried shrimps, rice flour, and various spices; *caruru*, made with fish, okra, peppers, oil, and various herbs; and *acarajê* (bean cakes fried in *dendê* oil) are examples of dishes adopted from the slaves. A visit to the market in Bahia reminds one of West Africa, and, for that matter, also of the West Indies. Trade with Africa, especially in wood for making sacred objects and in cloth and other products, continued through the nineteenth century.

Other aspects of the African heritage are to be found on the Northeast Coast. Perhaps the most spectacular are the religious cults corresponding to the Vodun of Haiti. Such cults are found along the entire coast of Brazil wherever there is a concentration of Negroes, but they are strongest along the Northeast Coast. Known as *candomblê* in Bahia, *xangô* in Pernambuco, and *macumba* in Rio de Janeiro, they are highly organized and follow a complex ritual. They are based essentially on religious

[4] Freyre, *The Masters and the Slaves*, pp. 342–43.

beliefs and practices of West African origin, but now mixed with Portuguese Catholic traditions. They are of growing importance in Brazil, and I will discuss them later in more detail in the context of national religious life.

In addition to such cults, there are the *capoeira* clubs: groups of men adept at the motions of the *capoeira*, which is at the same time a dance and a system of defense and attack similar to jujitsu. *Capoeira* was probably brought to the New World by slaves from Angola. Formerly, and sometimes even today, it was a deadly form of combat, with opponents using their fists, knees, heads, and feet to attack—it is said that sometimes razors were strapped to their ankles. As a form of dance and exhibit, which may be seen in Salvador at one of the *capoeira* clubs such as the Angola Sporting Club or the Club of Master Bimba, it is highly formalized and graceful. These clubs are led by a teacher or Master famed for his expertness. In the training exhibits, the opponents kneel before the Master and then "fight" to the rhythm of the *berimbau* (the African one-stringed bow with a resonator played by striking the string with a metal coin), a tambourine, and sometimes a rattle. The dancers keep time to the slow rhythm, but they attack each other stopping just short of a knee in the groin or a head in the belly. They pass gracefully beneath each other's legs and duck under the kick aimed at their face. The Master criticizes and judges, and the crowd applauds with low murmurs and comments rather than shouts or clapping.

The modern samba is known as the typical Brazilian rhythm and dance, and it is played and danced throughout the world. It developed from the *batuque* which was danced by slaves at night to African drums in colonial times. There are a series of special forms of this essentially African dancing and music, such as the *maracatu* of Pernambuco and the *sorongo* of Bahia and parts of Minas Gerais. Likewise, the ceremonial dancing and drumming of the African cults is almost identical with that of West Africa. The music of the Northeast Coast is becoming popularized, subject to the radio and even to television, but the African element remains strong and clear.

THE CACAO SUBREGION

The coastal forest lands on which the northeastern sugar cane plantations were established extend from Salvador almost to Rio de Janeiro. This *zona da mata* (forest zone) stretches inland and up the river valleys into the foothills of the mountains of Minas Gerais. Sugar cane was planted early in this area, but in desultory fashion; except for the zone near Campos in Rio de Janeiro state, the sugar industry was never a success as it was farther north. Perhaps this was due to the lack of the clayey *massapê* soil so favorable to sugar cane around Salvador. In any case, the coastal forests of southern Bahia and Espírito Santo state were regarded as a barrier to penetration and settlement rather than as fertile lands for plantation agriculture. The forests hid hostile Indians such as the Aimoré and Botocudo, who actually waged war on the settlers until late in the nineteenth century. For a time, the coast between Salvador and Campos was virtually abandoned.

Cacao brought from the Amazon Valley had been planted early in this region, but only in the middle of the nineteenth century did it begin to be planted as a cash crop. By 1907, a high-yield cacao tree was imported from Ceylon, and the developing chocolate industry in Europe provided a ready market. It was found that the humid forests of southern Bahia were a cacao habitat par excellence, there was a wild rush for cacao lands, and another Brazilian boom was underway.

In his novel *The Violent Land* (*Terras do sem fim*), Jorge Amado has portrayed the struggle for cacao lands which often ended in bloodshed. At first the land was cleared by small farmers, generally migrants from the Northeast. As the price of cacao rose on the international market, plantations took form, often through what was locally called *caxixe* (the fraudulent manipulation of documents), or even at times killings by hired gunmen. Local *coronéis* (bosses) acquired lucrative plantations for themselves, but they in turn were supplanted by business-men from the cities. Men speculated on "cacao futures," and money was plentiful. Plantations passed into the hands of city families and even of giant corporations.

Today Brazil is the world's second largest producer of cacao; the value of the crop was set at $135 million in 1954, but the industry is no longer a bonanza. It suffers now from crop dis-ease, erosion, soil exhaustion, and increasing competition from foreign producers. Bahian cacao is particularly vulnerable to new competition because of its dependence upon the extensive use of seasonal and unskilled labor. Unless the technology of production and plant care is improved along with transportation facilities, cacao may follow sugar, rubber, and other Brazilian cash crops in their boom and bust cycles.[5]

The way of life of the cacao zones has certain unique peculi-arities, relating mainly to the nature of the crop. Because of the recent occupancy of the area, there are few local traditions that reach far into the past. The population is made up for the most part of migrants who came within the last generation.

[5] See Leeds, *Economic Cycles in Brazil.*

Many of them are from the arid Northeast, especially from Sergipe, and they have introduced some of their homeland traditions such as the folk drama of *Bumba-meu-boi*. The majority of the people in the towns and most of the workers on the cacao plantations have had little opportunity to establish roots in their communities. Labor is highly mobile. During

Participants in the Bumba-meu-boi, *a folk drama*

one season, a worker may be employed on several plantations. There are no aristocratic landholding families with a tradition of *noblesse oblige*, as in the sugar region to the north. Instead, there is a commercial elite based upon wealth acquired over the last few decades. Monoculture has so definitely taken over that foodstuffs come almost entirely from outside the region. The continued influx of migrants looking for employment gives the cacao zone the air of a twentieth-century frontier.

The arid Northeast

Inland from this agricultural belt of the Northeast Coast lies the arid pastoral Northeast, which extends over large areas of the states of Maranhão, Piauí, Ceará, Pernambuco, Rio Grande do Norte, Sergipe, Alagoas, and Bahia. The limits of this cultural region are rather precisely defined by federal law as those of the so-called *polígono das sêcas* (drought polygon)— a special disaster area subject to periodic droughts accompanied by famine and mass emigration. This area has periodically attracted national attention, federal funds have been poured into it, and it has recently become a focus of the Alliance for Progress. It provides a classic contrast to the humid tropical forests of the Amazon Valley to the north and west and the agricultural Northeast to the east. It is a region covered by *caatinga*, a deciduous scrub forest mixed with cactus and thorny bushes. Low mesas and a few mountain ranges interrupt the otherwise flat or gently sloping terrain. With the exception of a few major rivers, the streams of the *sertão* are dry channels which are filled occasionally during the year when the headwaters are swollen by rains. Then, the stream beds fill swiftly and with little warning; in a few hours they are dry again. The rainfall is very irregular. Periods of drought may last from one to three years, and even in "good years" the rain comes in violent showers which turn the countryside only temporarily green. After a few days of hot sun and dry winds, the earth resumes its dusty brown. In a normal year it may rain four or five times a month in the rainy season (October to April). Although the annual precipitation averages between 20 and 40 inches over the entire region, the undependability of the rains makes much of the area unsuitable for agriculture. In many ways, it is reminiscent of the southwest United States.

The traditional economic activity of the arid Northeast is cattle grazing. Despite the importance of this activity in local life and the vast extent of the grazing lands, only 10 percent of

Vaqueiros *and cattle in Pernambuco*

Brazilian cattle are found in this region. The herds which are permitted to roam the thorny scrub are tended by *vaqueiros*, the northeastern version of the Brazilian cowboy. On many estates the *vaqueiros* are permitted to own a portion of the increase of the herds under their care. These cowboys are not exclusively herdsmen, but engage in a variety of collecting activities as well as in subsistence agriculture. They clear small garden sites and plant maize, beans, manioc, and cotton. The problem of keeping the cattle out of these clearings is a formidable one, since throughout the region it is the agriculturalist who must assume the responsibility for maintaining fences. The gardens are often lost for lack of rainfall or because too much rain falls at the wrong time. Some of the gardens are planted in the beds of dry streams to take advantage of the lingering moisture, but this too is precarious, since a sudden rainfall upstream may wipe out the garden in one hour. Many of the inhabitants of the region are squatters whose presence is tolerated by the landowner in exchange for herding and other services. As squatters, they are actively discouraged by the landlords from erecting permanent housing which might allow them to establish legal claims to ownership.

The livestock industry of the arid Northeast employs only the most rudimentary tools and techniques. In many districts the herds subsist mainly upon the leaves of shrubs and trees, and they tend to be emaciated even during the years of good rainfall. In the more humid districts, a primitive form of land rotation is practiced. The squatters and sharecroppers burn the *caatinga* and plant gardens for two or three successive years, after which the yield falls off beyond hope. Then the cleared area is planted in grass or *palma* (a thornless, watery cactus) and the owner of the estate grazes his herds on it until the *caatinga* once more takes over as the dominant vegetation. Selective breeding is impossible under the open-range conditions, and there is little, if any, veterinary care.

Collecting from wild stands is an important activity throughout the arid Northeast. It is indicative of a depressed and precarious economic situation. Several different kinds of palms, principally the *carnaúba* and the *licuri* (or *aricuri*), are exploited for their value as a source of wax for the international market. The *oiticica* tree provides an oleaginous substance used abroad in paint and varnish manufacture. These products enter the world market because of the marginal economic status of the Brazilian collectors, most of whom are squatters

Carnaúba *palms in Northeast Brazil*

and sharecroppers on the large estates where the trees are found.

At the higher elevations and along some of the more humid valleys, a number of commercial crops are grown. These, in order of importance, are cotton, sisal, and *mamona* (a source of castor oil). About one-third of the Brazilian cotton crop is produced in this region, but the fiber is now less important than cottonseed cake, which has become an important source of cattle feed.

A considerable but unspecified percentage of the population

of the arid Northeast is constantly involved in some form of migratory movement. Migrations of a regular or intermittent, temporary or permament type occur on a grand scale. Every year considerable numbers of *sertanejos,* as the inhabitants of the interior are called, leave their homes to participate in the sugar-cane and cacao harvests of the coastal region. The economic viability of these crops has become completely dependent on this influx of *sertanejo* labor for short periods during the year. In recent times, with the improvement of road transport, it has become possible for the *sertanejo* to range farther and farther into the adjacent regions in search of temporary jobs of all sorts.

Other *sertanejos* participate in migratory movements which involve absences from home of two or three years. Thus, a significant portion of rural labor in the state of São Paulo is performed by temporary emigrants from the Northeast. *Sertanejo* migrants are also widely employed in the building industry of the mushrooming metropolitan centers. In Rio de Janeiro and São Paulo, *sertanejo* construction workers sleep and eat right in the midst of the buildings which they are helping to put up. In addition to these temporary forms of migration, all of which involve a predominance of male migrants, whole families of *sertanejos* are moving in large numbers to other regions, chiefly São Paulo and Paraná. All of these migratory movements wax and wane in relation to the amount of rainfall each year. In times of drought, the migratory currents reach voluminous proportions and there is a general exodus from the region.

Droughts are recorded as far back as 1710–11, and every eight to fifteen years thereafter until the present. During the drought of 1877–79, the entire *sertão* was burned black by the sun, the cattle died, and there were no crops. One writer estimated that almost 500,000 people had died from starvation or from diseases connected with starvation during this single drought period.[6] Refugees, attracted by the beginnings of the rubber boom, began a movement from this region into the Amazon Valley. Since then there have been droughts of varying intensity in 1888–89, 1898, 1900, 1915, 1931–32, 1942–43, 1951, and 1958. Each time, the *sertão* has been turned into a virtual desert and a large number of people have migrated or died of starvation.

Despite its dust bowl qualities, the arid *sertão* is one of the most densely populated areas of Brazil, with more than 20 persons per square kilometer. Alagoas, with 39.3 per square kilometer, is the most densely populated state in the country. The population densities of Rio Grande do Norte, Paraíba, and Pernambuco are more than three times greater than that of the state of Paraná in the South, which has large areas of excellent agricultural land and only 10.53 people per square kilometer.

Since 1909, a federal government bureau (Inspetoria Federal de Obras Contra as Sêcas) has been constructing dams, drilling wells, and building irrigation systems and roads to modify the effects of the droughts which hit the region about twice in each generation. The government has spent large sums to make these areas habitable, while other regions with more favorable natural conditions are practically uninhabited. However, the *sertanejo* loves his semiarid homeland, and maintains that in between droughts it has a fine, healthy climate and rich land. As soon as the news that "it is raining in Ceará" reaches *sertanejos* who have left their land with a curse, they come trooping back again.

The arid Northeast is a region whose history is marked by

° H. H. Smith, *Brazil: The Amazons and the Coast*, p. 425.

the rise of fanatic religious movements. The dramatic story of the village of Canudos, which under the leadership of the religious fanatic, Antônio Conselheiro (Anthony the Counselor), battled federal troops until it was destroyed in a bloody massacre in 1896, has been told in a Brazilian masterpiece, *Rebellion in the Backlands* (*Os Sertões*), by Euclides da Cunha. Padre Cícero of the village of Juàzeiro do Norte in Ceará was another religious leader of the *sertão*. Although excommunicated by the Church, he was practically the supreme spiritual and political leader of the *sertão* in the first decades of this century. Large numbers of pilgrims still flock to his tomb each year. These movements are characterized by the appearance of a messianic leader promising to lead his followers to a promised land or "New Jerusalem," and they are said to derive from "Sebastianism" — the cult of the sixteenth-century Portuguese king who vanished in Africa while fighting the Moors. Functionally, such movements feed on the frustrations of the hostile environment and the semifeudal social system of the Northeast.

The *sertão* has also produced numerous outlaw bands, one of the most famous of which was led by Virgílio Ferreira da Silva, known as "Lampeão." From about 1920 until he was killed in 1938, Lampeão and his *cangaceiros* were the terror of the whole region. Like other bandit leaders in the area, Lampeão became a legend and the people of the *sertão* would not believe that he was dead until his severed head was exhibited publicly in several towns and finally donated to the museum of the Medical School in Salvador. Blind troubadours now sing folk verses in the market places of the *sertão* recounting the adventures of Lampeão and other famous *cangaceiros*. Like religious fanaticism, banditry seems to result from the constant frustrations of this harsh and unpredictable land.

In recent years, still another type of movement has appeared in the arid Northeast. This type is political and economic, but it is nevertheless a reaction to the ills of the physical and social environment. These are the so-called Peasant Leagues, so publicized in the United States in 1960 and 1961. In 1955, the peasant renters on a property known as Galiléia in the *município* of Vitória de Santo Antão, state of Pernambuco, organized themselves into the Agricultural and Pastoral Society of Pernambuco Planters to protest the steeply rising rents charged by absentee landlords. The society also aimed at mutual aid "to create a fund to help those who joined and pay the debts of those who were in arrears." [7] Alarmed by the threat of a peasant revolt, the owners attempted to evict them from the lands they occupied. Aided by the state deputy, Francisco Julião, the peasants entered into lengthy litigations to resist expulsion, and finally took possession of the property by legal expropriation. In the years that followed, other Peasant Leagues connected with the association formed at Galiléia arose throughout the Northeast. Francisco Julião became their spokesman and leader.

Julião has shown irrefutable leftist leanings; he has traveled to China and to Cuba, and he is outspoken in his admiration for Mao Tse-tung and Fidel Castro. The Peasant League movement has political implications which have caused considerable concern in the United States. It has been instrumental in calling attention both in Brazil and in the United States to the serious problems of the landless peasants in northeastern Brazil and to the dangers of generalized agrarian unrest or revolution. In 1959, the Brazilian government created a special agency, The Superintendency for the Development of the Northeast, known simply as SUDENE, under the leadership of the able

[7] Callado, *Os industriais das sêcas e os Galileus de Pernambuco*, p. 34.

economist Celso Furtado. SUDENE has sweeping powers, and
with ample funds from the Alliance for Progress and the Brazilian government it is carrying out a crash development program
for the entire Northeast. This region has long been a problem
area for Brazil, and is now becoming one for the Western
world.

THE SÃO FRANCISCO VALLEY SUBREGION

The São Francisco River, with its steady supply of water, cuts
through the arid semidesert of northeastern Brazil. For over
500 miles, between Pirapora where it emerges from the mountains of Minas Gerais and Juàzeiro in Bahia, it affords river
navigation through lands largely covered with *caatinga*. In its
lower course, the river drops abruptly over the Itaparica and
Paulo Afonso Falls, about 150 miles from the coast.

The area along the margins of this great stream has long been
considered a distinctive Brazilian region. The river itself has
been spoken of as "the river of national unity," for it provides
an interior link between the North and the South of the country. Thousands of people from the arid *sertão* travel upriver to
Pirapora in canoes, in flatboats propelled by poles, and in the
characteristic side-wheel river steamers, and continue by truck
or rail to prosperous São Paulo state. Most São Francisco river
towns are ports where the arrival and departure of steamers are
important events. As in the Amazon region, human habitation
tends to cling to the river and its tributaries. Because the annual
rise and fall of the river produces a narrow floodland where the
soils conserve sufficient moisture, a form of riverbank agriculture
(*cultura de vazante*) exists along the São Francisco. The people plant in the level flood plain or on the banks themselves as
the waters recede, and harvest before they rise again. Irrigation

is used in a few spots of the São Francisco flood plain between Juàzeiro and Paulo Afonso. For the most part, however, the river is disappointing as a potential source of irrigation. The flood plain is too narrow, and the lay of the land is such that irrigation techniques could be applied to large areas only at prohibitive expense.

As in the rest of the arid Northeast, the principal economic activity of the São Francisco Valley is grazing. Along the riverbanks and farther inland, there are great cattle *fazendas* which retain their enormous domains and traditional organization to this day.

In addition, like the rest of the arid Northeast, the São Francisco Valley is noted for its centers of religious pilgrimage. The shrine city of Bom Jesús da Lapa, to cite the most famous, with its image of Christ (to which miracles have been attributed) and its church installed in a cave, attracts more than a hundred thousand pilgrims each year. They come from the arid *sertão* of Bahia, Pernambuco, Ceará, and Rio Grande do Norte, as well as from the mountains of Bahia and Minas Gerais. They come by boat, by truck, by foot (spending sometimes more than a month en route), and even by airplane.

The São Francisco Valley is the focus of considerable national interest. The Paulo Afonso Falls on the lower course as well as the headwaters above Pirapora offer tremendous hydroelectric possibilities. The first stage of a great development plan, patterned in many ways after the Tennessee Valley authority, was the harnessing of a portion of the Paulo Afonso power to provide electric energy for the cities of Salvador, Aracaju, and Recife. And, in Minas Gerais, the great dam and electrical plant recently completed at Três Marias will generate 520,000 kilowatts. Further stages of the plan will provide power for the small communities along the river, and facilities for irrigating the São Francisco flood plain where that is practical.

The Eastern Highlands

This region may be roughly defined as including most of the state of Minas Gerais, the western part of Espírito Santo, and the southern part of Bahia. It consists mainly of hilly uplands, generally between 2,600 and 2,800 feet high, but it also includes the Serra do Espinhaço, a mountain range running from northern Minas Gerais through southern Bahia, which rises to 3,600 and up to 4,200 feet. The hilly uplands were probably once covered by semideciduous forest and the higher mountain areas by scrub woodland. By now the use of wood for charcoal and the clearing of lands for gardens and pasture, along with erosion, have modified the appearance of the countryside which is characterized by badly eroded, nearly bare mountainsides. The settlement of this region, as stated earlier, was accomplished during Brazil's second great boom—the gold rush of the eighteenth century. In 1698, an expedition of *bandeirantes* from São Paulo discovered gold in the southern part of the Serra do Espinhaço, and by 1729 diamonds had been discovered at Tijuca (now Diamantina) in the same mountain range. During the eighteenth century, this region produced 44 percent of the world's supply of gold. It has been said that because of the close economic ties between Portugal and Great Britain at that time, Brazilian gold financed England's industrial revolution.[8]

[8] By the Treaty of Methuen of 1703, Portugal agreed to kill its nascent textile industry if the English would buy Portuguese wines and lend support to the preservation of Portugal's colonies. Portugal became increasingly dependent on the products of English industry, which were purchased with Brazilian gold. See Furtado, *Formação econômica do Brasil*, pp. 49–50.

During this period, people poured into the Eastern Highlands. Colonials from São Paulo and the arid Northeast entered the area. Gold attracted a new wave of Portuguese immigrants; the Brazilian economist, Celso Furtado, estimates that between 300,000 and 500,000 Portuguese came to Brazil during the eighteenth century, more than doubling the number of Europeans in Brazil, which in 1800 was estimated at only one million.[9] And, as Furtado points out, this was a new type of immigrant; the mines exploited in the Eastern Highlands were not large enterprises, as in Mexico and Peru, but alluvial placer mines that could be worked by individuals and groups with little capital.[10] The gold rush coincided with the decline of the sugar plantations. The gold mines provided a new market for slaves imported from Africa, and many northeastern plantation owners sold their slaves to the miners.

Within a few decades after the discovery of gold, a number of urban settlements had been established in the Eastern Highlands, and some of them had grown into relatively large cities based upon wealth derived from the mines. The most famous of these cities was Vila Rica (now known as Ouro Prêto), which at one time had a population of close to 100,000. It had baroque churches, fine statuary, graceful public fountains, cobblestoned streets, and fine private homes. It was in Vila Rica and Congonhas do Campo that Aleijadinho ("Little Cripple"), the mulatto sculptor whose mother had been a slave, produced his magnificent figures in soapstone and wood. It was in Vila Rica at the end of the eighteenth century that the Inconfidência Mineira (Conspiracy of Minas Gerais), perhaps the most important early movement for Brazilian independence,

[9] *Ibid.*, p. 93n.
[10] *Ibid.*, p. 92.

developed, and that its leader, Joaquim José da Silva Xavier, known as Tiradentes ("Tooth Puller" or dentist), was hanged and quartered in the public square. Other towns grew near the sites of the mines and at likely localities for collecting the royal tax on gold. Rio de Janeiro became important as the gold-shipping port.

These cities and towns had a true urban ethos. They were generally situated in places ill-adapted to agriculture, and, as in most mining boom areas, food was hard to come by and expensive. Slaves were too costly to be put to work in agriculture; they worked in the mines, often according to a system which left them free to provide their owners periodically with a fixed amount of gold while gathering some for themselves. Many were thus able to purchase their freedom—a right long recognized in the Portuguese colony. The opulence of the central mountains benefited the grazing economies of São Paulo and Rio Grande do Sul and of the arid Northeast—for these states supplied meat and the tens of thousands of mules which were the most important means of transportation for food, merchandise, and gold.

The gold rush lasted about a hundred years; by 1821 an English traveler, John Mawe, reported that Vila Rica "scarcely retains a shadow of its former splendor." Throughout the highlands, once-important centers fell into decay. As Marvin Harris writes in his study of Minas Velhas in the state of Bahia, which had been one of these prosperous urban centers in the eighteenth century:

Wherever possible, the established urban centers adapted to the disappearance of their original *raison d'être* by evolving new basic economies. The old mining towns turned to handicrafts, cattle raising, coffee growing, mixed farming, fireworks manufacture, or whatever else the particular local environment would permit. Some of them managed to continue mining for gold and other precious and semiprecious minerals on a subsidiary basis. Most of these adaptations were makeshift and permitted little more than a marginal standard of living for the majority of people.[11]

Many people left the area entirely. Such centers did not turn altogether into ghost towns, mainly because they often continued as bureaucratic centers. Ouro Prêto continued as the capital of Minas Gerais until 1896, when the new capital of Belo Horizonte was completed. Today, with a population of about 15,000 people, Ouro Prêto is a national monument of narrow streets, colonial architecture, and memories of the past.

The Eastern Highlands are still endowed with a vast store of mineral wealth. Gold and industrial diamonds continue to be extracted from the subsoil in significant quantities. The lovely aquamarines and other semiprecious stones so avidly sought by tourists in Brazil come from this region. Zirconium, chromium, molybdenum, nickel, tungsten, titanium, and quartz crystals are sources of important mining industries. Minas Gerais has a great store of iron ore which is estimated at 23 percent of the world's reserves. Iron mining is now the country's most valuable extractive industry, and iron ore is the sixth most valuable export. These mines are supplying Brazil's rapidly developing steel industry. A new era of industrial expansion, once again based upon mining, seems to be in store for the Eastern Highlands.

Yet, despite the region's mineral wealth, stock raising and

[11] Harris, *Town and Country in Brazil*, pp. 15–16. The name Minas Velhas is fictitious.

agriculture are its principal economic activities. Minas Gerais ranks second in population among Brazilian states, but it also ranks high as a food-producing area. It produces corn, beans, butter, milk, and cheese, as well as coffee, oranges, manioc, and potatoes. In addition, it is said to have more cattle, pigs, and horses than any other Brazilian state. Much of this agricultural production is done by small farmers, but the majority is carried out on the *fazenda mineira*, the typical plantation of the region. The *fazenda mineira*, unlike the sugar plantation of the Northeast, does not tend to be monocultural. It is often remarkably diversified—planting coffee, food crops, and maize to feed animals, and raising a few pigs and some milk cattle. The accidental nature of the terrain allows, and possibly demands, a variety of uses. Again, contrary to the northeastern sugar estate, the tenants on the *fazenda mineira* are not concentrated in a plantation village, the residue of the *senzala*, but are scattered widely through the countryside. Many of them are sharecroppers and others work for wages.

The Eastern Highlands are also characterized by a large number of small towns with less than 5,000 people. These are interspersed among the rural holdings and serve as market places and bureaucratic centers for the enormous rural population. In 1950, Minas Gerais had but two cities with over 50,000 inhabitants out of a total of 1,095 urban centers. Many of these small towns and villages owe their origin to grants or *patrimônios* made by landowners to the Church with the express purpose of creating a town devoted to a particular saint. As Preston James points out: "While there is a certain religious prestige to be gained by such a grant, it is obvious that economic profit will also accrue, if only because of the supply of workers gathered together in the neighborhood." [12] Thus, the landowners guaranteed for themselves seasonal and temporary labor.

In recent years, motor roads have penetrated into the mountainous regions of the Eastern Highlands, breaking its isolation, but the quality of the roads and the hilly country make travel difficult and many of these small towns and villages are still relatively isolated. Yet, one of the great cities of Brazil, Belo Horizonte, was literally built in the region. Its site was selected on a wide sweep of sloping land, and its plan follows a pattern similar to that of Washington, D.C. It was inaugurated in 1896, and by 1920 there were over 55,000 people living there. By 1962, Belo Horizonte had over 650,000 people. It is a city of modern architecture and broad streets, with a new and dynamic university. In Pampulha, a nearby district, the well-known architect Oscar Niemeyer designed the church for which the famous painter Cândido Portinari painted murals which at first so scandalized both Brazilians and their visitors. Belo Horizonte was Brazil's first experience in planning a new city where none existed before.

Yet the people of the Eastern Highlands, and especially of the core state of Minas Gerais, are noted as the most conservative in Brazil. Several Brazilian writers speak of their conservative spirit and traditionalism.[13] Although the region includes mestizos from many parts of Brazil, it seems that the Lusitanian element has always predominated.[14] The Eastern Highlands, then, is the region par excellence in which to seek the traditional ideal patterns of Brazilian national culture.

[12] James, *Latin America*, p. 446.
[13] Diegues Junior, *Regiões culturais do Brasil*, pp. 255 ff.
[14] Alceu Amoroso Lima, *Voz de Minas*, p. 59, cited by Diegues Junior, *Regiões culturais do Brasil*, p. 245.

It retains the religious brotherhoods or *irmandades*. There is a middle class, even in the small cities, which persists in old patterns of behavior such as the *compadresco* system. Manuel Diegues Junior describes the importance of kinship—the *parentelas* or extensive kinship webs that still dominate local politics. Some thirty extensive kinship groups control politics in the area and extend into the federal arena with considerable force.[15] This is both one of the most vigorous and one of the most conservative regions in all of Brazil.

The Amazon Valley

During the nineteenth century, the economic spotlight slowly shifted from the mines of the Eastern Highlands to the coffee plantations of the Paraíba Valley and São Paulo. But that is a story to be told later as part of a larger scheme which involves the development of dynamic, industrial Brazil. For the moment, we will move in time to the end of the nineteenth century and in space to the far North of the country—the Amazon Valley. This was the scene of a dramatic boom and bust based upon wild rubber which began after the middle of the nineteenth century, gained momentum toward the end of the century, and "hit the skids" after 1912. It is a region that catches the imagination of Brazilians and foreigners alike. It has been called "Mysterious Amazon," "Green Hell," "Bread Basket of the World," and other colorful epithets. It is actually none of these, but it is one of the most romantic of all Brazilian cultural regions.

The Brazilian part of the Amazon Valley takes in the states of Acre, Amazonas, and Pará, and the northern portion of the

[15] *Ibid.*, p. 269.

state of Maranhão, as well as the federal territories of Amapá, Rondônia, and Rio Branco. The dense tropical forest that covers most of the Amazon Valley is by no means a vast swampy jungle. About 90 percent of the area lies above flood level. South of the town of Santarém, about halfway from Belém to Manaus on the mainstream of the Amazon, a range of hills rises over a thousand feet above the river. To the north, near the Colombian and Venezuelan frontiers, there are great stretches of grassy plains, and along the Venezuelan border there are mountains which rise above 8,000 feet. Throughout the entire Valley, patches of grassy savanná break the monotony of the forest, and near the Amazon River itself there are wide flood plains covered with coarse grass. Marajó Island, at the mouth of the Amazon, is as large as Switzerland and consists mainly of periodically flooded plains.

Contrary to popular opinion, the highest temperatures in South America occur along the Caribbean coast and in the Gran Chaco of Argentina, not in the Amazon. Santarém, which is only a short distance south of the Equator, has an average yearly temperature of 78.1° F, and at Manaus the yearly average is 81° F. The highest temperature recorded at Manaus for a thirty-year period was 99° F, the lowest 62° F. The climate is uncomfortable because of its monotony and humidity. The difference between the average daytime temperature during the warmest and the coldest months at Manaus is less than 4° F. The humidity runs as high as 80 percent or even 90 percent. Throughout the Valley rainfall is abundant; in Belém, the average is over 100 inches per year, in Manaus around 80 inches, and in the upper portions of the Valley as much as 100 inches. The rainy season, "winter" as it is called, lasts from January through June; actually these are only the months of heaviest precipitation, for it rains considerably during each month of the year, even during the "summer" dry season.

Transportation in the Amazon region is utterly dependent upon the waterways. The Amazon River itself is navigable for ocean-going steamers up to some 2,300 miles from its mouth,

Rubber-gatherer's hut on the Amazon River

and river boats ply all of its major tributaries. Three short railroads total about 620 miles; in 1955, there were only some 3,300 miles of automobile roads in the entire Valley, of which 36 miles were paved. There are two large cities; in 1961 Manaus had over 175,000 people, and Belém over 400,000. There are about 3,000,000 people in the entire region. At least half of these people live along the main rivers or along the *igarapés* (small streams), very much isolated from one another. They build their houses of planks or thatch on high spots along the banks or on stilts out of reach of the seasonal rise of the river. Each house has its own wharf alongside of which there is always a canoe, the family's only means of transportation.

Now and again, along the river, there is a larger wharf and, behind it, a long, low, wooden building. This is a *barracão*, a trading post, to which people from the scattered houses in the vicinity paddle every fifteen days or so (a *quinzena*) to buy or receive on credit canned goods, salt, a piece of cloth, kerosene, or another necessity. There, also, they sell the rubber, Brazil nuts, palm oils, *guaraná* (a seed used to make a soft drink), hardwoods, rosewood oil (used as a base for perfume), *timbó* vine (used for insecticides), animal pelts, alligator skins, or even just manioc flour produced from their own gardens. Periodically, river steamers stop at the *barracão* to load these products of the forest and to renew the trader's stock. These boats belong to one of the large exporting firms in Belém and Manaus known as *aviadores*. Just as the local trader extends credit to his collector-customers, so he receives credit from the *aviador*. The whole economic system of the Amazon Valley operates on credit and the forest collector and subsistence farmer remain forever in virtual debt slavery.

The story of rubber is an Amazon classic. During the latter part of the nineteenth century, a rubber boom took place which was in many respects like the gold rushes of Alaska, California, and Minas Gerais. In the stampede that ensued to buy forest rubber, enormous tracts of land were sold in Belém and Manaus, sight unseen and with faulty titles. The buyer would later visit his lands to find out whether he really was the wealthy owner of a tract of forest producing "black gold" or whether he had thrown away his money on worthless jungle. If his land had rubber trees, then labor was his great problem. Raids were made on Indian villages, and the subsequent enslavement and brutal treatment of Indians became an international scandal. Great numbers of men were recruited in the drought areas of northeastern Brazil and shipped in virtual debt slavery to the *seringais* (rubber fields) of the Amazon. The owner furnished supplies and assigned to each man several *estradas* ("roads" or paths leading to 150 or 200 rubber trees), each separated from the next by about 100 yards. From the trading post, situated strategically at the mouth of a tributary, the owner kept watch with rifles so that his gatherers could not escape downriver and intruders could not go upriver to buy from them.

Money was plentiful in the cities. Opera companies came directly from Europe to give performances in the diamond-roofed Opera House in Manaus. People still remember the good old days when dress shirts were sent to Portugal to be laundered and women ordered their frocks in Paris. As late as 1910, everyone looked to the future with the firm belief that the Amazon was blessed by God with a permanent world monopoly on rubber. Then the bubble burst. In 1876, an Englishman named Henry Wickham smuggled some rubber seeds out of Brazil to England. They were planted at Kew Gardens and from these plants the English started rubber plantations in Ceylon and Malaya. In 1910, the Far Eastern plantations produced only 9 percent of the world's rubber, but by 1913 they more than equaled the Amazon's production. By 1923, 93 percent of all the rubber used in the world came from these Eastern plantations. In 1940, Brazil exported only 12,000 tons of rubber as compared with over 40,000 tons in 1912.

During World War II, the Allies had to depend upon the Amazon Valley for a supply of natural rubber and the output rose once more. Today rubber is once again the most important commercial product of the Amazon. About 30,000 tons were produced in 1958, but this amount is insufficient to meet even Brazil's domestic requirements.

The pattern of life of the Amazon peasant has remained little changed by the ups and downs of prices on the world market. He continues to eke out an existence from the gathering of forest products and from subsistence agriculture. His way of life draws heavily on elements inherited from the Indian. Although only 10,000 to 20,000 tribal Indians are left in the Brazilian Amazon today, the Indian has contributed more to the life of this region than to that of any other part of Brazil. The Amazon population is mainly of American Indian racial stock, although most people also have some European and Negro ancestors. Only a few Negro slaves were imported into the Valley, and the number of European colonists was small. In the Amazon, so many names of places, animals and birds, and so many popular expressions have been borrowed from Tupí-Guaraní that the educated Brazilian from the South needs a glossary when he reads about the region.

The principal food crops of the region—corn, beans, peppers, peanuts, and manioc—are native to America. In the Amazon, manioc is the staff of life. The basis of all meals, *farinha dágua*, a flour prepared from the poisonous variety of the plant, is the local bread, the necessary complement to any meal.

In the Amazon, popular Catholicism is strongly flavored by surviving Indian customs. Although they consider themselves good Roman Catholics, many Amazon peasants believe in American Indian supernaturals and call on medicine men (*pagés* as they are called in the regional Portuguese) to cure them by traditional methods. These *pagés* cure the sick by sucking or massaging out of the patient's body an object which is thought to have been placed there by magic. The medicine men inhale great gulps of tobacco smoke and blow clouds of it over the patient, sing, and dance, keeping time with a gourd rattle. As they sing, they call on their familiar spirits to aid them in the cure.

The Amazon Valley accounts for about 45 percent of the total area of Brazil. However, less than 5 percent of the Brazilian people live in this vast region. Present conditions in the Amazon certainly qualify it as one of the world's greatest underdeveloped regions. Even in relation to the rest of Brazil, the Amazon makes a poor showing. Illiteracy in the state of Amazonas is 65 percent of the population over ten years of age, infant mortality is shockingly high, diet is seriously substandard both in caloric intake and in quality, the collecting economy is stagnant and utterly at the mercy of world-market price fluctuations, and less than 1 percent of the area is under cultivation. Even this small part is exploited with the most primitive tools and techniques. Thus, in 1940, the last year for which data are available, of the 500,000 plows in Brazil, less than 200 were being used in the Amazon Valley.

Some authorities are inclined to view this region as a place of great potential agricultural and population growth. Others are inclined to believe that the poor soil, humid climate, and prevalence of disease (especially malaria) doom the Valley to remain forever a "Green Hell," a "Green Desert," or "Green Opium" (referring to the fancies of the optimists). Is this an underdeveloped or undevelopable part of the world?

There is no doubt that the natural environment of the

Amazon contributes to its present backwardness and poverty. Yet none of the many obvious natural barriers to development can be reckoned as insurmountable from a purely technological standpoint. Tropical diseases can be and are being corrected, and the effects of the climate can be mitigated by modern architecture, refrigeration, and air-conditioning. It must be remembered that never in the history of the Valley has modern technology been brought to bear upon its natural problems. Never has Amazon man had the use of the kinds of knowledge, skills, and equipment which are now available in the more advanced regions for the exploitation and control of the physical world. Actually, a modern tropical technology has never been applied anywhere on a large scale. Much of that technology has not even been developed as yet. Nutrition, agronomy, modern engineering, and other applied sciences have been concerned for the most part with solving the problems of temperate countries. Brazilian students of engineering, agronomy, and medicine still study largely from books written by temperate-zone authors. It is clear that in order to achieve the "conquest" of the Amazon, a whole new set of applied sciences must be developed to meet the challenge of tropical conditions. While it is possible to be optimistic about the ability of modern science to come up with appropriate technological solutions, there is little prospect that this is going to occur in the near future, or that Brazil will be able to afford such a tropical technology.

The fact is that at this time there are few compelling reasons (other than humanitarian ones) for Brazil to attempt to develop the Amazon Valley on a large scale. Brazil, even without the Amazon Valley, is an underpopulated country. There are vast stretches of Mato Grosso and Goiás, infinitely richer by natural endowment than the Valley, in which development programs can achieve greater results with the expenditure of less time, ingenuity, and money. As long as Brazil has other frontiers, it is difficult to conceive of the advantages to be derived from encouraging further population growth in the Amazon. It is also difficult to conceive of the source of the political and economic effort for making the Amazon more habitable, as long as government and private capital continue to reap richer rewards in the other frontier regions. This situation would change, however, if, as many Brazilians insist, the Amazon were found to contain oil. The search for oil is being pushed at the moment and several wells have been drilled, but with no conclusive results. In the federal territory of Amapá, just north of Belém, the presence of rich manganese deposits and other minerals has provided a compelling reason for rapid development. Macapá, the capital of the territory, has increased enormously in population and in urban facilities. A railroad has been built and a port equipped to export the ore. A hydroelectric plant is being installed. But, in fact, nothing has changed; this is but another extractive industry. In the meantime, efforts to improve the local standard of living must depend largely upon government programs, for which there is little enthusiasm in the regions from which the funds and trained personnel must be drawn.

The South

The Brazilian South is in reality a series of cultural regions or subregions, each of which has its own version of Brazilian national culture. There is cosmopolitan Rio de Janeiro, whose florescence and preeminence as a port dates from the era of the gold boom in the mountains of Minas Gerais and the arrival of the Portuguese court fleeing from Napoleon. There are the dynamic city and state of São Paulo, with their tremendous pride in progress and energy. There is the region of European immigration in Santa Catarina, Paraná, and Rio Grande do Sul, with people of German, Italian, and Polish descent. There are the wide pampas of the extreme South with their *gaúcho*, the southern Brazilian cowboy, and with a goodly touch of Hispanic influence. And, there is the new frontier near the boundary with Paraguay, where land is being cleared for the first time and where new settlers arrive every day. Each of these regions and subregions must be described separately.

Yet the Brazilian South, taken as a whole, should be set off from the North. The two zones contrast just as our own South contrasts with our North—almost as if the map were turned upside down. In Brazil, it is the North which has the heritage of plantations and slavery, and even today it is semifeudal and agrarian; while the Brazilian South has modern cities, industry, immigrants, mechanized agriculture, and a developing middle class. Southerners in Brazil feel about the North somewhat as North American Yankees feel about our South. The North is poor and a problem to the modern South. Northeasterners flood Rio de Janeiro and São Paulo in a manner similar to the migration of southern Negroes to the northern cities of the United States; they do so not to escape racial discrimination, but to escape poverty and exploitative economic situations reminiscent of those which prevail in our South.

THE INDUSTRIAL CENTER

The industrial heartland of modern Brazil is found in and around the two great cities of Rio de Janeiro and São Paulo. Within 200 miles of each other, these two cities have more than 3 million people each. They are connected by railroad, a modern highway, and airplane flights every half-hour. The Paraíba Valley between São Paulo and Rio de Janeiro is becoming the industrial center of the nation. At Volta Redonda in the Paraíba Valley, 50 miles from Rio de Janeiro, lie the great steel mills of the Companhia Siderúrgica Nacional. These government-owned mills are the largest in South America, producing over a million tons of steel in 1962. In an area of about 300,000 square kilometers between and around these two cities live well over 20 percent of all Brazilians. The area has a population density of 51 per square kilometer compared to an average of only 6 for the whole nation. While the per capita income is estimated at about $200 for Brazil as a whole, it has reached $400 in this region. Most of Brazil's modern universities, research laboratories, trade schools, museums, theatres, and other cultural institutions are found here. In short, this is the part of Brazil where modern Western technology has been introduced most successfully. From this center, Brazil's own brand of modern Western culture is spreading to the rest of the country.

This industrial heartland of Brazil does not form a self-conscious, unified region such as New England in the United States. In fact Rio de Janeiro and São Paulo are traditional rivals—the latter the commercial and financial capital and the former, until recently, the political, diplomatic, and bureaucratic center. The *paulista* criticizes the *carioca* of Rio de

Janeiro as lazy, placid, and untrustworthy; while the *carioca* portrays the *paulista* as a crass materialist. Despite their relative proximity, each city has its zone of influence. The state of Rio de Janeiro, the minuscule state of Guanabara (formerly the Federal District) and the eastern Paraíba Valley constitute the immediate sphere of Rio de Janeiro. The zone of influence

Copacabana Beach in Rio de Janeiro

of São Paulo is much wider. It includes the whole state of which it is the capital and extends into parts of Minas Gerais, Goiás, Mato Grosso, and Paraná, following the railroads that were built from São Paulo (and its port city of Santos) early in the twentieth century.

Every Brazilian hopes someday to visit the magnificent city

of Rio de Janeiro. People want to migrate to São Paulo to make money, and Brazilians are patriotically proud of their new capital of Brasília. But Rio is the showplace of Brazil, with its beaches stretching in sweeping curves, elegant modern apartments with breathtaking views from their balconies, mountains rising almost straight up from the ocean, magnificent harbor, and exciting night life. Everyone recognizes pictures of such familiar scenes as the Sugar Loaf and the statue of Christ that stands above Rio on the Corcovado (Hunchback) Peak. And then there is Maracanã Stadium where championship soccer is played (seating almost 200,000), the exciting activities of Carnival, and the annual racing season, which attracts people from all over Brazil, the Argentine, and Europe. In keeping with the beauty and spirit of their city, the people of Rio are known for their sharp sense of humor and their cosmopolitan air.

For those who have lived in Rio de Janeiro, it is also a city memorable for its monumental traffic jams. Squeezed as it is between the mountains and the sea and bay, there are few throughways from one part of the city to another and the rush hour is a mad struggle to get to or from work. One also remembers the sprawling *favelas* (shanty towns) situated high up on the mountainsides, often with breathtaking views. One remembers frequent electric blackouts, the leaky and inadequate water supply, the rickety taxicabs, the antiquated *bondes* (streetcars), now finally being replaced by electric buses, and the streets that are constantly being dug up for one reason or another. The shortage of telephone lines is such that one must buy one's instrument and line at a very inflated price from a private party, and telephone lines are literally inherited. Then, there is the periodic shortage of food—of milk, meat, or beans

—which supports an active black market. But the *cariocas* are an amazingly tolerant and patient people. They say that the only way to live in their great city is with a sense of humor. Only now and again do their tempers flare up at the irritations of a city without adequate public services—at times when the trains to the suburbs ran unbearably late, they have burned passenger cars, thus contributing to the system's deterioration, and when the cost of movies for students (who have a cut rate) was increased, they have overturned streetcars. Otherwise, the *cariocas* love their confusing and beautiful city.

Rio de Janeiro lacks the massive industrial base of São Paulo, but all the major companies have offices there. In addition, its seaport is always busy and it is one of the country's principal financial centers. Although it is no longer the national capital, the running of the federal government is still perhaps its most important business. All of the federal ministries still have offices in Rio, with by far the majority of the federal employees. Only a minority have moved as yet to the new capital, and the main offices of nearly all federal agencies are still located in Rio. In time, Rio will perhaps lose out as the bureaucratic center of the nation, but this will take a generation or so. Legislators, functionaries, diplomats, and others connected with the government find Brasília dull and isolated, and they are not anxious to move there. For years to come, Rio will be the cosmopolitan capital of Brazil, if not legally, at least in the minds of most Brazilians. In newspapers and magazines, and in popular language, Brasília is *Novacap* (New Capital) while Rio de Janeiro is *Belacap* (Beautiful Capital).

With an estimated population of over 3,300,000 in 1960 (estimated at over 3,775,000 in 1962), the city of São Paulo is unquestionably the financial and industrial capital of Brazil.

Beyond the city itself are the port city of Santos with over 250,000 people and such dynamic smaller metropolitan centers as Campinas (population in 1960, 180,000), Ribeirão Prêto (population, 120,000), and Araraquara (population, 60,000), to mention but a few. São Paulo is said to be one of the most rapidly growing cities in the world, and its industrial center

Downtown São Paulo near the famous Viaduto do Chá

one of the most rapidly developing. Situated about 2,500 feet above sea level, the city has a pleasant climate. Hydroelectric power is plentiful, and communications with the agricultural areas over motor roads and by railroad are better than in any other part of Brazil. Its industry is highly diversified, including textiles, furniture, pharmaceuticals, chemicals, clothing and shoes, paint and cement. It is the site of Brazil's new automobile industry, which produced over 200,000 vehicles in 1960.

São Paulo is at once the Detroit, the Chicago, and the New York of Brazil.

The phenomenal growth of São Paulo and the wealth of its zone of influence are relatively recent. From soon after the founding of the initial São Paulo nucleus in 1554 until about the middle of the nineteenth century, the life of São Paulo was characterized by *bandeirismo*—a word used to indicate the predominance of adventure and exploration over an economy based upon grazing or agriculture. This word derives from the *bandeirantes* (flag bearers), groups of adventurers organized in São Vicente and later in São Paulo who penetrated into the heartland of South America seeking gold, diamonds, the "land of eternal youth," and slaves. Such groups were composed of Portuguese, *mamelucos*, and domesticated Indians. They often spent one, two, or more years marching through the backlands, stopping to plant gardens for food, ravaging Indian villages, and procreating children with Indian women. The great period of the *bandeirantes* was between 1580 and 1640, when individual *bandeiras* traveled from São Paulo south to the Río de la Plata and into Paraguay, west to the Guaporé, Madeira, and Tapajós rivers, and north to the Amazon. Much of unexplored Brazil at the beginning of the twentieth century, even the River of Doubt discovered by Teddy Roosevelt, had been traversed by these expeditions.

These *bandeiras* did little for the economic prosperity of São Paulo. In fact, it was one of the poorest *capitanias* in the colony. Their expeditions did, however, pay off in several ways. Through their travels, they extended the frontiers of Brazil beyond the boundaries originally set by the Treaty of Tordesillas. They brought to São Paulo thousands of Indian slaves, many captured in raids on Jesuit missions, to be sold to planters in the Northeast. In the late eighteenth century, they finally discovered gold and diamonds in Minas Gerais, Goiás, and Mato Grosso. They did provide São Paulo with its proud *bandeirante* spirit of adventure and daring which *paulistas* like to think has been carried over into modern industrial life. Until almost 1850, however, the city of São Paulo remained but a "village turned toward the backlands." [16] Gold in Minas Gerais brought some activity to the region. In June and July of each year, the town of Sorocabana was a great market place for mules and cattle from south Brazil destined for the mining area. As late as 1883, the city of São Paulo was still an old colonial town of irregular, narrow, and mostly unpaved streets, with a population of only 35,000 people. At the same time, the whole state contained less than a million and a half people devoted mainly to grazing and to subsistence agriculture.

The revolution which was to make São Paulo the most progressive part of Brazil was, however, already underway. Coffee had already been planted on a profitable commercial scale in the Paraíba Valley between Rio de Janeiro and São Paulo. By 1860, coffee plantations had moved into the region around Campinas, which by 1885 supplanted the towns of the Paraíba Valley as the center of coffee production. Coffee farms rapidly moved north and northwest into São Paulo state where the famous *terra roxa*, a deep porous soil which is purplish-red in color, was found to be highly suitable for this crop. By 1899 Brazil was producing 9 million sacks (60 kilograms each) of coffee, and by 1906, 20 million sacks, although the world consumption was only 12 million. With considerable flux in the world market and price difficulties, the coffee production of Brazil rose steadily until the great crash of 1929, when with a

[16] Diegues Junior, *Regiões culturais do Brasil*, p. 370.

production of 26 million sacks (1928) the price of coffee dropped from 24.8 cents per pound in March of 1929 to 7.6 cents in October of 1931. Since then the volume of coffee production has not increased, but coffee trees have been planted far to the west in Paraná, and coffee is still Brazil's first export commodity in value. The city of São Paulo early became the hub of this coffee boom, and over the decades of this century coffee was the chief basis for its mighty growth.

Several fundamental changes in regional and national society accompanied the São Paulo coffee boom and were intimately related to the newly arising way of life. In 1888 Brazil finally abolished slavery. The *paulistas* had never been slavocrats on a large scale, and they had already foreseen this event. In need of labor for their coffee farms, São Paulo had stimulated immigration since 1882; from 1886 to 1936, almost a million and a half immigrants, mainly Italian, Portuguese, Spanish, German, and Slavic people, came to São Paulo. Since 1908, approximately 200,000 Japanese have entered Brazil, and the majority have come to São Paulo. Most of these immigrants were at first employed on coffee plantations on a wage or sharecropper basis. Soon, however, many of them made their way to the city or were able in one way or another to acquire farms of their own. Now, in the last two decades or more, these foreign immigrants are being replaced on the coffee plantations and on the low rungs of industrial labor by thousands of Northeasterners who migrate to São Paulo each year. Thus, São Paulo became a veritable melting pot and the European immigrants, especially the Italians who were most numerous, have influenced the *paulista* variety of Brazilian national culture.

The coffee plantations of São Paulo were in many ways

similar to the sugar plantations of the North. At least at first, plantations in the Paraíba Valley had their *casas grandes* (mansions) and *senzalas* (slave quarters). And, as Stanley Stein shows, a coffee aristocracy analogous to the sugar aristocracy of the North arose in the Paraíba Valley.[17] But the development of coffee farming was based upon free labor. The slave was replaced by the *colono*. Typically, coffee *fazendas* are tended by tenants or *colonos* who are obligated to clear the forest and plant coffee. In return, they make use of the land while the trees grow, planting maize, beans, rice, and other subsistence crops between the trees. Once the plantation begins to produce, either the tenant is forced to move on or he and his family remain as permanent laborers responsible for a set number of trees and receiving a share (one-third to one-half) of the produce. When a larger labor force is necessary during the harvest, day laborers can be recruited from among the small farmers and itinerant Northeasterners looking for work. The São Paulo coffee farm is not family-owned like the *engenho*-type sugar plantation of northeastern Brazil, but is a business enterprise more similar to the giant corporation-owned *usina*, although the capital investment is generally not as large. Still, the coffee plantation must have its drying platforms, tanks, canals, husking and sorting machines, and houses for the overseers and workmen. A coffee *fazenda* is a distinctive type of Brazilian community.

It seemed that the coffee boom was over after 1930, but this proved not to be so, for since World War II fortunes have been made in planting and trading in coffee. It may be said, however, that since then coffee has played an important but declining role in the economy of the region; thus, unlike

[17] See Stein, *Vassouras*.

the sugar, gold, and rubber booms, the rise of coffee as a commercial crop has not been followed by an era of decadence. The São Paulo boom goes on unabated. Several factors have led to the continued growth of the regional economy of São Paulo. As coffee began to decline, new crops were emphasized in the agricultural economy. The state of São Paulo today not only produces about half of Brazil's coffee, but is also the largest producer of cotton, rice, sugar, potatoes, and other food crops. Coffee plantations, some of them falling low in productivity, have been broken up and sold to small farmers who follow a European type of mixed agriculture. Wealth earned from coffee has been invested in urban real estate and in industry, which form the basis of São Paulo's new economic growth. Large amounts of foreign capital have been invested in São Paulo, especially since World War II; advertisements announce Goodyear tires, Coca Cola, Esso gasoline stations, Kolynos toothpaste, and thousands of other products of European and North American origin, now produced in Brazil. They indicate the degree of international influence in Brazilian industry.

São Paulo is an international city, but retains its own individual spirit. The people are busy, they walk quickly, and they brag of their *bandeirante* spirit and enterprise. They complain of the social and economic drag of the other regions of Brazil, citing the old Brazilian saying that "Brazil is made up of one locomotive and twenty box cars"; São Paulo is, of course, the locomotive, and the other states are the box cars, of which there are now twenty-one. *Paulistas* are also proud of their laboratories and scientific institutions, such as the Butantan Snake Farm and the Biological Institute; these organizations and the University of São Paulo are the most advanced in

Brazil, if not in all of South America. The professional soccer clubs of São Paulo and Santos pay their players the highest salaries in Brazil and thus have the majority of the outstanding players. The *paulistas* point with pride to the large number of supermarkets of the North American variety and to the ample supply of other consumer products and facilities. Suburban districts such as Brooklin Nova are growing up around São Paulo, with middle-class homes bought on long-term mortgages. Domestic servants are relatively expensive and hard to find and keep. In São Paulo, one has a glimpse of the future Latin American society with all of its potential for a good life and many of its problems.

THE EXTREME SOUTH

The three states of Paraná, Santa Catarina, and Rio Grande do Sul have been spoken of as "another Brazil." They never shared in the aristocrat versus slave or worker complex of the North. Colonized first by Portuguese from the Azores and then by Europeans of various countries, the South developed a way of life more similar to that of the North American pioneers than to that of the *bandeirantes* or the planters of northern Brazil. This region has never had an economic boom and bust comparable to those of the northern regions, but has steadily grown in prosperity. The people of the extreme South are different from the Brazilians of the North, but they also differ among themselves. In the South there are two traditions, one symbolized by the *gaúcho* of the *estâncias* (pampas cattle ranches) and the other by the European homesteader.

The *estância* is the equivalent of the Texas ranch in the United States, and there are certain analogies in its historical past. The *estância* arose in a border state where Spanish influence is strong and where Spain might easily have taken over political control. Brazil's most southern states were not really incorporated into the colony until quite late. *Bandeirantes* from São Paulo traveled south into the region in the sixteenth and seventeenth centuries, and the Jesuits established the Eastern Missions, an extension of their Paraguayan establishments, in the late seventeenth and early eighteenth centuries. However, Portugal had a weak hold over the South which was endangered by Spanish penetration from the colonies to the south and west. So, in the eighteenth century, the Crown imported immigrants from the Azores to secure its hold over what is today the extreme South of Brazil. Unlike the situation in northern Brazil, this was a planned program of colonization. The Azoreans were to come in couples with their passage paid by the Crown and with a specific list of tools made available to each family during the first year. Just how many came is not known. As a colonization scheme, it seems to have been a failure. As a population and political scheme, it must have been a success. The coastal region of Rio Grande do Sul and Santa Catarina was occupied by these people of Lusitanian origin, and through them the backlands were guaranteed for the Portuguese.

On the pampas, another way of life developed, one which was quite different from the sedentary existence of the Azoreans on the coast, namely, that of the *gaúcho*. The pampas of South America, like the Great Plains of the United States, were an ideal habitat for cattle and horses, both brought to the Americas by the Spaniards. Just as cattle and horses replaced the buffalo in North America, these same animals replaced the vicuña and other animals on the South American plains. Just as the North American cowboy became a typical figure of our West, so did the *gaúcho* become the typical figure of the South American plains. The pampas of South America extend from Argentina, through Uruguay, and into Brazil. The figure of the *gaúcho* is similar in all three countries, but in Brazil he speaks Portuguese and shares many Brazilian culture traits.

European cattle literally spawned on the pampas after they were introduced by the Jesuits and Spaniards from the Spanish colonies to the south. They were hunted almost like wild animals by horsemen who were the offspring of Portuguese men and Indian women, and who sought the hides which could be exported, not the meat, which was left rotting on the plains. These *gaúchos*, as they came to be called, derived much of their technology and way of life from the pastoral regions of Iberia, but they also owe much to the American Indian tradition. For example, their *bola*, made of heavy weights connected with leather ropes which entangle the animal, is an American Indian instrument. The *gaúcho* has a characteristic garb: plus-four-like pants, a wide hat, a broad belt with silver decorations, a knife, and leather boots which can be extended up and down like accordions.

As a stereotype, the *gaúcho* contrasts sharply with his counterpart, the *vaqueiro* of northeastern Brazil. Euclides da Cunha has described the contrast in essentially accurate, if somewhat romantic terms, in his classic *Rebellion in the Backlands:* "The southern Gaucho, upon meeting the vaqueiro . . . would look him over commiseratingly. The northern cowboy is his very antithesis. In the matter of bearing, gesture, mode of speech, character, and habits there is no comparing the two." Whereas the vaqueiro is downcast, defeated by his environment, the *gaúcho* "awakes to life amid a glowing, animating wealth of

Nature; and he goes through life adventurous, jovial, eloquent of speech, valiant and swaggering." His clothes are "a holiday garb compared to the vaqueiro's rustic garments. . . . His horse, inseparable companion of his romantic life, is a near-luxurious object, with its complicated and spectacular trappings." [18]

In time, the wide expanse of the pampas was divided into great latifundia and granted to individuals. From these land grants arose the great *estâncias*. The meat was prepared in the form of *charque*, that is, it was cut in slabs, dipped in brine, salted, and allowed to dry in the sun. Meat prepared in this manner (much of it still is) may be kept almost indefinitely without refrigeration and may thus be shipped to distant parts of the country. The meat plants or *charqueadas* became typical industrial and social centers of the Brazilian pampas. They gave rise to small nuclei of about 400 people, to which were added periodically the cowboys who came to deliver cattle. These *charqueada* villages offered the opportunity for extensive miscegenation between the Portuguese, the Indians, and the Negro slaves.

Nowadays, Rio Grande do Sul still produces *charque*, although often by more modern drying methods that involve the use of steam rather than sunlight. However, in recent years, sheep have come to outnumber cattle as the chief livestock in the area. The *estâncias* now provide both sheep and cattle for modern packing plants in Pôrto Alegre and other urban centers. Considerable progress has been made toward scientific breeding, veterinary assistance, and modern marketing techniques. The modern *estância* is a business enterprise, but it retains much of the old ranch tradition; it is controlled by an administrator, and there is a highly formalized division of labor

[18] Cunha, *Rebellion in the Backlands*, pp. 91–92.

among the cooks, houseboys, cowboys, horse trainers, fence riders, and others, which parallels closely the way of life on our Western cattle ranches.

Although literally the word *gaúcho* refers to the cowboy, it is applied to all native inhabitants of Rio Grande do Sul. A Brazilian writer remarks: "Generally, we see him [the *gaúcho*] with his typical customs, habits, and psychology in the midst of the plains or in the frontier region, but he also lives in the city, where he shares in urban life without losing the influence of earlier life and his love of the plains." [19] Although the population of the *estância* area proper is quite small, the *gaúcho* spirit has influenced the outlook of the inhabitants of Pôrto Alegre, a city of well over 600,000 people with a rapidly expanding industry; of the rice farmers in the flood plains of the Jacuí River, who produce about 25 percent of Brazil's rice; and even of the descendants of the European colonists in the region. Elsewhere in Brazil, the *gaúcho* is thought of as aggressive, boisterous, and belligerent, in contrast to the more courtly, graceful, and retiring Brazilian of the older and more aristocratic regions of the North. In contrast, the southern *gaúcho* thinks of himself as proud, energetic, active, and more productive than the lackadaisical Northerner with his aristocratic airs. The more rapid progress of the South is pointed to as proof of this superiority over the North.

Not all of the South is pampa. Much of it consists of hilly uplands, mountains, and inland plateaus. Curitiba, the capital of Paraná state, is situated on a high plateau about 3,000 feet above sea level. Much of this area was once covered by semideciduous forests, and, at higher altitudes, by pine trees. The

[19] Bezerra dos Santos, "People and Scenes of Brazil," *Revista Brasileira de Geografia* (1945), 137–38.

climate is semitemperate; in the highlands, frosts are common
in the winter and now and again there is a light snowfall. It is
in these areas, vaguely similar to their homelands, that European colonists settled in the nineteenth century. The first influx occurred between 1824 and 1859, when more than 20,000
Germans were settled in forested lands just north of Pôrto

European colonists in southern Brazil

Alegre in Rio Grande do Sul. Beginning in 1850, additional
German groups were settled in the areas of Blumenau and
Joinville in Santa Catarina. Between 1870 and 1890, Italians
began to settle in Rio Grande do Sul, especially in the vicinity
of Caxias. Still later, groups of Poles and Russians formed
colonies in the state of Paraná.

The descendants of these European immigrants have multiplied rapidly—much more rapidly than the Brazilian population of Portuguese descent which surrounds them—and they

have spread out to influence large areas of the South. Despite the relatively small scale of the immigration, it was estimated, just before World War II, that 600,000 people in the state of Rio Grande do Sul, 300,000 in Santa Catarina, and about 126,000 in Paraná, were of German descent. Today, in Paraná, there are probably more than 200,000 people of Polish descent.

The adjustment of these European immigrants and their descendants in southern Brazil contrasts strongly with that of immigrants in other parts of Brazil. It contrasts also with that of the Luso-Brazilian population which they encountered. Most of the immigrants to other regions of Brazil—São Paulo, Espírito Santo, and other states—were initially integrated into the Brazilian economy as sharecroppers and wage earners on large agricultural estates. They encountered a landed aristocracy interested mainly in commercial crops. Even where small farms have come into being in the hands of European immigrants, there is an emphasis upon commercial crops such as coffee, rice, and cotton, and the Japanese have specialized in truck farming to feed the cities. Only in the European colonies of the South has the European mixed-farming system been fully transplanted to Brazil. In these areas, one finds small farms worked by the owner and his family which produce a balanced variety of crops, livestock, and dairy products. The people also churn butter, manufacture cheese, sausages, wine, and candles, bake bread, do carpentry, and tan hides. They use traction animals to pull a plow and, among the Polish colonists especially, to pull a four-wheeled wagon similar to those seen in the rural zones of the United States not too long ago. In keeping with this system of agriculture and with their own traditions, their houses look European. They are made of wood or brick with steep roofs covered with flat tile, and contrast strongly with the adobe walls and straw-thatched roofs of rural Brazilian houses.

This unique adaptation was possible because the colonists to south Brazil entered a regional society which lacked a plantation system, and because they were settled in colonies, often financed by the Brazilian government and often helped by their home governments. They did not come as individual families, to be submerged in the masses of Brazil. This system had its benefits, but it also meant that the European colonists generally lived aloof and isolated from the Luso-Brazilians. They continued to speak their native languages, and created veritable cysts within the Brazilian nation. Brazilian standards of living, Brazilian educational facilities, Brazilian agricultural methods, and all they could see around them offered little incentive for assimilation. In fact they learned to look down on their Brazilian neighbors, who, in turn, looked down their noses at these strangers and their strange customs.

The Germans resisted assimilation most tenaciously. They were proud of their German heritage, their way of life, and their German schools. Before World War II, at least three-fourths of the people living in and around the city of Blumenau spoke German, and it was difficult to communicate in Portuguese. In 1938, the Brazilian government prohibited instruction in any language but Portuguese—a law aimed chiefly at the Germans. During World War II, the Brazilian government closed German clubs and schools, for Nazi propaganda was rife among German-Brazilians. Young men from the South, some of whom spoke Portuguese with difficulty, were required to do their military service in the North where, among the lovely *mulatas*, they learned the national language. The rate of assimilation has naturally increased.

Nowadays, the descendants of Europeans would like to become Brazilians. Their home countries lost out in World War II, and Brazil has changed. Brazilians now have a higher standard of living and are building schools. As late as 1956, there were German schools in Brazil, staffed by German teachers, for the children of German immigrants in Paraná state; such schools were functioning with the connivance of local authorities. They were unlike schools for North American and British children in the big cities, which followed as closely as possible the Brazilian system. These schools taught excellently in German, and their curriculum had nothing to do with Brazil's educational system.

The influence of these Europeans in the South has not been limited to the agricultural zones. Within the last few years, Italians and Germans have developed a wine industry which has expanded from a regional to a national market. European artisans have expanded their small shops into small weaving, metalworking, chemical, and leather industries. In fact Emílio Willems estimates that almost 80 percent of the industrial activities of Rio Grande do Sul and Santa Catarina were developed by people of European immigrant extraction.[20] The presence of these European immigrants has influenced the social structure of the region. The small landholders, the artisans and technicians of German and Italian origin, came to form a middle class, intermediate between the owners of great cattle ranches and the lowly *peões* or cowboys. This middle class was typically European, lacking the disdain for manual labor of the middle-class groups in northern Brazil. As they moved into the urban centers, they took over bureaucratic and administrative posts and broke the political monopoly of the Luso-

[20] Cited in Diegues Junior, *Regiões culturais do Brasil*, p. 352.

Brazilian landed class. Italian and German names are today common in the political life of the South and appear frequently on the national scene. Preston James aptly summed up the influence of the European colonist on southern Brazil when he wrote:

Although the dominant theme of the region is Brazilian, it is a new kind of Brazil set off from the rest of the country by the presence of a considerable number of people who know how to engage in the hard physical work of pioneering in the forests and who are content with the relatively modest profits of an economy which is not speculative.[21]

The Brazilian West

The last of the great cultural regions to be discussed and the last region of Brazil to be occupied and developed is the West. As early as the sixteenth and seventeenth centuries, *bandeirantes* from São Paulo penetrated deep into the Brazilian hinterland, and in the eighteenth century settlements had already been established in Mato Grosso (Cuiabá) and in Goiás, near gold mines. In the seventeenth century, cattle were introduced in Goiás and Mato Grosso and multiplied rapidly, especially in the great *pantanal* (swampland) of southern Mato Grosso. But this does not mean that the Brazilian West was settled. Many of these early settlements either died out or became isolated towns cut off from the rest of Brazil and surrounded by miles and miles of uninhabited lands. Until the era of the airplane, it took literally weeks to reach Cuiabá, the capital of Mato Grosso, by railroad and then by boat up the Paraguay River. The states of Mato Grosso and Goiás account for 22 percent

[21] James, *Latin America*, p. 514.

of the total territory of Brazil, but as late as 1950 they contained only 3.3 percent of its population.

Great parts of the Brazilian West are veritable frontier zones, while others are almost completely uninhabited even today. The territory lying between the Araguaia, Xingú, and Tapajós rivers in the states of Mato Grosso and Pará is even today only partially explored. The Indian tribes of this area are among the few remaining untouched primitives in the world. Several tribes, such as the Chavante and Kayapo, have established peaceful relations with Brazilians only during the last decade. Unknown tribal groups have been discovered, only to disappear again into the vast plains and the deep forests. It is at the headwaters of the Xingú that the Vilas Boas brothers (Cláudio, Orlando, and Leonardo) have carried out their expeditions, discovering and pacifying Indian groups over the last twenty years. The Brazilian government has now set aside a large area as an "Indian Park," both a reservation for Indians and a national game preserve.

A frontier way of life prevails on the fringes of this wild country. Here and there, diamonds and gold are still to be found in riverbeds, and when a new *garimpo* (placer mine) is discovered, a boom town springs up, attracting placer miners, merchants, gamblers, prostitutes, and others. Many parts of the region lie practically outside the effective limits of the Brazilian state. Law and order are maintained by self-styled leaders, such as ranchers or traders, who sometimes take it on themselves to form a posse of their followers to capture an adulterer or murderer. The criminal is seldom delivered alive to legal authorities. I may cite as an example a man I knew, Lúcio da Luz, who lived along the Araguaia River in the early 1940s. *Coronel* Lúcio was wanted for murder upriver in Goiás and downriver in Pará. He lived surrounded by thirty or forty men who worked for him, planting manioc gardens and rounding up his cattle which ran half-wild on open plains. He was the law; on one occasion, when one of his workmen ran off with another's wife, Lúcio sent an armed posse to catch the pair. The following day, the two were found, riddled with bullets, and buried on a beach. By 1955, Lúcio had become a *fazendeiro* (rancher).[22] He had married off one of his daughters by one of his many concubines to a young man from São Paulo. Lúcio, with his son-in-law's help, had laid legal claim to a vast tract of land. His cattle were estimated at "over ten thousand" head, and annually he sent some to market over the trails to the city of Anápolis in Goiás. The charges against him in Goiás and Pará seem to have run out or to have been forgotten. He could travel to the city from time to time. His home, however, still looked like an arsenal, and he and his men normally carried revolvers. Brazilian civilization was penetrating into the region, but slowly.

A distinction needs to be made between the semioccupied land of the West on the one hand, and the frontier and pioneering zones on the other. Vast areas, as stated above, are totally uninhabited or but thinly populated by pastoralists and subsistence agriculturalists. Much of the West has been thus occupied for centuries. The isolation of most of the area is profound, subsistence is difficult, and social services (medicine, education, and the like) are rudimentary or entirely absent. Not all of this area, however, is a pioneer zone. Pioneer zones are found within the area mainly as enclaves, wherever soil conditions, lines of transportation, or planned cities make for

[22] The word *fazenda* refers to any large agricultural property, e.g., a ranch or a plantation.

special circumstances; the pioneer zones of the West are characterized by rapid economic development, rapid immigration, and rapid social change. It is not enough to speak of the expansion of the Brazilian West in general; one must seek out those islands or enclaves which are true frontiers.

One of these frontier areas is western Paraná, where coffee

Main street in Maringá, a southern frontier town

has now arrived from São Paulo state. The prevailing vegetation is dense, subtropical forest which is being rapidly removed to make room for coffee. Unlike the situation on the coffee frontier of earlier times, some of the trees are being cut for lumber rather than merely burned. The land is being sold for medium-sized farms, but the crops are still largely speculative —coffee and cotton. The truck is a crucial instrument in this frontier region, bringing in supplies and even new immigrants and taking out coffee and other products. The land is being sold by government-regulated companies which are required to sell in small parcels; thus, for the present, medium-sized farms seem to predominate. But speculative purchases by landowners who do not occupy their land, and frequent consolidations by resale, may mean that soon the small parcels will be gobbled up by large holders.

This pioneer zone looks like a Hollywood version of our early Midwest. Cities spring up within a few years. Londrina, the principal urban center, is located upon a site that was virgin forest in 1932. It had a population of 33,000 by 1950, and is now well over the 80,000 mark. Maringá, just beyond Londrina in the march of the frontier, received its first settlers in 1945 and by 1960 had over 47,000 people. In these centers, miles of streets are laid out through seas of mud which in a few years are transformed into paved streets. Maringá was planned to contain eventually 100,000 people. Its main street is five miles long, and in 1953 it had an ultramodern movie house seating 1,800 which was filled to capacity every night. There were sixteen banks and, indicative of the breaking of traditional Brazilian patterns, there were churches of eight different and highly competitive evangelical Protestant sects, plus the usual Catholic cathedral and a Buddhist temple for the Japanese. Many of the structures were temporary, for example, a wooden barrack served as a hospital. A hospital, it was explained, was very necessary, for each night victims of knife and gun fights were brought in. The main street had cafes that were so similar in appearance to those of our Old West that one expected Gary Cooper to swagger out the door, or to shoot it out with Billy the Kid. Buses and trucks were much in evidence, bringing people mainly from northeastern Brazil.

Less dramatic than the western Paraná area are the pioneer zones to the north. One of these is southern Mato Grosso. Traditionally, this was an area where cattle were grazed on un-fenced ranges. During the last twenty years, the railroad from São Paulo has been extended through the area to Campo Grande, to Corumbá on the Paraguay River, and on to Santa Cruz and La Paz in Bolivia. With transportation came people and an expansion of grazing and agriculture. Mines of iron ore and manganese were exploited. Campo Grande became a lead-ing commercial town of over 65,000 people (1960), and Corumbá grew from a sleepy town on the riverbanks to a shipping and commercial center of the Brazilian Chaco and a gateway to Bolivia with over 38,000 people (1960).

Likewise, there is a pioneer zone in Goiás, especially north and west of Anápolis. Some 50,000 people migrated into this region between 1940 and 1950.[23] According to Preston James, this pioneer zone of Goiás has not been too successful, for after the forests were cleared and the land cultivated, soil erosion was so great that the crop yields declined abruptly. Some farmers then rented their land for cattle grazing and departed. Yet migrants continue to arrive and to occupy the remaining areas of relatively good soil. One of the problems of this northern part of the West relates to the soil. Most of the land which has been occupied in the Western pioneer move-ment was formerly covered by forests, and this land is generally fertile until the primitive crop system robs it of its essential elements. But much of the West is what is called *campo cerrado*, a plains country covered with low scrub vegetation. There is considerable difference of opinion as to the agricultural and grazing potentials of such lands, but it is quite clear that this region is far from being another Great Plains of the United

[23] James, *Latin America*, p. 534.

States. The ultimate fate of the *campo cerrado* of the Brazilian West involves a dilemma similar to that of the Amazon Valley. With technical innovations and sufficient capital, the *campo cerrado* could certainly be made productive. On the other hand, there is a question of investment priorities. Preston James has summed up the situation very succinctly:

> If modern agricultural methods can be used to transform these lands into productive farms, or even if improved pastures could be developed on them, a large new resource base would be made available. . . . [But]—even if modern agricultural methods could be successfully applied to the campo cerrado, there is the question whether the same amount of capital and human effort applied to the wornout lands close to the big cities might not prove vastly more worthwhile.[24]

Brazilians do not follow his logic. In fact, Brazil is now highly committed to the development of the West. It is in the West, in the midst of *campo cerrado*, that they have built their new national capital of Brasília. The very presence of Brasília in the West changes the whole picture. Since the establishment of the Republic in 1889, a section in each successive constitution has authorized the establishment of a national capital on the plateau of Goiás. For many years, maps of Brazil have shown a square in this heartland labeled "Future Federal District," but President Juscelino Kubitschek turned the law and the vague plans into reality. On April 21, 1960, the federal capital was formally moved to Brasília—a city constructed in the wilderness in three years, and now containing more than 100,000 people. There is considerable argument in Brazil as to the wisdom of this great effort. The cost upset the Brazilian economy. Deputies and senators still refuse to live there, and

[24] *Ibid.*, p. 535 f.

absenteeism is so high that a quorum is often not possible in either house of legislation. But Brasília has changed the complexion of the Brazilian West, and of all Brazil, in many ways.

First, there is the city itself, planned by Brazilian architects according to the most daring tenets of their trade. The city plan was drawn by the Brazilian architect Lúcio Costa. The

Alvorada Palace in Brasília

scheme has the outline of a great airplane. A residential axis (the wings) extends on either side of a monumental axis (the fuselage) where the public buildings are located. The city is planned to hold ultimately half a million people. It lies about 4,000 feet above sea level. There is a large artificial lake providing water for the city, and, one hopes, helping employees to assuage their nostalgia for sea beaches. In Brasília, people live in "super-blocks." Each super-block will have a school, a supermarket, a health center, and a social club with a swimming pool and playground. Many of these super-blocks have been built, and the public services are in the process of being installed, for Brasília will be a long time a-building. A new university, the University of Brasília, was founded in 1962. The plans for this new center of higher education, which began to function in April of 1962, indicate that it may be Brazil's outstanding university and research center in years to come. The public buildings which house the ministries, high courts, and houses of legislation, as well as most of the other buildings in Brasília, were designed by Oscar Niemeyer, one of the architects responsible for the United Nations building in New York City. His undisputed talents have been indulged on a lavish and probably unprecedented scale, but his version of modern architecture can be monotonous, and to a layman it seems notably lacking in consideration of detail. One wonders whether the buildings in Brasília would have space for the employees of the various ministries if they ever really transferred all of their activities there. Brasília will soon be one of the most beautiful and daring modern cities in the world, but there are a minority of Brazilians who regard the move as a waste of capital that might have been used more effectively for the development of their country.

On the other hand, Brasília stands as a monument to Brazilian enterprise and capacity to produce; Brazilians are proud of what has been achieved in so little time. To complete the move of the capital by April of 1960, roads were built with remarkable speed, providing communications from Brasília to Anápolis and Goiânia in Goiás state, and from there to São Paulo; from Brasília to Belo Horizonte; from Brasília to Belém at the mouth of the Amazon River; and from Brasília to the distant state of Acre on the Bolivian boundary. Telephones were connected both locally and by long-distance microwave with other parts of the country. Railroads are being pushed on to Brasília. This new system of communications in itself has changed the map of western Brazil. And, as one might suspect, there is a land boom not only near Brasília, but along the new ways of communication.

To build the city, concrete, some of which was flown inland from the coast, was poured at night. Thousands of workers, mainly from the arid Northeast, came to Brasília looking for employment. They went to live in a kind of shanty town two or three kilometers outside Brasília which has come to be known as the Free City (officially it was called the *Núcleo Bandeirante*) and which is as unplanned and confusing as Brasília is planned and orderly. The Free City was allowed to grow as a temporary workers' camp to be torn down in a few years, but it may have become a permanent fixture. People from the Northeast continue to flow into the area looking for work, although the tempo of construction has slowed down. The Free City is the unplanned slum containing all those things that city planners tend to forget in their utopian dreams.

The building of Brasília has not been without its scandals: there have been several investigations of Novacap (Company of Urbanization of the New Capital of Brazil), and many well-known names have been involved. They were accused of getting rich through building contracts. But Brasília is growing and is acquiring self-consciousness as a community. The inhabitants of Brasília are now called *candangos*. *Candango*, said to be originally a Bantu word used by African natives for the Portuguese colonists, was used in Brasília to designate the Northeastern laborer who came looking for work. It is now

7

(7

211

used with pride by those who make this new city their home, for there are many public employees who are happy to live in Brasília, where they do not suffer from transportation problems, find schools for their children, live in apartments with low rents (subsidized by the government) in which water and electricity are plentiful, and lead quiet lives far from the agitation of Rio de Janeiro. Brasília has made Brazil aware that civilization need not be but a crust on the coast, and has opened a new era for what was but a few years ago the Wild West.

❧3❧ SOCIAL CLASSES

THE unity of Brazilian national culture is broken in each local community by the existence of well-defined social and economic classes. In each cultural region of Brazil, there are differences in speech, dress, etiquette, and custom, deriving from differences in social class. Differences in behavior are often determined more by social class than by regional factors; the upper classes of the extreme North and the extreme South share more behavior traits with each other than they do with the low-class *caboclos* (rural peasants) or *peões*, respectively. In fact, it is generally in the folkways, in the behavior of the rural and even urban lower class, that regionalism is felt most strongly. The influence of ecology, major crops and industries, folk traditions, and regional events is exerted mostly on the *povo* (people), as the various lower-class segments are universally called. The middle and upper classes share national ideal patterns of how one ought to behave in any given circumstance, and they share what I have called the Great Tradition or written tradition inherited from Europe. But the distance is great between the *povo* and the middle and upper classes in any region of Brazil, and to understand the country one must understand something of this diversity resulting from social classes.

It is not easy for North Americans to understand the Brazilian class system. In the United States, we live according to what has been called an open class system. The position of an individual or a family in a highly competitive prestige system depends mainly upon income, education, dress, tastes, and housing. These material factors, however, are rather easily modified in our highly mobile society. Within one generation, all of these attributes may be changed, for better or for worse. In Brazil, membership in a social class is determined by these same material factors, but until very recently Brazil was a highly stable society and people were seldom able to change their circumstances. The son of a poor man was poor and the son of an illiterate remained illiterate; thus membership in a social class was, in a sense, hereditary. People were very conscious of family as a criterion for placing an individual in his proper class, and they tended to marry within their own class, thus perpetuating class solidarity.

In sociological parlance, the traditional Brazilian class hierarchy was a two-class system, weighted heavily at the extremes and with few intermediary positions. Upward mobility has always been difficult. Even today, in most Brazilian communities, the man with a clean suit, a white shirt, and a shine on his shoes is a man who has been to high school, has servants in his home, does not engage in manual labor, and comes from a family which has belonged to the upper or middle class for several generations. Likewise, a man who is badly dressed and performs manual labor is illiterate and belongs to a family that has always been lower class. Brazilians are expert at discovering the class of any stranger in their midst—they ask about his family, watch for signs of deference to the upper class, and take notice of his dress and speech. They are often confused by North Americans—a man may dress well, have a

high school diploma, and earn a high salary, all of which are
high-status attributes, and yet drive a tractor, which automatically places him in the lower class.

Thus, it might be said that traditionally there were only two
social classes in Brazil: an upper class consisting of landowners,
merchants, professionals, government officials, and bureaucrats,
and a lower class of manual laborers and artisans. The upper
class consisted of patrões (employers), while the lower class
included their extrafamilial dependents—household servants,
field hands, sharecroppers, and other employees. This two-class
system is not entirely a thing of the past, but, as indicated
above, most Brazilians still fall into one of the two traditional
hierarchical categories. This is particularly true of small communities and even of the great cities in the more traditional
North Brazil. Perhaps there has always been a relatively small
group in Brazil who might be called middle class, particularly
in the South where European patterns are strongest, but as I
shall discuss later the development of a large middle class is
something new for Brazilian society.

All observers of the Brazilian scene since World War II agree
that the traditional Brazilian class structure is changing in a
significant and fairly rapid fashion. To me, the direction of
change is quite clear. New social sectors and even a new
social class are appearing, and the quality of the relationships
among all classes is being affected by the growth of impersonal,
large-scale, industrial forms of wage employment, and by the
exigencies of a mass society. Brazil is no longer a stable society
without social or economic mobility, but a highly dynamic
society in a state of rapid flux. The traditional lower class is
splitting into an agricultural peasantry, a new factory in the
field proletariat, and a rapidly expanding metropolitan lower

class which includes industrial workers. A new metropolitan upper class whose power stems from the ownership of industrial plants and commercial enterprises is taking the place of the traditional elite. A new middle class consisting of salaried professionals and white-collar workers is appearing, particularly in the large cities. These changes seem to have gained momentum during the last decade or so. To understand their significance on the Brazilian scene, however, one must understand the traditional patterns they are affecting.

The traditional upper class

At the turn of the century, Brazil was clearly a stable, if somewhat isolated society. Slavery had just been abolished and the monarchy had been replaced by the republic. Throughout Brazil, a group of "traditional families" gradually supplanted the nobility and the landed gentry of the empire and came to dominate the country's economic, political, and social life. To a large extent, they carried on the aristocratic traditions of the empire and preserved the paternalistic attitude of the old upper class toward the lower classes. Some of these traditional families were descendants of the nobility of the empire—Baron Taubaté, Baron Rio Branco, and a hundred other titles handed out by the emperor to one generation. Other families achieved prominence after the advent of the republic through newly acquired wealth or political position. By the turn of the century, both groups had fused through intermarriage into a clearly defined upper class into which admission was difficult, though of course not impossible. Members of this traditional upper class could list the names of those who belonged to it, not only in their own region but in other parts of the country as well. The genealogies and family connections of friends were known and recounted. Membership in one of these good families was often an indispensable prerequisite to economic, professional, political, or social success. Although I have used the past tense, this group is not extinct; such traditional families are still important in Brazil. Their names continue to appear in high business circles, in political and public life, in the diplomatic corps, and in the intellectual life of the country. The members of these families can still list the important names, and they are still genealogical experts.

Although often highly patriotic and public-spirited, members of this traditional upper class suffered from what the Brazilian writer Viana Moog has called *mozambismo*, that is, a tendency to deprecate everything Brazilian and to look with almost worshipful eyes toward Europe, especially France. They were all highly literate, often poets, and writers of florid prose. They lived in mild but polished luxury with many servants. Their children went to private schools—to Sacré Coeur and Notre Dame de Sion for girls, or Santo Inácio (Jesuit) for boys. They read French magazines and novels and they followed Brazilian literature. They traveled more than most people of equivalent income in other parts of the world, for they felt that Brazil was isolated, and they sent their children abroad to study and above all to learn foreign languages, especially French, which was their second language. They valued traditional Brazilian customs and ceremonies, such as Carnival and St. John's Eve, but stood somewhat apart from them. This class valued a stable and closed society in which their privileges and special rights were guaranteed. Indeed, the educational system of Brazil reflects to this day the aristocratic and European values of the traditional upper class. Brazil's secondary schools and universities are patterned after the classical tradition of France and are aimed at training a small elite.

In discussing the traditional Brazilian upper class, one must distinguish between the social scene as seen by an impartial observer from the outside, as seen by one of the good families of a large city, or as seen by the inhabitants of a small town or provincial city. Each small town and provincial city has its traditional upper class made up of landowners, bureaucrats, and merchants who constitute the elite in terms of the local hierarchy. This local upper class is among the most important social sectors in the nation. Its members control the rural vote and economic life of the masses of rural people. They share the social values of the national elite, avoid any form of physical work, and in their home town make the most money and enjoy considerable leisure. They own an abundance of clothing, including such items as raincoats, sweaters, nylon underclothing, and umbrellas; they live in big houses, have a separate bed for each child, and maintain servants to cook, wash, and carry water; they own radios, horses, or cars, and most of them have traveled and are familiar with the life of the big cities. In many regions the identity of the local upper class remains constant throughout a large number of small communities; that is, the elite is made up of the same families, interrelated by marriage, over a wide area.

Nowadays, however, the relations of this local upper class with the metropolitan elite vary more widely. From the point of view of an objective observer, it is the metropolitan upper class that now constitutes the true national elite. In some cases, the local and the metropolitan upper class are still one and the same: the sugar and cacao *fazendeiros* of Bahia and Pernambuco, the coffee planters of São Paulo, and the rich ranchers of

Rio Grande do Sul move with ease between their estates and their fine houses or luxury apartments in Recife, Salvador, São Paulo, or Pôrto Alegre.

⸕ Local elites from marginal or depressed economic areas, however, today find themselves in an anomalous situation when they travel to the metropolitan centers. Many local celebrities who command the allegiance of scores of *agregados* (squatters who pay some sort of labor service to the owners), and who are treated with an elaborate display of respect wherever they go in their rural community, can only afford to stay in a second-class *pensão* (boardinghouse) when they visit the metropolis, and are utterly cut off from the social milieu of the metropolitan upper class. Their plight is indicative of the vast gulf which has opened up between the standards of material consumption which denote luxurious living in the backward rural areas and those of the modern metropolis. With the exception of families who derive their income from commercial export crops under boom conditions, it is becoming increasingly difficult for Brazil's rural elite to live according to the highest national standards, which call for the large-scale consumption of expensive "São Paulo-made" products and services, in the face of the dizzy upward spiral of wages and prices.

The plight of members of the local elite, who turn out to be "small fish" when they swim into the "big pond," reflects the process which has been shifting the locus of Brazil's socio-economic power from the paternalistic landed gentry to the owners and managers of impersonal industrial corporations. But the Brazilian landed gentry are not disappearing; their influence has simply paled in comparison with the wealth and power which can now be obtained through other means. Many of them have become industrialists, politicians, and successful businessmen in Rio de Janeiro and São Paulo. They have married their daughters to the new rich and maintained their aristocratic standards. While the rural upper class occupies an intermediate position in terms of wealth and sociopolitical power, it is not part of the middle class. Even though its members may appear shabby today in a metropolitan context, back home in their own communities they are regarded by the lower class as immensely wealthy and powerful figures.

The traditional lower class

The great majority of Brazilians have always belonged to the lower-class rural groups. They are generally illiterate and in some way dependent upon the upper class. They earn their living as workers on cane fields and coffee plantations, cowboys on the pampas of the South and the ranches of the Northeast, rubber collectors in the Amazon Valley, sharecroppers on large estates, squatters living by subsistence agriculture on other people's land, renters of land, and even sometimes small peasant owners. Except perhaps among the small landholders in southern Brazil, the standard of living of this rural lower class is miserably low. Fresh meat and bread are luxuries; they consume manioc flour, sometimes flavored with a few beans, dried beef, or salted fish. Many actually live in semistarvation. It is to this large rural lower class (and even its counterpart in the cities) that hurried shipments of beans, wheat, powdered milk, and other surplus foods have been sent from the United States as part of the Food for Peace program. Especially in northern Brazil, this chronic hunger is part of the Brazilian scene.

For most of this rural lower class, economic security and

social well-being are conceived as flowing from the paternal ministrations of the local elite. Everyone should have a *patrão*. Essentially, this *patrão*-worker relationship was, and still is in many localities, an economic relationship between employer and worker, landlord and tenant, or creditor and debtor. It was also highly exploitative, for the wages of the lower classes, however paid, were notoriously low. Yet the traditional *patrão*-worker relationship was something more than an economic bond. It involved a sense of *noblesse oblige* and paternalism on the part of the employer, a survival from the times of slavery and the monarchy. On the part of the worker, it involved a sense of loyalty to the *patrão* and, needless to say, political support, if and when the worker could vote.

A *patrão* was not always an actual employer. Land-holding peasants might be tied to a storekeeper through debts or past favors. Frequently the local political boss, the *coronel* (similar to a Kentucky Colonel) was a sort of *patrão* to his followers, who had received favors and expected future favors. A lower-class worker without a *patrão* of one kind or another was a man without a protector in time of need. The *patrão* provided some measure of social security—generally the only form available to the worker. This relationship could be a highly intimate one where the upper-class *patrão* and the lower-class dependent had close, warm ties and treated each other as individuals, not as members of a different group. Sometimes the lower-class individual, long after he had left the employment or the land of his upper-class *patrão*, returned to seek advice, favors, or new employment.

This "*patrão* complex" is not a thing of the past. It is still the basic form of relationship between people of different social classes in most of the communities of northern Brazil, and it is far from extinct in São Paulo and even in the extreme South. A study of a family-owned plantation in the Recôncavo region of Bahia, carried out a few years ago, showed this *patrão* complex in almost pristine traditional form. On this plantation the owners were clearly members of the old traditional upper class, descendants of the sugar nobility of slavery times. Most of the permanent workers had been born there or on neighboring plantations.

The workers were paid in cash, and their relationship with the owner was basically that of employee to employer. Yet, at the same time, this relationship had paternalistic, highly personal overtones, and was often based upon a lifetime of close acquaintance. When the plantation owner returned from a stay in the city, he came loaded down with small purchases requested by the workers. The workers' wives called upon the wife of the *fazendeiro*, or plantation owner, on her return. They were not asked to sit down, for a rigid barrier of social class was maintained, but the lady of the house asked after their children, each of whom she generally knew by name. They in turn inquired about her relatives who lived in the city or about her children who were away at school. The owners were *compadres* to several of the workers, that is, they had stood as ritual sponsors to some of their children at baptism; as elsewhere in Latin America, this ritual kinship involves a series of mutual obligations and rights between two couples— the godparents of the child and the child's own parents. On his own birthday, and on Christmas Eve, the plantation owner organized a festival for the workers on his plantation. Under these patriarchal conditions, it was rare for a worker to leave a plantation and seek work elsewhere.[1]

[1] H. W. Hutchinson, *Village and Plantation Life in Northeastern Brazil*, especially pp. 57–62.

Another highly traditional form of the *patrão* complex is that which exists between the rubber gatherers and small subsistence farmers and the local trader in the Amazon Valley. The economic bond based upon the extension of credit by the trader to his customer-debtors has been mentioned in my description of the Amazon Valley as a region. But, as usual, the relationship between the *patrão*-trader and customer-collector extends beyond the strictly economic sphere.

The people attached to a particular trading post often form a neighborhood within which there is mutual help and constant visiting. While such families are in perpetual debt to the trader, they are also tied to him in other ways. Often the trader and his wife are their *compadres* in the same way that the plantation owner described above was the *compadre* of his field hands. Generally, the rubber gatherer owes past debts to his *patrão* and *compadre*. Perhaps the trader has continued credit advances in a year when the collector of wild rubber was ill. Perhaps the trader sent a sick member of the collector's family on the river boat that comes to load rubber and restock the trading post. The regular trading day is also a day of social intercourse, when the men drink and the women gossip in the building that serves at once as a home for the trader, as his store, and as a social center. Likewise, on the trader's birthday, on a saint's day, or on election day, dances and festivals are held at the trading post. The trader-collector relationship is not merely an economic bond; in the Amazon Valley, if a trader's collector-customer succeeds in paying off his debts and takes his produce elsewhere, the trader is apt to regard this as an act of personal disloyalty.

These lower-class rural Brazilians, who are called by a variety of names depending on the region, such as *caboclos* (in the Amazon and generally), *tabaréus* (in Bahia), and *jecas* (in São Paulo), almost universally seek a stable *patrão* relationship, whether in the rubber forests of the Amazon, the coffee plantations of São Paulo or Paraná, the cattle ranches of the pampas or the dry Northeast, or the maté forests of southern Mato Grosso. Yet they are but loosely attached to the soil and are often seminomadic. The lack of land, the periodic droughts, and the general poverty of the region keep forcing these Brazilians out of the Northeast. They move seasonally from the arid *sertão* to the sugar-cane coastal strip, looking for harvest work. They go to the coffee *fazendas* of São Paulo and to the cities of the South seeking employment, and often return after a year or more. Often they simply move about their own region, vaguely hoping to improve their lot and to acquire a better *patrão*. People are attracted by such 'boom crops' as *babassu* nuts and Brazil nuts; they also seek out localities where large building projects might provide employment, such as Brasília or the Paulo Afonso hydroelectric plant. This is not just "local milling around," to use T. Lynn Smith's words,[2] but mostly internal migration resulting from downright poverty in the rural zones. It is not a new phenomenon on the Brazilian scene, as shown by accounts of nineteenth-century travelers such as Herbert H. Smith, Ferdinand Denis, and Auguste de Saint-Hilaire. .

Today spatial mobility is greater than ever before. It is spurred by the development of the southern part of the country, by the many construction schemes tied to economic development such as the Três Marias hydroelectric project in Minas Gerais, and by the rapid construction of private housing in all the big cities of Brazil. Trucks, buses, and new roads

[2] T. L. Smith, *Brazil: People and Institutions*, p. 257.

provide facilities for migration never before available. A common sight on the roads of northern Brazil is the truck called *pau de arara* (parrot's perch), a vehicle with narrow benches which may transport from forty to sixty people, on its way over a thousand miles of dirt roads to Rio de Janeiro or São Paulo. Carrying men, women, and children, these trucks sometimes overturn and the fatalities are numerous. Such accidents seldom make the front pages of the newspapers. Higher in economic and social status are the buses which travel from Recife, Fortaleza, João Pessoa, and Bahia to Rio de Janeiro and São Paulo; few rural workers can afford the fare (about $18 from Recife to São Paulo) for the six-day trip. Perhaps over 200,000 people migrate each year from the Northeast to São Paulo state, and the numbers that move about locally to the coastal cities and to centers of construction must be almost as large.

The traditional *patrão* system of the hinterland has not been strong enough to tie *caboclos* to the land. Brazilians talk fervently and urgently about land reform, and a motion to this end has been placed before the legislature. Brazilians hope thus to relate rural Brazilians to the land and to increase production, but there is tremendous opposition among the landholding class and little real agreement among the proponents of land reform as to exactly how it is to be carried out. For the moment, the rural Brazilian lower classes stand in a state of limbo, rather than ferment, between the stagnation of the old *patrão* system and the rapid development of the nation.

The rural proletariat

Brazil has always had an economy based primarily on cash crops and commercial plantations. Only in the last two decades or so have there been large mechanized plantations, and even today it is doubtful whether Brazilian plantations are as large and as mechanized as those of Puerto Rico, Cuba, or the Far East. On the large sugar plantations and in the sugar mills of São Paulo, Bahia, and Pernambuco, on the large coffee plantations of São Paulo and Paraná, and on a few large cacao plantations in southern Bahia, the workers form a new segment of the Brazilian population which I shall call "rural proletariat," to use the term coined by Sidney Mintz in his studies of Puerto Rico.[3] They are wage workers in a modern sense, and no longer have a *patrão*. They are employees of an impersonal corporation, and their immediate supervisors are hired administrators. It is true that the shareholders of many of these corporations are relatives, and that corporations sometimes are but family affairs. Still, the corporation must be run strictly on a business basis, and there is little possibility of continuing the traditional *patrão*-worker relationships.

In the study cited earlier, Harry W. Hutchinson describes the transition from the old order to the new on a sugar plantation in the state of Bahia, for this process of change could be observed during his stay. He writes:

These two new managers [employed by the corporation] have put the relations between management and labor on a strictly business basis and have removed all elements of paternalism. Upon taking over, they dismissed most of the older, higher-level factory, field, and office workers. Administrators, mechanics, and bookkeepers, most of whom had twenty years or more of service, were dispatched. New people came to take their places and some of the vacancies were filled by promotions. Time clocks were installed, and the new system of authority was reinforced all the way down the line. Social

[3] Sidney Mintz, "The Culture History of a Puerto Rican Cane Plantation, 1876–1949," *Hispanic American Historical Review* (1953), 224–51.

legislation—a new factor in rural, agricultural Brazil—was invoked to take the place of paternalism.[4]

The workers on these modern agricultural establishments are more numerous and more heterogeneous than on the smaller, traditional, family-owned plantations. The field hands, the overseers, the office workers, and even the executives no longer form a closely knit neighborhood where each knows his position in the hierarchy. They come from many different places and they frequently move on after a while to seek work elsewhere.

These large plantations are generally closely integrated into the national marketing system. By necessity they must have transportation and communication facilities linking them to the ports and the metropolitan centers. The workers' houses are generally provided by the company, and the settlement takes the form of a company town; there are stores, a school, a chapel or church, and usually a soccer field and a club as well. Often there is electricity and a water-supply system. The corporation generally supplies medical assistance through a clinic or a small hospital. The workers are protected by social legislation, at least in theory, and labor unions are active. Many of these workers are recent migrants from distant rural zones and many are illiterate. They hardly know how to cope with this new impersonal world and its many regulations. They no longer have a protective, though exploitative *patrão*. They must depend on politicians and labor leaders for help in securing their rights. They are vulnerable to charismatic leaders, even demagogues, who promise protection in an impersonal world. It is not surprising, therefore, that the Peasant Leagues

[4] H. W. Hutchinson, *Village and Plantation Life in Northeastern Brazil*, p. 180.

and other movements are rife in the sugar-producing zone of the Northeast, but not in the deep backlands. It is this coastal segment of the rural population that has broken most sharply with the traditional institutions while failing to evolve new ways of coping with the society that is taking form.

The urban lower class

The same kind of stirring, but certainly of a more intense sort, is characteristic of members of the lower class who break away from the two-class system of the rural zones and move into the cities. Brazilian cities have been growing at a much faster rate than the total population of the country, and the urban trend is almost frightening, so fast are the slums growing. During the last twenty years, migrants of all classes from the rural zones have filled the cities. The great ambition of all small-town youths has been to move to the metropolis where life is more stimulating and there is greater economic opportunity. The majority of rural migrants to the cities belong to the lower class, however, and continue to do manual labor. Many have come from great distances, most often from the arid Northeast, directly to Rio de Janeiro or São Paulo. Single males may go straight into construction work and live in the skeletons of the very structures they are helping to build. At night they sleep in hammocks as they did at home, and often they cook their meals over open fires in the reinforced concrete structures. Whole families also migrate from distant areas, but more often from nearby rural zones. As nearby rural inhabitants move into the city, their places are often filled by migrants from more distant regions. Thus, migration to the cities takes place by steps, rather than all at once.[5] Nevertheless, these migrants bring their rural way of life into the city, for studies of small communities relatively close to Rio de Janeiro and São Paulo reveal an outlook as rustic and rural as that of communities in the deep interior.[6]

It seems clear that the members of this enormously swollen urban lower class do not form an urban proletariat in the European sense of holding urban values and being born and bred to the city. They are like peasants living in an urban center. Many of them live with a false dream of someday returning to their small town or farm after they have saved enough money—and many do return, but not with the savings they had expected. Others remain and acquire a veneer of urbanity and a taste for city things. They are paid poorly by North American or European standards, but sometimes they earn three or four times more than in the rural zones.[7] Furthermore, they have steady work instead of the intermittent employment which is generally all they can find at home, and in the city it is easier for women to find work. Many of these rural migrants can buy radios, alarm clocks, phonographs, wrist watches, nylon hose, and other commodities which are symbols of the good life at home. They can look forward to an occasional movie, the parade on Independence Day, soccer games, and the excitement of Carnival. The city has above all *movimento* (motion or activity), something all rural Brazilians yearn for.

The city also has misery, dirt, and crime. The great metropolitan centers are foci for all the pressures deriving from inflation. Food prices are exceedingly high relative to wages, and

[5] See Unzer de Almeida and Mendes Sobrinho, *Migração rural-urbana.*
[6] See Willems, *Cunha: tradição e transição em uma cultura rural do Brasil;* Pierson, *Cruz das Almas: A Brazilian Village.*
[7] Lambert, *Os dois Brasís,* p. 44.

Backyard in the Favela do Esqueleto, Rio de Janeiro

housing is perhaps the most inflated of all economic items. Some migrants find housing in the remote suburbs, sometimes two hours away from their work by decrepit buses or trains. Many end up in shanty towns—*favelas* as they are called in Rio or *invasões* as they are called in Bahia. All Brazilian cities have miles of such shanty towns in one form or another, as do most Latin American, African, and Asian cities.

The *favelas* of beautiful Rio de Janeiro are perhaps best known. All told, over 650,000 people are said to live there. These *favelas* consist of a jumble of rude shacks made of wood, cardboard, scrap metal, and other odd bits of materials. They are crowded together, sometimes only a few feet apart, on the steep hillsides which rise above the city. Sometimes the view is beautiful, as indicated by the scenes from the movie "Black Orpheus," which was filmed in Rio. The shacks are often perched most precariously on steep slopes, supported by fragile wooden piles; sometimes, in a heavy tropical rainstorm, several come tumbling down, killing the inhabitants. The alleyways between the shacks are, of course, unpaved, and the houses follow no regular order. Sewers are totally lacking, and the only way to dispose of human waste and garbage is a copious rainfall. These *favelas*, of course, emit an overpowering stench, especially during the dry periods, which plagues not only the *favelados* (residents of the *favelas*), but also those who live nearby in what are often fashionable neighborhoods. *Favelas* also lack a public water supply, except at a few points where the city may have set up a public fountain or where the *favelados* may have opened up a fire plug of their own accord. In Rio, a common sight is that of women and children carrying water up the steep hillside in kerosene tins, an onerous task that keeps them busy several hours a day.

There is no public illumination in the *favelas*. Oddly enough, however, many houses have electricity—a few weak bulbs, radios, and even television sets. The electricity is obtained from enterprising subcontractors. These subcontractors string wires from their own homes near the edge of the settlement to the shacks of their clients, who pay them a rate said to be several times that of the light company. A similar group of entrepreneurs provide postal service. Since the houses in the *favelas* have no legal addresses, the inhabitants have their mail delivered to an individual, usually a small shopkeeper, whose existence is recognized by the post office and who charges them for the service. One of the most remarkable features of these *favelas* is the large number of small shops, reminiscent in many ways of similar establishments which abound in the small towns of the backlands. These shops are generally unlicensed and have no access to wholesalers. Instead, they buy from retail stores and street markets and then resell at higher prices to their customers. These buy from the *favela* shops because credit is extended to them on a weekly or even monthly basis, and because they feel more at ease dealing with the local shopkeeper, who is often a *favelado* too.

Life in a *favela* follows that of a closely knit neighborhood. Some time ago, middle- and upper-class Brazil was shocked by the description of *favela* life provided in a book called *Child of the Dark (Quarto de Despejo)*[8] by Carolina Maria de Jesus, a woman who raised three children in a São Paulo shanty town. The public was also charmed by her elegant prose, and the book became a best seller. She describes the gossip concerning the "private lives" (nothing can be private in a *favela*) of the neighbors, the criminals who are harbored in the *favela*, the local leaders, and above all the constant battle for enough to eat. Carolina herself made a living collecting and selling old newspapers, rags, and the like. She and her children often went on scavenging expeditions for food; she was very angry with a butcher shopkeeper who threw poison on the scraps and old bones in his

[8] Literally, "garbage dump."

garbage to cut down on flies, for this had been one source of food for her family. Carolina, like many *favela* women, was without a husband; she had had several lovers by whom she had several children, but in such precarious economic conditions men are apt to be unstable and transient. Carolina was very critical of the loose sexual life around her and of women she called prostitutes. She was unhappy about the immoral language which her children heard. She was not a popular neighbor, and on the day her book was published, her neighbors threw stones at her as she regally moved out of the *favela*.

Such *favelas* come to be established in a characteristic manner throughout Brazil. They begin with an invasion (hence their name, *invasão*, in Bahia); a number of squatters suddenly occupy a piece of vacant property, which for one reason or another is of low value but lies within the city. In Rio, for example, the hillsides had no water or sewers, and in Bahia the valleys were hot and full of mosquitoes, so the invasions took place on the hills of Rio and in the valleys of Bahia. Such invasions generally take place at night and are well organized. A landowner awakes one morning to find several shacks on his property. To dispossess the inhabitants of the shacks he must enter into litigation. Brazilian law holds that squatters can be evicted only if they are compensated for the "improvements" they have made. Meanwhile, more shacks are built. The case lingers in court, and the bill of indemnities grows. Some landowners give up soon and lease the land to the invaders, who promptly put up more shacks which they sublease to additional builders.

Often politics enters the picture. A local politician looking for support suggests that the city expropriate the land and divide it among the invaders. The owner is apt to agree—at least with his upper-class *pistolão* (literally "pistol," but meaning "pull") he can get a high evaluation for his land. When this happens a hillside or a valley may become covered with hundreds of shacks within a period of months. According to Andrew Pearse, the Rio de Janeiro *favela* called "Skeleton" (*O Esqueleto,* named after the skeleton of an unfinished hospital at its center) had its beginning in the early 1940s. By 1948, it had 5,732 inhabitants. In 1956, on the basis of an aerial survey, its 75,000 square meters were judged to contain 25,000 people.[9] As such *favelas* become permanent parts of the great cities, a further step is taken. The residents begin to improve their property and to build more permanent dwellings. This is especially noticeable in Bahia, where shacks are turned into adobe houses; next, a painted façade is added, and then the municipality paves the streets and allows electricity and other services to be brought to the area. Finally, the *invasão* that was a slum becomes a permanent residential district for the better-off members of the city's lower class.

This greatly expanded urban lower class has its own subculture, sharply set off from the world of modern apartments, up-to-date commerce, universities, and car-lined avenues that surrounds them. It is a subculture that is essentially rural— many of its members keep chickens and pigs. Social institutions such as the *patrão* complex with its highly personal paternalism have disappeared. Members of the lower class live in the impersonal city without the kinsmen and lifelong friends of their rural neighborhood and without upper-class protectors. They hardly understand the city and modern mass society; they

[9] Pearse, "Integração social das famílias de favelados," *Educação e Ciências Sociais,* II, No. 6 (1957).

are bewildered by the complexities of bureaucracy. Now they must get help through Brazil's well-conceived but badly applied labor code, from the labor union, or from the inspector of the Ministry of Labor. This class is as yet remarkably free of concepts implanted by the extreme left. They are Catholics easily influenced by the Church. They are traditional Brazilians who are for the time being relatively mild and passive, but they might easily learn to be violent. They are vulnerable to any new and hopeful set of political promises. They are illiterate, hungry, and sick, and they can see all about them luxury and ostentation.

It would be foolhardy to think that the glamor of the metropolis and the pleasures of a transistor radio will long continue to compensate for the privations of life in a *favela*. Second-generation *favelados* not only lack the sense of discovery and adventure of their rural-born parents, but they are fast acquiring new and expanded standards of material expectations. There are generally no schools in the *favelas*, but a number of children attend schools on the fringes, thus creating a problem for educators. Many learn to read and write. Others are not in school and, in any case, a school session takes up only three or four hours out of the day. These children are thus "on the loose," subject to all the possibilities of crime and vice. Although the *favelas* are the object of missionary and charitable efforts and aid programs financed by the state, municipal, and even federal governments, the basic instability of the Brazilian economy remains and, until this is corrected, more *favelas* will arise than these well-meaning projects can ever cope with.

The new middle class

Since the early nineteenth century, Brazil has had a small group of people who might be classified as middle class. These were originally the families of men who were clerks in government offices or who had other white-collar occupations. As already described, small towns and cities included a provincial elite distinct from the landed gentry. Traditionally, the army has been a means of upward mobility and has been dominated by the middle class. Since the mid-nineteenth century, the immigration of Europeans, especially to southern Brazil, has added to the small Brazilian middle class. Until very recently, this middle segment has been relatively insignificant in numbers and might even be said to have been actually the lower and poorer fringes of the upper class.

Everyone who has known Brazil for the last two decades agrees that the middle class has increased many times over and is rapidly expanding. This is reflected in an enormous increase in demand for consumer goods, in the expansion of middle-income housing, and in the heavier pressure on all public services. Perhaps the best index of middle-class expansion is the increase in white-collar jobs, for the middle sectors still consider manual labor in any form as a lower-class occupation. The tremendous expansion of federal, state, and municipal civil service has opened up many white-collar positions, and government employment has been perhaps the most single important road to membership in the middle class. With the growth of industry and commerce, numerous jobs have become available in offices and stores. Furthermore, opportunities in the professions have increased with Brazil's population explosion and with the increased buying power of its people. There is an urgent need for chemists, nurses, engineers, and the like. The expanding economy calls for white-collar workers and specialists, as well as for labor. The new middle sector has new demands, and is becoming at least superficially similar to the middle classes of the United States and Europe.

This growing new class finds itself in a difficult situation. Its members have learned to expect a higher standard of living than they can actually afford. They live in a world of radio, television, cinema, and theater; in fact they probably go to the movies more often than the average middle-class North American. They have learned to want and even to need telephones, electric refrigerators, washing machines, typewriters, automobiles, and a multitude of industrial products and gadgets. They want better and more modern houses, and they are extremely conscious of and eager for good clothes. They are prey to modern advertising and fads, for they read *Manchete*, a magazine patterned after *Paris Match* and *Life*, and *O Cruzeiro*, a sort of Brazilian *Saturday Evening Post*. Both are as filled with advertising matter as their foreign counterparts.

Few of these middle-class Brazilians earn enough to acquire what they have been taught to regard as modern necessities, and the public services fall far short of their minimum demands. A few professionals and some successful businessmen can afford to buy cooperative apartments or homes in the suburbs, a Brazilian-made automobile, and electrical appliances; however, the salaries of the lower echelons of the new middle class are exceedingly low in relation to their aspirations. A study of clerks and other low-ranking commercial employees carried out in 1948 showed that they spent 40 to 45 percent of their total income for food alone.[10] By 1962, with spiraling inflation and a shortage of basic foodstuffs such as wheat, beans, and corn, the percentage of income spent on food was certainly higher. In early 1962, a monthly salary of 60,000 cruzeiros (approximately $150) was considered good for an office worker; at the same time, however, an apartment in a middle-class neighborhood rented for at least 15,000 or 20,000 cruzeiros ($40 to $50) per month, an electric refrigerator sold for 100,000 cruzeiros ($250), a man's suit was 10,000 to 15,000 cruzeiros ($30 to $45), and a Brazilian-made Volkswagen was 800,000 cruzeiros ($2,000). It is not surprising that many middle-class families buy on time and that so many are in debt. Nor is it surprising that so many wives and unmarried sons and daughters must work and contribute to family support.

The frustrations of this expanding middle class are also reflected in the public facilities crisis. Brazil is now expropriating the telephone and light systems which in the past were run by private corporations, mainly English, Canadian, and North American. Because the middle class could not afford to pay higher rates, the companies have not been allowed to raise the tariff, and as a result they have provided utterly inadequate services. At the present rate of installation, it would take ten years to supply telephones for those now on the waiting list in Rio de Janeiro. In Recife and Bahia, the telephone services function badly or not at all. As late as 1962, there were less than 3,000 telephones in Bahia, a city of almost 650,000 people. A new national company was formed to take over from the foreign concessionaire and install a new system with more modern equipment. This company was established on the basis of

[10] Costa Pinto, *Pesquisa sôbre o padrão de vida do comerciário no Distrito Federal (Rio de Janeiro)*, p. 107.

shares; each telephone line is held by a shareholder. Shares sold initially for 60,000 cruzeiros, but even before the new company had completed installations they were reselling for 200,000 cruzeiros (approximately $500 as of June, 1962). The new telephone system calls for only 20,000 lines. It will not be sufficiently large or inexpensive to satisfy the demands of the middle sectors in this old city.

Members of the Brazilian middle class value education as a means of social and economic mobility, but here again they are frustrated. Although primary education is free in Brazil and there are public secondary schools, at least two-thirds of the secondary schools in operation are private. Tuition is not expensive by North American standards (between $10 and $15 per month in a Catholic secondary school), but it is another heavy drain on the pocketbooks of members of the middle class, who are eager for their children to secure secondary and even higher education in order to consolidate or improve the social position they have won. It is the middle-class family, above all, that sends its children to secondary schools; for example, in a sociological study of 1,353 students in seventeen different middle schools (*ginásios*) in São Paulo, it was found that 73 percent came from families whose fathers had middle-class occupations (businessmen or lower-prestige professionals), while 18.6 percent belonged to the upper class (i.e., their fathers were landed gentry, high-prestige professionals, or industrialists) and only 8.4 percent were lower class (their fathers being manual laborers or artisans).[11] Facilities for secondary education have increased many times over during the last decade, but this growth is far below the demands of the

[11] Brandão Lopes, "Escôlha ocupacional e origem social de ginasianos em São Paulo," *Educação e Ciências Sociais*, I (1956), 43–62.

middle class, and, according to most Brazilian educators, not in accordance with its needs.

The Brazilian middle class can hardly be said to have a distinctive ideology comparable to that of its European and North American counterparts. Its members may call themselves *classe média*, but in fact they identify with and share the aristocratic social values of the traditional upper class. Except in the extreme South where European influences are strong, the Brazilian middle class has a deep disdain for manual labor in any form. In the same study of secondary schools cited above, more than 60 percent of the students hoped to become engineers, physicians, lawyers, or plantation owners—the four prestige occupations of traditional upper-class Brazil. According to the Brazilian sociologist who carried out the study, this indicates "the permanence of traditional Brazilian values relating to work in an environment in which economic development demands new specialties." [12] Likewise, it is customary for middle-class families, even though they may have a hard time making ends meet, to have at least one domestic servant. And, although it cannot be shown statistically, they attempt to offer hospitality that often reaches an ostentatious level far beyond their means. In short, they tend to aspire to the aristocratic values of last century's landed gentry which are out of keeping with modern Brazil.

In a sense, middle-class families are culturally the most conservative sector of Brazilian society. Because they are insecure in their position, they make a point of preserving traditional Brazilian values and attitudes. Yet they cannot maintain many of these values and patterns of behavior, either because the world is changing around them or because they lack the eco-

[12] *Ibid.,* p. 61.

nomic basis to support them. They believe that a woman's place is in the home, yet their daughters and even their wives often work in commercial and government offices. They value close ties with kinsmen, but many members of the middle class have been forced to migrate from small towns to cities leaving their relatives behind, and others through economic and social mobility have lost touch with their lower-class kinsmen. Members of the middle class emphasize the value of a humanistic education, but at the same time they are highly materialistic. They want badly a higher standard of living, and they are aware of the importance of technology and of a scientific education. They value honesty in public office and in government, but they are not above seeking a special favor from an official or government employee for themselves or for a relative; it is part of the normal course of life to make use of a "pull" (*pistolão*). They are patriotic and nationalistic, but they put an exaggerated value on anything French or North American. These are the people who flock to English language courses in all Brazilian cities and who follow the lives of American movie stars in Brazilian fan magazines; but, at the same time, they may be highly critical of the United States, even articulately anti-American, and full of misconceptions about the United States. Yet the United States represents, at least materially, the type of society to which they aspire.

The new upper class

In the nineteenth century, the elite groups of Brazil's small towns and the elite groups of the big cities were, for the most part, either one and the same or at least equivalent in status. A wealthy *fazendeiro* was wealthy both in his own community and in the capital of his state. The greatest fortunes came from having many slaves and *agregados* who tended cattle ranches or sugar or coffee plantations. While not all *fazendeiros* maintained houses in the big cities, most of them had relatives who lived there. These relatives, brothers, cousins, and in-laws, were the city elite; they dominated state and national politics, they monopolized the legal and medical professions, and they set the standards of dress, etiquette, and erudition. If they were not themselves *fazendeiros*, their exalted positions were either directly or indirectly based on agrarian fortunes accumulated by some member of their family.

In the twentieth century, the descendants of this traditional upper class have gone several different ways. With the growth of industrial standards of consumption, part of the old elite have lost their upper-class connections in the metropolitan centers, but linger on as great seigneurial figures amid the technological stagnation and poverty of the backlands. Another portion of the group, the big-city bureaucrats and professionals, have diverged from the elite and merged with the upper echelons of the expanding middle class. Yet another portion, by diversifying investments, industrializing and nationalizing their rural holdings, and intermarrying with the industrial capitalist elements who now dominate the upper class, have managed to preserve their influence and power on the national scene.

The traditional families of the beginning of the century are still important in Brazilian life and their names continue to appear in high business circles, in political and public life, in the diplomatic corps, and in the intellectual life of the country. But during the last twenty years an increasing number of people from the middle class have moved into the upper class through acquired wealth, political influence, education, or professional competence. The Vargas regime brought many new names to national prominence. The expanding economy of the last twenty years has opened up numerous opportunities for amassing new wealth, and rags to riches stories are often heard in Rio de Janeiro and São Paulo. Many of the European immigrants who arrived in Brazil during the late nineteenth or early twentieth century have prospered and even made great fortunes. Such names as Matarazzo in industry, Jaffet in industry and banking, Lunardelli in coffee, Santos Vahlis in real estate, and Klabin in paper manufacturing represent but a few people of non-Luso-Brazilian origin who came to be of very great importance in their respective fields. Many second-generation immigrants have entered the scientific, artistic, and even political life of the country.

Many of these new upper-class members are *arrivistas*, or upstarts, and, like the new rich everywhere, they often shock the traditional upper class, and even the middle class, by their ostentation, their manners, and their unscrupulous methods. It might almost be said that many in this group have no traditional values. They have achieved their exalted positions by astuteness and hard work, not by inheritance or family position. These are, as Gilbert Freyre has pointed out, "transitional figures," arising out of the rapid changes in the economic system. As he also points out:

The transitional figure is just as common among Brazilians of Portuguese origin as among those of non-Portuguese origin. Their transition has been from the agrarian North to the industrial South, from country to city, and sometimes from positions of weakness and poverty to positions of power and wealth. In such circumstances, moral controls break down, and the influence of one's ancestral environment, whether it was a farm in Brazil or a farm in Italy, no longer affects one's behavior.[13]

Such people have only partially understood the values of the Brazilian gentry and, in fact, they may be said to aspire only partially to traditional Brazilian upper-class values. They are far more interested in acquiring the many material comforts of the rich of New York and Paris than the traditions of the old, family-oriented Brazilian upper class, yet they continue a long Brazilian tradition of ostentation and luxury.

It must not be thought that this new upper class stands apart and is rebuffed by the traditional families of Brazil. Nor must it be thought that all of its members behave as *arrivistas*. Many are as malleable and mobile socially as they have been economically and politically. One has only to look at the increasing number of non-Portuguese names in the society columns of the large cities and at the frequent announcements of marriages between traditional upper-class families and the new upper class to understand that their success is not confined to the market place or the political arena. The new upper class is, in fact, rapidly fusing with the old traditional upper class to form a new dominant segment of Brazilian society. This is taking place even in the traditional sugar plantation area of Bahia. Harry W. Hutchinson describes vividly how a new upper-class family, the "Helvetians," took over control of an important sugar mill from the old traditional family, whom he calls the "Condes":

Usina São Pedro was described earlier as a family corporation, owned and directed by members of one extended family [i.e.,

---

[13] Freyre, "The Brazilian Melting Pot," *Atlantic Monthly* (February, 1946), 107.

the Condes]. At one time in the past five years, this family was obliged to take into the corporation a large amount of capital representing a second family enterprise, considerably larger in scope than the first. Within a short period the second family achieved complete control of the factory through a series of financial manipulations. As a result, Usina São Pedro passed from the Conde family's ownership and direction and is now just one element of a large commercial firm. . . . The second family, the Helvetians, is a second-generation immigrant family. . . . The Helvetians have taken a place in the upper ranks of Bahian society, representing new money and economic power. Their history is important. The original immigrant married into a Bahian family of "good name" and all of his sons have done the same. One of them married a daughter of the *Coronel*, founder of the Usina São Pedro. It was through this marriage that the transfer of the factory was channeled.[14]

This process is not a new one in Brazilian society, for the traditional upper class has never been a truly closed social class; it has always been fed through the assimilation of newcomers from the lower and middle classes and from abroad. During the empire and early republic, the aristocracy was enlarged by newcomers who soon became part of the traditional upper class by intermarriage. In the past, it has been the traditional upper class that has absorbed the newcomers, thereby preserving and transmitting its aristocratic values. Nowadays, newcomers into the upper economic and social echelons of society are more numerous than ever before. As a consequence, the dominant segment of Brazilian society may take a new form, one more like that which prevails in the United States, where the values of the power group derive from commerce, industry, and capital rather than from politics and land-owning.

[14] H. W. Hutchinson, *Village and Plantation Life in Northeastern Brazil*, p. 179.

Race and social class

So far, the social and economic classes of Brazil have been described as if they were racially homogeneous, as if Brazil were not a multiracial society. Actually, one cannot understand social and economic stratification in Brazil without referring to race relations, for in Brazil race and class relations are historically and functionally interrelated. The traditional Brazilian two-class system was closely associated with the two-fold racial division of the Brazilian people. The landed gentry, the traditional upper class, was predominantly of Caucasoid ancestry, as its descendants still are. The slaves, the peasants, manual workers, and dependents of all kinds were historically of Negroid, American Indian, or mixed ancestry. In modern Brazil, the newly formed classes and social segments continue to have racial overtones. In general, as one moves down the social hierarchy, the number of racially mixed or otherwise nonwhite individuals gradually increases.

At no point in the social and economic hierarchy does one encounter a homogeneous group. Individuals of mixed ancestry occur even among the upper classes, and many whites are found in the lower social strata. In fact it is one of the most cherished national themes that Brazil is a racial democracy. Since the abolition of slavery in 1888, there has been no legal form of racial discrimination or segregation in Brazil. Innumerable individuals of Negroid or mixed physical appearance have filled important roles in Brazil's national life since the time of the empire. All books on Brazil cite names of Negroes and mulattoes of importance, such as the baroque sculptor Aleijadinho, the great nineteenth-century novelist Machado de

Assis, the abolitionist journalist and statesman José do Patro-
cínio, the politician Nilo Peçanha (who was president of the
republic in 1909–10), the twentieth-century poet Mário de
Andrade, and the psychiatrist Juliano Moreira, to cite but a
few. The world championship soccer team of 1962 covered the
whole spectrum of skin color: Pelé, the "King of Soccer," who
is a Negro, was injured but was competently replaced by
Amarildo, a mulatto. Several players were clearly white. This
tradition of racial democracy is a source of great pride to
Brazilians. More than any country in the Western world,
Brazil is recognized, cited, and applauded as proof that racial
democracy can work. But the facts of Brazilian race and class
relations are not as simple as that. They require some explana-
tion, sometimes even to Brazilians themselves.

Basic to the understanding of race and social class relations
is the Brazilian concept of "race." The official statistics use
only four categories, namely, *branco* (white), *pardo* (brown),
prêto (black), and *amarelo* (yellow). However, the people in
the street have other racial categories which vary from one
region to another. In one small town in the Eastern Highlands
described by Marvin Harris, they recognized in addition to
"whites" and "Negroes" five other types: *moreno, chulo, mulato,
creolo,* and *cabo verde.* Harris describes these types:

The *moreno* has wavy hair with the skin coloring of a heavily sun-
burnt white. The *mulato* has crisp, curly hair and is darker than
the *moreno.* The *chulo* has crisp, rolled hair and his skin is the
"color of burnt sugar or tobacco." The *creolo* has fine wavy hair,
is almost as dark as the *chulo,* but has smoother skin. The *cabo
verde* has very straight hair and is the color of the Negro.[15]

[15] Harris, *Town and Country in Brazil,* p. 119n.

In some localities the system of popular classification is much more complex[16] while in others it is somewhat simpler, but everywhere in Brazil intermediate types between white and Negro are recognized, these types are ranked in terms of attractiveness and acceptability from the most Caucasoid to the most Negroid, and criteria other than skin color, such as nose shape, hair type, and lip thickness are also used to classify an individual.[17]

The existence of recognized intermediate types is important to the understanding of the Brazilian race-class system and to its functioning. To put it simply, a twofold Jim Crow system could never work in Brazil. A mulatto is not a Negro, and a *moreno* (dark white) is not a mulatto. If Brazilians wanted to install a Jim Crow system, they would have to provide at least four or more sets of schools, hospitals, sections on public transportation, and restaurants. Our North American South can hardly afford a two-race system of segregation, and certainly Brazil could not afford a fourfold or sixfold system.[18]

To be accurate, however, the picture of Brazilian racial democracy must be drawn in relation to the racial composition of the population as a whole and to that of the various social and economic classes. The 1950 census classified 61.6 percent of all Brazilians as white, 11 percent as black, 26.6 percent as brown, and the small remainder as yellow. It should be remembered that the census data reflect racial identity as reckoned by the respondents and sometimes by the census taker;

[16] See H. W. Hutchinson, *Village and Plantation Life in Northeastern Brazil*, pp. 118–20.

[17] See Wagley, ed., *Race and Class in Rural Brazil*.

[18] The hierarchy of types in Brazil is very much like that prevailing among North American Negroes, who accord each other beauty and prestige to the extent that their skin color and type of hair, lips, and nose, approximate that of the whites.

a survey by objective anthropological standards would certainly show a larger percentage of mixed types. A study of color and occupation making use of 1940 census data underlines the correlation between class and color throughout the country.[19] The white 64 percent of the male population over ten years of age accounts for 90 percent of those engaged in the professions, private teaching, and cultural and private administrative activities, for 76 percent of those in public administration, and for 79 percent of those in commercial and financial positions. The Negro 14.7 percent accounts for only 2.5 percent, 8 percent, and 5 percent of these prestige categories, respectively.[20] Another set of data shows equal disproportion. The 342,000 males classified as employers include 3.48 percent of the whites but only 0.74 percent of the browns and 0.55 percent of the blacks. To look at it in a slightly different way, whites account for 81 percent of these employers, browns for 11.8 percent, and blacks for 5.7 percent.[21] There is no reason to believe that these ratios have changed strikingly in the last twenty years or so, although the social mobility of people of color is a noted fact in some parts of the country.

These figures do not tell the entire story, for the population of the various regions of Brazil is dissimilar in racial composition. In the Northeast coastal region and in such areas as the coast of Maranhão, Piauí state, and the São Francisco Valley, the percentage of people of color is unusually high and whites predominate only in the middle and upper classes. On the other hand, in states such as São Paulo, Paraná, Santa Catarina, and Rio Grande do Sul, over four-fifths of the population are white

[19] *Estudos sôbre a composição da população do Brasil segundo a côr*, IBGE.
[20] *Ibid.*
[21] *Ibid.*

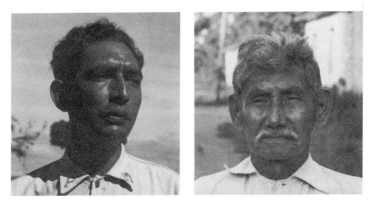

Brazilians of mixed racial origin—Negroid, American Indian, Caucasoid

Primitive tribesman of the Xingú River headwaters

Brazilian descendant of West African slaves

in all social and economic classes. And in the Amazon Valley, where there were few Negro slaves, where Negroes often came as free men and artisans, and where the Indian was the exploited laborer, the majority of people in the lower classes are of the American Indian physical type. But for Brazil as a whole,

Amazon caboclo *man and wife, primarily of American Indian racial origin*

Small-town lady of Portuguese origin

Northeasterner from the arid sertão

and speaking generally, the old Brazilian rule of thumb still stands: "The darker the skin the lower the class and the lighter the skin the higher the class."

The claims for a Brazilian racial democracy must be judged also against widely documented color prejudice in almost every part of the nation. This color prejudice is expressed in many ways, some subtle and some overt. Almost all studies of race relations in Brazil have cited the traditional derogatory sayings about Negroes. This example was recorded by Harry W. Hutchinson in a small community of the Recôncavo region of Bahia:

Negro doesn't marry, he gets together.
Negro doesn't accompany a procession, he runs after it.
Negro doesn't sit down, he squats.
Negro in white clothes is a sign of rain.
Negro doesn't hear Mass, he spies on it.
Negro at a white man's party is the first to grab and the last to eat.
Negro's intelligence is the same size as his hair [i.e., short].[22]

Similar sayings involving derogatory stereotypes have been recorded in widely separate Brazilian communities and are part of the Brazilian cultural heritage. They portray the Negro as inferior in intelligence, dependability, morality, honesty, and physical appearance. Attitude questionnaires and social-distance tests reveal similar prejudice against the Negro, and in a milder and sometimes somewhat different form, against the mulatto as well. White Brazilians indicate in verbal responses some resistance to working with Negroes, living with them, dancing with them, accepting them into the family, and marrying them

[22] H. W. Hutchinson, *Village and Plantation Life in Northeastern Brazil*, p. 122. A slightly modified version of the same was recorded by Marvin Harris for the Eastern Highlands (*Town and Country in Brazil*, p. 118).

—generally in about that order of intensity. Many of the overt derogatory statements about Negroes heard in Brazil are as shocking as those heard in the Deep South of the United States, although the social-distance tests show less reluctance to associate with Negroes at all levels.

Furthermore, there have been and still are overt forms of discrimination in terms of skin color, although this is strictly illegal. North American Negroes have been surprised to find that there were no rooms available in Brazilian upper-class hotels, although reservations had been made. Until recently it was well known in Brazil that the Foreign Service excluded people of darker skins (some have now been admitted) and that the traditionally upper-class Naval Academy accepted only white candidates. Certain private schools, both primary and secondary, were until recently homogeneously white or accepted a brilliant mulatto or two on scholarships as a matter of principle. Then, too, there was (now discontinued) a way of warning dark mulattoes and Negroes that they need not apply for openings as clerks or office workers—an advertisement reading "Needed: young lady of good appearance for office position" could be inserted in the newspaper, and it was clearly understood what "good appearance" meant.

The existence of color prejudice and even of discrimination does not mean, for several reasons, that the Brazilian racial democracy is a myth. First, there is obviously a wide gulf in Brazil between what people say and what they do, between verbal and social behavior. The emotional tone surrounding color prejudice is generally lighthearted and amused, and mixed with a liberal sprinkling of earthy appreciation. Oracy Nogueira records the heckling of a football team by fans in racial terms so strong that they would have caused a race riot in the United States.[23] Marvin Harris tells of a white man in the community of Minas Velhas who stoutly maintained that a Negro, even if he was a *doutor* (a professional) should not be associated with, but who bowed and scraped when he actually met a Negro engineer.[24] Also, set against the derogatory attitude, there is a certain pride in the "Brazilian race" and even in the *prêto* (Negro): everyone who visited Brazil in recent years has seen the huge billboard featuring Pelé, the black soccer player, with his arms about a little white boy, obviously his ardent fan. Derogatory attitudes and stereotypes remain in the Brazilian tradition and can be called on in any competitive situation (if there is no other way to get at your competitor you can always call him a *prêto*), but they generally lack conviction as determinants of behavior.

Secondly, many of the stereotypes and attitudes are survivals from slavery times and are shared by the southern United States and the West Indies. There is a vast difference, however, between the social effect of these attitudes and stereotypes in the United States and in Brazil. In the United States, they are aimed against all people of known Negro ancestry, regardless of physical appearance. Thus, such attitudes, derogatory stereotypes, and forms of prejudice and discrimination are aimed against a large group that varies from Caucasoid to Negroid in physical appearance. It is a group determined by ancestry and descent, not by any objective physical anthropological standards of measurement. In Brazil, on the other

[23] Oracy Nogueira, "Relações raciais no município de Itapininga," in Bastide and Fernandes, eds., *Relações raciais entre negros e brancos em São Paulo*, p. 507.
[24] Harris, *Town and Country in Brazil*, p. 125.

hand, the criterion is physical appearance. As the Brazilian sociologist Oracy Nogueira puts it, in Brazil there is "race prejudice of mark" (i.e., prejudice of appearance) rather than "race prejudice of origin." Color and other physical characteristics such as hair, lip, and nose type are visible marks and symbols of one's social class, and probably of one's slave ancestry. But through miscegenation succeeding generations can and do become lighter. Color prejudice or "prejudice of mark" decreases as the skin lightens.[25]

In fact demographic figures indicate that the numbers of whites and browns are increasing at the expense of the blacks. From 1940 to 1950, for example, the percentage of those classified as *prêto* was reduced from 14.6 percent to 10.9 percent. This has been called the bleaching process in the Brazilian population. Much of it can be ascribed to the tendency of census takers to "classify lighter," but some of it is biological. The chance has always been very good at all levels of the social and economic hierarchy for frequent licit and illicit sexual unions between people of different colors. This does not mean that unions between very dark-skinned and very light-skinned individuals are common. Such unions, whether in marriage or concubinage, are considered socially undesirable and cause embarrassment to the individuals concerned. Rather, it is common for an upward-moving individual, generally a male, to take a spouse several shades lighter. Color differences between spouses are most acceptable in the lower classes, but tolerance for marriages between white and not-quite-white partners is a traditional and enduring part of Brazilian national culture.

[25] Nogueira, "Skin Color and Social Class," in *Plantation Systems of the New World*, pp. 164–79.

Thirdly, perhaps the most important difference between race relations in Brazil and in the United States is that color is but one of the criteria by which people are placed in the total social hierarchy. Before two Brazilians decide how they ought to behave toward each other, they must know more than the fact that one is dark-skinned and the other light-skinned. A Brazilian is never merely a white man or a man of color; he is a rich, well-educated white man of a good family or a poor, uneducated white man from the *povo*; he is a well-educated mulatto with a good job, or a poor, uneducated Negro. Other criteria, such as income, education, family connections, and even personal charm and special abilities or aptitudes come into play when placing a person in terms of the prestige hierarchy or even of social class. Above all, these multiple criteria determine who will be admitted to hotels, restaurants, and most social clubs; who will get preferential treatment in stores, churches, nightclubs, and travel conveyances; and who will have the best chance among a number of marriage suitors.

As a matter of fact, a Brazilian's perception of an individual's racial classification is influenced by all these social criteria. I have told elsewhere how people in a small Amazon community refused to classify the most important lady in town as the dark mulatto she was, but made her white, and how the same townspeople refused to see the town drunk as "white"—"How could he be a white?" they said.[26] Brazilians cannot ignore the obvious, and no one would have the courage to call a wealthy, highly educated Negro a white, but they might politely call him a *moreno* (brunet). Yet the amusing Brazilian statement, "Money whitens the skin," is not unmeaningful. It is easy to

[26] Wagley, *Amazon Town*, p. 134.

lower or to raise the color status of people from one grade to
another according to criteria other than color. Thus, a *pardo*
who is a professional, has a good income, good manners, and
thus good social connections, will be raised to *branco*. In Bahia,
there are two amusing terms for such people, namely, *branco
da Bahia* (white from Bahia) and *branco da terra* (white from
the country). Likewise, a *pardo* who is poor, illiterate, and
marginal is apt to be classed as a Negro. It is this interplay
between skin color and social criteria that makes Brazilian
census data on race so dubious.

This means, in effect, that there are no Brazilian social
groups based on skin color alone, although, to the casual visitor,
this would not seem to be true. Are not the "Samba Schools,"
the beautifully costumed groups who come down from the
favelas and the suburbs of Rio de Janeiro to dance during
Carnival, homogeneously Negro? It seems that all the participants in a *candomblé* ceremony in Bahia are Negroes. One can
visit social clubs throughout the country in which all of the
members are exceedingly dark in skin color. There is in Brazil
an Association of Men of Color, and St. Benedict is the patron
saint of many religious brotherhoods whose members are black
or nearly so. However, if one looks closely at the members of
these associations, it becomes apparent that there are different
shades of darkness, and even a few very light-skinned people.
But that is not the point. The essential point is that these are
people of the same social class and incidentally of similar skin
color.

Generally, when an individual improves his social and economic situation, he soon moves upward to another club or
association more in keeping with his new status. The Brazilian

sociologist Fernando Henrique Cardoso makes this point in an article describing the results of his studies of race relations in southern Brazil. He describes the pride shown when one of the members of a club made up of Negroes graduates from normal school or another school of higher learning or is appointed to an important position. The members of the club hold a dance or a luncheon in his honor. "The orator," he writes, "recalls that the success of the young *doutor* is also a success for the Negro race. The young *doutor*, who is now called by this title, will in all probability soon stop coming to the club which is thus honoring him, since henceforth he will formally act as if he belonged to another social level." [27]

Thus, in Brazil, race relations and social class are intertwined in an intricate manner. They are not separate phenomena as they are apt to be elsewhere. There is no middle-class Negro society separate from white middle-class society. But this does not mean that color prejudice and discrimination can be entirely reduced to class prejudice; it is not simply that the colored populations have not improved their status because the socioeconomic system of Brazil has afforded them few opportunities for upward mobility. It would seem that their physical appearance is an added disability, although negligible as compared to other countries. For nowhere in Brazil does one's physical appearance, one's race, constitute an impossible barrier to upward mobility.

Race discrimination is thus relatively mild and equivocal in Brazil, but class discrimination produces disabilities and inequalities of a sharp, incisive nature that can be shocking to North Americans. Some of the more subtle aspects of the rela-

---

[27] Cardoso, "Os brancos e a ascenção social dos negros em Pôrto Alegre," *Anhembi*, XXXIX (August, 1960), 585.

tions between the upper and lower classes have been described by the Brazilian anthropologist Thales de Azevedo for the traditional city of Salvador in Bahia. He writes:

The people of the lower class are obliged to address the superior group with the title *Dona* for women and *O senhor* for men, terms which indicate subordination in this context, no matter what the physical type or age of the speaker might be. In the inverse situation [i.e., upper class addressing lower class] the title *Dona* is much less used because it expresses subordination of the speaker, but *O senhor* remains obligatory because it keeps anyone at a distance. An "inferior" person cannot, except with offensive intent, use *você* [second person for "you" and less intimate than *tu*] to address the members of the superior group—a mode of address common in horizontal and intra-class relations. . . . The greetings with kisses among women, the little goodbye signal made with the fingers, the handshake and embrace between men are rarely employed in asymetrical relations [between classes]. They always require the initiative of the superior and in these cases the inferior always limits himself to letting the superior take his hand without responding with a clasp of his own. Other mechanisms . . . regulate the spatial relations of people and limit the expressions of intimacy. A member of the lower class may be received into the house of the upper- or middle-class person, but rarely will he sit in the living room or at the dinner table; if food is offered him, he eats in the kitchen, in the pantry, or even at the dining table— but separately, after or before the others.[28]

Azevedo stresses the fact that marriages seldom cross class lines, that clothing is different, that speech is different, and that treatment before public authorities differs for the two groups:

A *popular* [i.e., member of the lower class] caught in a crime by a policeman is taken to a filthy prison without facilities where he

[28] Azevedo, "Classes sociais e grupos de prestígio na Bahia," *Arquivos da Universidade da Bahia*, V (1956), 86.

may be treated with brutality and where his companions are criminals, bums, alcoholics, and beggars. The individual of the upper class . . . in the same circumstances almost always finds a way of avoiding immediate arrest; if arrested, however, he is taken to the police station discreetly in an automobile . . . he may then be taken to the hospital rather than the prison on the pretext that he is ill . . . while persons with higher educational degrees have the legal right to be held in a special prison.[29]

These are but a few details of class discrimination, and they could be extended at length. Such details, however, are reflections of a profound gulf between the Brazilian middle and upper classes and the masses of the people. More important are the differences in living standards and in access to education and other services. While the middle class suffers from its inability to acquire the accessories of modern living, and the upper class spends less than it used to in Paris and New York, the masses of the Brazilian people cannot afford the basic essentials of life. They cannot buy bread, meat, clothes, shoes, education, shelter, and medicines for themselves and their children. Under such conditions the issue of racial discrimination is scarcely a vital one. Lower-class whites and lower-class colored people are both segregated and discriminated against. Brazil is accurately described as a racial and political democracy, but by no stretch of the imagination is it as yet a social democracy.

Thus, the cleavage between social and economic classes works strongly for diversity in Brazilian national culture. One would think that Brazil would be ripe for a violent class revolution and that interclass tension and conflict would be widespread and intense. Although there are signs of peasant uprisings in the Northeast and some lower-class discontent throughout the

[29] *Ibid.*, p. 89.

country, the lower classes of Brazil are surprisingly passive, resigned, and tolerant. They are hungry, but they participate in religious processions and in Carnival, and they share the enthusiasm of the rest of the country for soccer. They accept the traditions and the ideal behavior patterns formed by the middle and upper classes. They would like to (but cannot for pecuniary reasons) live like their more fortunate compatriots, marry like them, dress like them, and eat like them. They do not have a culture apart from the upper class—they share in Brazilian culture, although largely in a vicarious way.

❦4❦ THE COMMUNITY

IT has been suggested that the Brazilian is almost a man without a community.[1] This statement was not meant to be taken literally, for, of course, all human societies are communities of one kind or another. It merely implies that the Brazilian community is amorphous, not easy to define, lacking in *esprit de corps* or community spirit, and split by divisions of social class. Brazilian metropolitan centers are as heterogeneous, sprawling, and complex as elsewhere, but they lack many community services found in other parts of the Western world. In the rural zones of Brazil, there is nothing comparable in cohesiveness to the corporate, landholding Indian and mestizo communities of the Andes and of Guatemala and Mexico. The village and its lands do not form a community as they do in Europe. The Brazilian rural community takes several different forms throughout the country, but in none of them can it be said to provide a solid grass-roots foundation for Brazilian national unity. Instead, like regionalism and social class, the Brazilian community actually encourages diversity in Brazilian national life.

What then are the forms of the Brazilian community? It is of course easier to begin with the simpler forms of the rural zones, where the majority of Brazilians live. In 1950, almost 70 percent of the Brazilian people lived in isolated homesteads,

[1] T. L. Smith, *Brazil: People and Institutions*, p. 497.

small hamlets or villages, and towns with less than 2,000 inhabitants. In one sense Brazil's population is, as T. Lynn Smith has put it, "one of the most rural in the entire world." [2]

The rural community

The Brazilian states are divided into countylike *municípios*, each of which has a county seat called a *cidade* (city), even though it may have only a few hundred inhabitants. Each *município* is further divided into districts or *distritos de paz*, whose headquarters are called a *vila* (village). The administrative and political functions of these formal units will be described in a later chapter. It must now be said, however, that these units seldom, if ever, coincide with the rural community. Occasionally a district and its village may form a community; almost invariably, however, a *município* contains several communities, one of which may have the *cidade* as its center.

In simplest terms, the Brazilian rural community consists of a village or small town and a cluster of neighborhoods which are in several ways tributary to it. It is a geographical area which is only vaguely delimited in the minds of its inhabitants. It is a local trading area—people come periodically to the village or small town to buy and sell. It is often a religious area—people from the rural zone come to the village church for baptisms, marriages, and even Mass. Rural people may be tied to townsmen by kinship and ritual bonds. If the community center happens to be the official administrative center of the *município* or of a district, they go there to settle their legal and political affairs. The inhabitants of the village or town which serves as the community nucleus are of course quite aware that

[2] *Ibid.*, p. 162.

they are members of that community, but even then their
allegiance may not be strong, for townspeople and villagers
move easily from one community to another. People from the
tributary rural neighborhoods generally know to which community nucleus they are attached by informal bonds, but again
this attachment may be weak. There are neighborhoods that
seem to waver, giving their allegiance to more than one community center, attending a market at one place this week and
at another next week. As T. Lynn Smith has pointed out, the
Brazilian community is basically similar to the rural community of the United States.[3]

The greatest community spirit is found within the rural
neighborhoods. These neighborhoods are composed of small
groups of farmers, collectors of native products, fishermen, and
workers on small or medium-size agricultural and pastoral
estates, depending on the economic activities of the locality and
region. The neighborhood includes from twenty to forty families who may be closely interrelated. Generally it is not a concentrated hamlet, except on agricultural estates, and it seldom
has any formal organization. Yet it may support a chapel and
the patron saint may be the basis for the organization of a
religious brotherhood whose officers provide a kind of formal
leadership within the group. The people of a neighborhood are
generally homogeneous; they are fishermen, sharecropping agriculturalists, or landholding peasants, and they are not divided
by class differences. Nowadays, a neighborhood may have a
rural school and a small store. Mutual aid and exchange of
labor is common, often in the form of the *mutirão*—a kind of
work party for clearing, planting, or harvesting fields. Neighborhood families will also attend the wake of a kinsman or neigh-

[3] *Ibid.*, pp. 498–99.

bor, and accompany the body in a procession to the cemetery in the village or small town. Above all, the people of a neighborhood live in face-to-face contact, but they are necessarily dependent for many services and many aspects of their life on the larger community. These neighborhood groups are the most tightly knit sectors of the Brazilian rural community.

Brazilian rural communities, however, differ in relation to a number of factors including size, regional location, whether or not their community service center is a county seat, and above all the type of neighborhoods which they contain. Furthermore, the Brazilian small town is not generally a rural settlement; rather, it is characterized by what Marvin Harris has called an "urban ethos." [4] There is a tremendous social distance between most inhabitants of the concentrated centers and the people of the rural neighborhoods. In addition, the rural neighborhoods are of many types—they may include squatters, free farmers, sharecroppers, collectors, or wage workers. The type of rural neighborhood fundamentally affects the form of the whole community. Let us describe and analyze the Brazilian small town, and then turn to the various possible types of neighborhoods of which it may be the center.

THE COMMUNITY NUCLEUS: THE VILLAGE AND SMALL TOWN

Brazilian villages and towns have never been as standardized in their ground plan as those of Spanish America. Even so, traditionally, they have all had a *praça* (the Spanish plaza or American square), but there was no efficient Council of the Indies to establish a neat gridiron pattern of streets radiating from a central plaza as in Spanish America. Thus many Brazilian towns "just grew," seemingly without any plan, but the

[4] See Harris, *Town and Country in Brazil*.

Iberian town pattern is still recognizable. Generally, if the town is large enough, there is more than one *praça*—the others were added as the town grew in size. In the old and traditional town of Monte Serrat in the arid *sertão* of northern Bahia, for example, there are two *praças*. One is surrounded by the church, the city hall, the police station, the small hotel, and the homes of several prominent families. Three blocks away there is a second *praça* where the school is situated along with several general stores and the homes of other prominent families.[5] A larger town might have three or more squares.

Radiating out and intersecting are the *ruas* or streets. Nowadays, as a rule, the squares and the main thoroughfares leading off the squares are paved with cobblestones, concrete, or asphalt, and people give you directions such as "near the end of the asphalt." Other streets, obviously less important, are unpaved; the Beco de Lama (Mud Alley) in Minas Velhas in the Eastern Highlands had a name of dual significance, for it was certainly muddy in the rainy season and it housed the local prostitutes.[6] The houses are built flush with the street and close together. Each has a *quintal* (backyard), but only the most modern houses have any space between their façade and the sidewalk. Despite the solid front which such a street presents, it is not monotonous, for each house is painted differently—white, brown, pink, or blue. The houses are solidly built of adobe or *taipa* (wattle and daub), with ceramic tile roofs. These houses are larger than they seem from the street, for they typically stretch back in a series of rooms opening from a central hallway. Away from the *praças* and their nearby streets, the houses of a typical Brazilian small town tend to

[5] Zimmerman, *Monte Serrat*. The name Monte Serrat is fictitious.
[6] Harris, *Town and Country in Brazil*, p. 36.

be of poor quality. They are often only huts made of adobe with thatched or precariously tiled roofs. The outskirts of many villages and small towns are often similar to urban shanty towns.

Brazilian small towns are apt to contain monuments of one kind or another—a commemorative plaque of some historical event or a bust of Getúlio Vargas or some local hero. The most important square is often a public garden where roses or other unlikely flowers are planted. Although even in small towns Brazilians in recent years have come to appreciate their lovely tropical and semitropical plants, most public gardens look as if the gardener had once seen pictures of Versailles, or remembered the gardens of Portugal. Typically, the most imposing structure on the main square is the church, and on or near the most important square are public buildings such as the town hall, the post office and telegraph station, and the state tax collector's office. There is usually also a bar where people (chiefly males) take coffee, soft drinks, and occasional alcoholic drinks, and typically the bar is also a billiard parlor where young men play snooker. Traditionally, on Sunday evenings, the square was the scene of "footing," as the strolling of young men in one direction and young girls in the other around the square was called. Nowadays, in most small towns, there is a cinema which attracts the young people, and "footing" has all but disappeared.

One of the most complimentary statements that might be made about a Brazilian small town is that it has *movimento*. This seems to mean more than just commercial activities and a busy social life, but it means these as well. It also means noise and general bustle. A town of any importance has one or more public address systems, often in competition with one another. Records are played; public announcements are made of births, deaths, birthdays, and marriages; advertisements are broadcast for products and stores; and political announcements and campaign speeches are carried through these loudspeakers. They operate at a volume which is deafening to the unaccustomed ear but which is part of the concept of *movimento*. Many Brazilian small towns depend on diesel-run generators for their electricity, and current is cut off during many hours of the day and at 10:00 or 11:00 P.M. The visitor then gets some relief from *movimento*.

Brazilian small towns are above all bureaucratic and commercial centers. If the town is the seat of a *município*, there are federal, state, and municipal employees and office holders. If it is only the seat of a district, the bureaucracy is smaller but still exists. In Minas Velhas, a municipal seat of about 1,500 people in the mountains of southern Bahia, there were well over fifty people occupying civil service positions ranging from federal tax collector and sergeant of the state police down to the municipal street cleaner. It is a safe guess that in most small municipal seats at least 20 percent of all families receive at least part of their income from the public coffers. An even higher percentage of townsmen are involved in commerce in one way or another.[7] If the town is fairly large, that is, 4,000 or 5,000 people, it probably has a public market with permanent stalls, each specializing in certain products—like leather goods, religious objects, vegetables, meat, and cereals. Peasants and family farmers sell their products to the owners of these market stalls who act as entrepreneurs, but usually there is a weekly *dia de feira* (market day) when the stalls are filled with food and the housewives do their shopping. In relatively small towns that lack a daily public market, market may be held on

[7] *Ibid.*, pp. 45–46.

one of the squares once a week, and the farmers bring their produce into town to sell directly to the consumers.

The strength of this commercial tradition cannot be under-estimated in interpreting Brazil, for even in Rio de Janeiro there are street markets which are moved about the city on trucks and which are set up at night on specific days of the week in such cosmopolitan districts as Copacabana and Bota-fogo. They block traffic and scatter filth on the city streets. These urban *feiras*, similar in most ways to those of the Bra-zilian small town, are frequented not by rural migrants but by sophisticated *senhoras* from modern apartments who believe that they get fresher vegetables and better meat at lower prices than in their supermarkets and neighborhood stores. In Bra-zilian small towns, the *dia de feira* is an event; it is often the only day when one can buy eggs, vegetables, fresh meat, and similar products. The *dia de feira* is an old tradition; in fact the Portuguese language calls the days of the week by market terms. Monday is *segunda feira* (second market), and so on through Friday. Only Saturday and Sunday have day names.

Brazilian commercialism does not stop at the public market or weekly fair. Municipal seats with as few as 2,000 inhabitants frequently have from twenty to thirty general stores selling the same kind of merchandise. They sell canned goods, cloth, axes, hoes, bush knives, thread, pots and pans, rope, and hun-dreds of other items, as well as beans, rice, dried meat, and other food staples. The stock of any small-town store is gen-erally limited, for these retailers lack credit to build up their inventories. On the other hand, they sell on credit to towns-people and rural peasants, and their sales are small though fre-quent. It is common for a customer to buy 2 cents worth of salt, 10 cents worth of dried beef, and one pound of manioc flour, all to be charged to his account. Then, too, in small towns, everyone is a merchant. It is common to see a few oranges, a half-dozen eggs, or some vegetable oil of local manufacture placed on a window sill for sale; there are also small shops with little more than a few boxes of matches, some *cachaça* (white rum), salt, and kerosene for sale. The number of commercial transactions in any Brazilian small town is enormous. Everyone sells something to everyone else.

Obviously not all of the merchants make much money, and not all small-town public employees are white-collar workers. But each Brazilian small town has its upper class, people who are essentially white-collar workers. These people are the local leaders. They are usually, but not invariably, of Caucasoid ancestry. They are profoundly urban in their ethos. These bureaucrats and small businessmen are generally more aware of events in the distant big cities than of the life of the peasantry in the surrounding rural zones. They employ household servants; follow fashion styles and dress in suit, tie, and hat; maintain social clubs; and, if they can afford it, send their children to be educated in the city. They look down upon the poorer townspeople and especially upon the rural peasants, who are referred to as *caboclos, matutos, caipiras, tabaréus,* and other terms that carry the connotation of hick and yokel. Such people feel greater solidarity with relatives and friends of similar social status in other towns and in the cities than with their townsmen of lower status. The class structure of the small Brazilian town means that it is almost impossible to solve local problems through voluntary or cooperative agencies.

In all small towns, there is an avid interest in politics. The local upper-class leaders are directly concerned with changes in political regime, since so many of them hold government posts. There is hardly anyone in this sector of a small-town population whose brother, sister, cousin, or some other relative is not dependent on political events. Thus, generally, two or more political parties split the allegiance of the townspeople, promoting intense feelings of hostility between close neighbors and sometimes between kinsmen. Even the local priest may be involved; in two small towns which were studied by anthropologists, the local priests were leaders of political parties and were bitterly criticized by the opposing party members. Political rivalry becomes unbelievably tense. In one small town during the political campaign of 1950, each political party frequented one of the *praças*, and to frequent a bar on one square was tantamount to supporting that political party. People stopped speaking to one another. They painted names and slogans on each other's houses, and there were physical fights.

Marvin Harris describes vividly the extremes which political strife can reach in a Brazilian small town:

Passengers on a flight from Salvador [in Bahia] to Bom Jesus da Lapa will see an impressive sight as they approach a small mountain town called Macaúbas. A plane lands here only once or twice a week, but when it does it has the choice of two separate airfields located on opposite sides of the town. One airport was built by partisans of the UDN and the other by partisans of the PSD. When our field group landed in Macaúbas, we had to wait for the mail to be turned over to the pilot. Shortly after the plane landed, a truck full of townspeople drove up amid a swirl of dust. These were the airport's partisans. Fifteen minutes later, a lone figure carrying the mail pouch trudged into view. This was the mail clerk who, unfortunately, was of the opposite party and had to walk. In this same town there are two separate public address systems. Loudspeakers placed on opposite sides of the squares and streets simultaneously blare out propaganda for the respective parties. One barber cuts only UDN hair, another only PSD hair; one bar wets only UDN throats, another only those of the PSD.[8]

Sometimes, political schism is less amusing and political feuds develop that stretch on for years, even in-between campaigns, and which lead to deaths through ambush and other forms of violence. The political leaders are of course members of the local upper class, but poor townspeople and even peasants follow such leaders and are thus divided by politics. Along with divisions of social class, political schisms make any cooperative endeavor almost impossible in most Brazilian small towns. A man in Minas Velhas expressed these difficulties in organizing a cooperative: "Here in Minas Velhas this kind of thing will never work. Politics make it impossible for those who join to cooperate in spirit. In fact, any measure for the common good is difficult in this city because of politics." [9]

The Brazilian small town in which so many Brazilians live is not, then, a homogeneous, neighborly, democratic community close to the soil in its way of life. The idea of a New England town meeting would be a joking matter in most Brazilian small towns. In Brazil, the small town is but an extension of the urban scene—a highly stratified society based on differences in the prestige accorded to various types of occupations, widely different degrees of wealth and power, differences of racial type, differences of education, and differences of family background. These same small towns are guardians of old Brazilian traditions, both good and bad, including the *compadrio* system, large families and a large *parentela* (kin group), and the festivals of Sts. John and Peter. Brazilians regard the

---

[8] Harris, *Town and Country in Brazil*, pp. 197–98.
[9] *Ibid.*, p. 206.

small town of their childhood with affection but they like to move out of it.

RURAL NEIGHBORHOODS

Each small town, as stated earlier, is the nucleus of a number of rural neighborhoods. In fact, it is the type of rural neighborhood that determines the nature of the total community of which the town or village is a part. Broadly speaking, there are only two types of rural neighborhoods in Brazil —those composed of a number of peasant families and those made up of workers on medium- or large-scale plantations of one kind or another. But there are many subtypes of both groups. Peasant neighborhoods vary depending on the subsistence activities and on the system of land tenure. Plantation neighborhoods differ according to the commercial crop that is produced (i.e., sugar, coffee, cacao, cotton, or cattle), which often determines how the people are remunerated and even how the settlement is patterned. Over the centuries, in the various regions of Brazil, a large variety of man-land patterns of relationship have arisen and have determined the nature of rural neighborhoods.

Whatever its type, however, the rural neighborhood consists of a number of families who live in face-to-face contact. As stated earlier, there is far more *esprit de corps* among the members of a neighborhood than in the community as a whole; in fact, after the family, the rural neighborhood is the basic social unit. T. Lynn Smith describes it succinctly:

Brazilian neighborhoods owe their integration to a wide variety of causes: to the visiting and mutual aid among families who live near one another; to the pooling of efforts in order to secure and maintain a church or a chapel or a school; to a mutual dependence upon a landed proprietor, a sugarmill, a cotton gin, a gristmill, a co-operative marketing association, a creamery or cheese factory, a rail-road station, or some other economic agency; to the grouping to-gether in close proximity of farm families who are intimately knit together by ties of kinship, national origins and language, and re-ligion; or to the fact that a few families have been thrown into close and constant contact among themselves, and isolated from the larger world, by establishing their residences in a small mountain valley or cove, a fertile and watered area in the midst of a barren region, on a small island, or even on a large fazenda or plantation.[10]

The nature of the Brazilian peasant community is closely re-lated to the process by which its peasantry arose. The Brazilian peasant differs profoundly from his European counterpart. Ex-cept for those European colonists who came in the nineteenth century, Brazilian peasants are not mixed farmers in the Euro-pean or early North American sense. European peasants char-acteristically produce staple grains and vegetables in conjunc-tion with livestock-raising and dairying. Use of the plow is general in Europe. Fertilization with manure permits a com-pletely sedentary agriculture. Houses can be constructed of permanent materials such as wood and stone, and the farm site can be passed down intact from generation to generation. Peasant families in Europe are often almost self-sufficient—they churn butter, make cheese, wine, and candles, weave cloth, bake bread, tan hides, and perform a hundred other household tasks. They often live in nucleated landholding villages, and there is a strong sense of village allegiance which emigrants carry with them long after they have left their native village. This is particularly true of present-day Portuguese immigrants to Brazil.

Most of this European peasant farming tradition was lost in

[10] T. L. Smith, Brazil: People and Institutions, p. 497.

the transfer of the Portuguese from the Old World to the New. The Brazilian peasant rarely combines agriculture with stock raising. He may have a few chickens, a pig or two, or even an occasional cow, but there is hardly enough meat for his family. Except in a few special localities, Brazilian peasant families do not weave, make butter or cheese, bake bread, or perform most of the other household arts of Europe. They either do without these products or purchase them with cash. To buy such foods and manufactured necessities, the Brazilian peasant must have a crop surplus to sell for cash or to trade in the market. Seldom does the Brazilian peasant fertilize his land, and in large parts of Brazil the plow is practically unknown. In reality, peasant agriculture consists mainly of horticulture; it follows slash-and-burn techniques closer to aboriginal than to European patterns. The peasant has tended to be seminomadic, planting and collecting in one locality until land exhaustion or other factors force him to migrate. Thus peasant homes generally have a temporary look, built as they are of adobe, wattle and daub, or palm leaves on a wooden framework. People have tended to locate their homes in isolation from one another, close to their gardens and to new sites suitable for clearing. The nucleated peasant village is relatively rare in Brazil, and peasant communities are generally made up of households scattered over extensive areas.

Part of this break with the European peasant farming tradition was due to the New World environment. Barley, rye, apples, grapes, and other temperate zone crops are not easily grown in much of Brazil, especially in the tropical North, which was the first region to be colonized. The general absence of wheat explains the loss of bread-making. The Eastern Highlands, however, extend the semitemperate zone of Brazil to within twelve degrees of the Equator, and many temperate crops can be grown in these highlands. Furthermore, maize, perhaps the world's most important food crop for livestock, grows everywhere in Brazil. There are other native crops such as beans, manioc, and peanuts that amply substitute for Old World plants. As always, climate has had its influence, but the absence of the European peasant farming tradition clearly results from a breakdown in the mechanism of culture transfer, rather than from the obstacles of the New World environment.

In fact not until sugar cane was planted along the Northeast Coast did the colonization of Brazil take on an agrarian character. Previously, colonization had been limited to forts and trading posts. Even the planters of sugar cane were hardly agriculturalists. Rather, they were businessmen, entrepreneurs, and administrators. Not they but their slaves, at first Indians and then Africans, actually tilled the land. This has been true of most producers of commercial crops, such as coffee, cacao, and cotton. In the first centuries, few Portuguese came to Brazil and very few were peasants. The majority were traders, petty noblemen, and bureaucrats, and they treated the land as if it were a factory, an industrial or business enterprise.

Until the nineteenth century, the Brazilian peasantry consisted mainly of non-Europeans and mestizos. The people who worked the land as farmers, hunters, and collectors were assimilated Indians, escaped and manumitted slaves, and people of mixed ancestry. These people quite naturally depended on aboriginal patterns to exploit the land; they lacked European models to follow. They occupied much of the land outside the orbit of the commercial plantations, but their hold on the land was, and still is, most precarious. Early in the colonial period, large tracts of land were granted by the Crown to individuals who could prove they were of *fidalgo* lineage. Through such grants, and subsequent resale and inheritance, vast areas of the Brazilian hinterland became privately owned. Such owners were city folk, and unless their land produced sugar or some other profitable crop, or else contained gold or diamonds, they paid little attention to their holdings. But their land did not remain totally uninhabited. The growing mass of mestizo peasants occupied some of it and exploited it in many ways. They planted *roças* (subsistence gardens of manioc, maize, and beans); they herded half-wild scrub cattle; they collected products of the forest such as palm nuts, Brazil nuts, and rubber; they fished and hunted for food and for pelts. They occupied the land as squatters, as *agregados*, and later as sharecroppers and sometimes as *sitiantes* (independent peasant owners).

It was not unusual for a landowner in the city to learn that his land had been occupied by hundreds of squatters. If the land could be made at all productive, the owner needed labor; thus, rather than expel these people, he tried to transform them into sharecroppers or wage laborers. Sometimes, owners of relatively productive land granted parts of it for the formation of a *vila*, to guarantee for themselves a labor supply beyond that provided by sharecroppers or permanent wage laborers.[11] Many small villages owe their existence to this procedure.

Thus a large variety of peasant neighborhoods arose throughout Brazil. In agricultural areas, such neighborhoods often consist of a group of houses not too close to one another. There

---

[11] José Artur Rios, "The Cities of Brazil," in Smith and Marchant, eds., *Brazil: Portrait of Half a Continent*, p. 201.

may be a chapel, a small store, and even a school at some central point. The people consist of thirty to fifty families and speak of themselves as "one big family." They may be *meieiros* or *parceiros*, as sharecroppers are called. They plant dry rice, cotton, tobacco, cacao, or other cash crops which they share with the landowner, who generally markets their produce and grants them advances of money and goods. They are also allowed their own plots of subsistence crops (manioc, beans, and maize), but sometimes they must give labor in return for such favors. In other regions, these peasant neighborhoods may be based on grazing or even on the collecting of tropical products. In the arid *sertão* of the Northeast, cowboys are sharecroppers—raising cattle on the land of an absentee owner and taking one-fourth of the herd increase as their share. They are allowed to graze their own herds on the land and, in addition, they plant small gardens. On the small subsidiary streams of the Amazon, there are neighborhoods of rubber collectors who are allowed to gather latex from several "roads" (i.e., trails of 100 or 150 wild rubber trees) by a trader who may or may not be the legal owner of the land. In addition, such people fish, hunt for food and pelts, and sometimes plant small gardens. Each Amazonian neighborhood of this type generally has a chapel, a patron saint, and a religious brotherhood that provides some formal leadership to the unit. Its members are tied to the trader, who advances them goods and food during the year and receives rubber in exchange. Likewise, throughout Brazil, there are neighborhoods of fishermen, collectors of *carnaúba* palms (Ceará), *babassu* nuts (Maranhão), coconuts (Northeast Coast), and other products.

The Brazilian peasantry has never been self-sufficient, and it has always been involved directly or indirectly in a cash economy. Thus the peasant is dependent on the town—he goes to town sometimes to sell his products, sometimes for religious festivals, sometimes to register a birth or have a child baptized or a daughter married, sometimes to vote if he can sign his name, sometimes to bury his dead, and sometimes just to watch and hear *movimento*. A peasant's term for going to town is *ir ao comércio* (go to the commerce) or *vamos à rua* (let's go to the streets). Yet most peasants have a profound distrust of townsfolk. Many do not register the birth of their children or legalize their weddings (although church weddings are prized more highly); they do not manifest much interest in local, state, or national politics except to please a *patrão*; and they stand back in awe in front of the town upper class and even its lower class. Townspeople often make fun of them because they are shy, lack town manners, and dress differently. Townspeople in the Northeast, for example, laugh at peasant women who smoke pipes—and at both sexes because they have the habit of squatting instead of sitting on chairs or benches. However, the town and the nearby countryside are clearly symbiotic; neither the peasants nor the townspeople could carry on life as they know it without one another.

PLANTATION NEIGHBORHOODS

The plantation system which was introduced into Brazil along with sugar cane in the sixteenth century also deviated drastically from any Old World agrarian system. In the New World, the plantation became a capitalistic enterprise based on the production and sale of a cash crop through slave and then through wage labor. In the Old World, the large landowner often extracted his income by means of feudal rents, while the peasants used the land to produce food crops. Not so in the New World, where the landowner used the lands to produce sugar, cacao, coffee, and sometimes cotton. This involved a large capital outlay to purchase and maintain slaves and later to extend credit and pay wages to free laborers. As stated earlier, the planter was a businessman, an entrepreneur, and an administrator rather than an agriculturalist. This highly commercial system of exploitation of the land, along with the crops that were produced and the system of labor supply that was used, determined the various subtypes of plantation neighborhoods in Brazil.

Sugar cane was Brazil's first commercial crop, and has the longest history. We can therefore use sugar plantations to illustrate patterns of plantation neighborhoods, but what has occurred on sugar plantations holds true in a very general way for coffee and cacao plantations. Earlier, we distinguished two subtypes of sugar plantation neighborhoods: the *engenho* and the *usina* types. *Engenho*-type neighborhoods are inhabited by workers (formerly by slaves) on family-owned plantations who are related to the landowners by traditional personal bonds as well as by economic ties. *Usina* neighborhoods are made up of the class we have earlier called the rural proletariat—people who work for impersonal managerial employers.

Earlier, in describing the Northeast Coast region, life on an *engenho*-type sugar plantation was described as it was during slavery. It was mentioned that with the abolition of slavery and with the introduction of the large steam-powered *usina* in the nineteenth century the *engenhos* tended to give way to the larger corporation-owned plantations. Today, of course, slavery has ended, but *engenho*-type plantations survive throughout Brazil. In *Village and Plantation Life in Northeastern Brazil* Harry W. Hutchinson describes Fazenda das Moças, a relatively small family-owned plantation in the Recôncavo region of Bahia which closely approximates the typical *engenho* neighborhood. At the time of his study (1950), Fazenda das Moças was owned by Dona Sinhá, a widow and a member of a local aristocratic family whose members are well known as sugar growers. The property extended over approximately 700 acres, about 50 percent of which was planted in sugar cane and the rest in pasture and subsistence crops. Of course, Fazenda das Moças was not truly an *engenho* any longer for it lacked any kind of mill; the cane was sold on contract to the nearby *usina*. But it did retain many aspects of the old *engenho* system. Dona Sinhá lived most of the year on the plantation and escaped to the city only during the heavy winter rains to stay with her children who were studying there. She and her family had an intimate, highly personalized relationship with the resident workers, along the traditional lines which were described earlier in reference to the rural lower class. She was clearly their *patrão* and felt a protective responsibility for their well-being.

The plantation neighborhood contained over 200 people, men, women, and children, who provided a working force of sixty to seventy men and boys. Although Dona Sinhá was present much of the time, she had an overseer, Seu Paulo, who was skilled in growing sugar cane and who directed the workmen and helped manage the plantation. Besides the overseer, there was also a foreman (*feitor*) who supervised the field hands and saw to it that the owner's and overseer's orders were carried out. These two men received monthly salaries; the only other salaried employee was the *vaqueiro* who cared for the oxen, milk cows, and horses and who also mended fences and performed other small tasks. The remainder of the resident workers, the *moradores* (residents), were paid by the task:

weeding, "carrying seed" (i.e., transplanting cane), or cutting the cane. They were given a house and also had the right to plant a small subsistence garden, usually on marginal land. Sometimes a workman might own an ox or burro which he was allowed to pasture on plantation lands and which he might rent to the owner for transportation during harvest time. In the slack season, a resident worker had the right to seek temporary employment elsewhere in the neighborhood, but his services had to remain at the disposal of Fazenda das Moças.

On the plantation there was a definite hierarchy of power and prestige descending from the owner and her family, through the overseer and the foreman, to the cowboy and the resident workers. Yet there was a strong sense of belonging. This was most noticeable in the attitude toward the migrant workers, generally from the arid Northeast, who came each year when they were needed during the harvest. Their services were secured through an *empreiteiro* (contractor), they left their families behind and lived temporarily in barracks, and they had little to do with the resident workers, who regarded them with suspicion as outsiders.

The actual plantation village of Fazenda das Moças contained, besides the owner's house and a house provided for the overseer, forty-five dwellings for resident workers and their families. These were oriented in a row forming a street; they were really apartments joined together under a common roof, similar in many ways to the houses flush on the street of a small town. The little plantation village had a school with rooms for classes and living quarters for the schoolteacher. There was a *casa de farinha*, a structure where the workmen's wives manufactured manioc flour, the staple in their diet. At

*A family of workers on a sugar plantation
in the state of Pernambuco*

the end of the street there were long barracks for the migrant workers. Next there were sheds to protect the tractor, jeep, plow, and other tools. The little settlement did not have a chapel as many others do; now and again the padre came to baptize children, offer First Communion, or perform marriages. The school also served as a temporary chapel. Neither did Fazenda das Moças have a store. The workmen and their families were dependent for many services on the larger community of which the town was the center.

It was, however, a tightly knit neighborhood. Life among the residents was close; some were kinsmen and others were tied to each other by ritual kinship as godparents to each other's children. Men cooperated in planting their little subsistence plots or repairing their houses and their wives worked together in the arduous task of making manioc flour. Most of them had spent a lifetime together, for the turnover of resident labor was small. Thus they felt each other's problems and sorrows strongly. Their problems and life situations were known to the family owner and to the overseer, who shared their neighborhood life in many ways. Nothing could bring this home more clearly, I think, than this excerpt from the diary of Dona Sinhá cited by Hutchinson:

"Dona Sinhá, there is a man here looking for you." "What is it my son?" "I have some boils coming out all over my body." Some sulfa and a little ointment do the trick, and just in time, for here comes Seu Paulo, the overseer.

"The oxen of Pedras, the neighboring plantation, invaded the cane fields last night. Also those of Seu Cosme." "I'll telephone the *usina* immediately." "Also, there are no wagons at the loading post." "I'll find out about that too."

The tractor driver comes, complaining that there is no oil. I get that from the storeroom. Now there are two men on the veranda wanting to know about the last payday, when they claim their money "came out wrong." Going through the pay sheets, that was straightened out.

Now, while there is no one else, I'll go out and look over the fields. I look at the plantings, feel the earth which I love. But it doesn't satisfy me. Something is missing. We are backward and retrogressing, passively. This place puts an inertia in the heart of a person, a desire to stop fighting, to find everything fine and as it should be—the ragamuffin Negroes, poorly fed, ignorant and rude, their dirty children with protruding stomachs and the white pretending that there is progress, his house full of company, electricity, radio, telephone . . . poetry of Baudelaire . . . but in the end, Zero! Sometimes I feel a tremendous anguish. . . . Deep down there is a clash against these indefatigable overseers, mulattoes, and Negroes with their boots, *senhores da fazenda*.[12]

There are many family-owned plantations throughout Brazil similar in many respects to Fazenda das Moças. There are cattle ranches in the extreme South, cacao plantations in southern Bahia, and mixed farms in Minas Gerais where a variety of crops and even dairy farming are the central occupation. There are even coffee plantations owned by families which form what I have called *engenho*-type neighborhoods. They differ from each other, of course, depending upon the crop that is produced, the method of remuneration of the workers, and regional history. But the social values and the traditional patterns of social relations between *patrão* and worker are essentially those described for Fazenda das Moças, and these values and relationships are an inheritance of the past.

In recent years, family-owned plantations have tended to give way before the impact of larger agricultural enterprises. I have called these larger and more complex plantations *usinas*,

[12] H. W. Hutchinson, *Village and Plantation Life in Northeastern Brazil*, p. 61.

although, as stated, this term applies in fact only to sugar cane plantations. Again, sugar plantations offer us the illustration which may be extended with certain modifications to coffee, cacao, cotton, and other one-crop plantations. The first power-driven sugar mills came to Brazil late in the nineteenth century. As we have said, they were known as *usinas* (factories) but also as the *engenho central*, indicating the centralization of the refining process in the factory. They were of course more efficient than the little *engenho* mills, and these began to disappear; the family-owned plantations sent their cane to the *usina* for processing. Little by little, the corporations administering the central factories went into the business of sugar-cane growing. They bought out family-owned farms and incorporated them into larger agricultural schemes. The result has been large factories in the field, infinitely more complex, efficient, and impersonal than the family-owned, *engenho*-type plantations which survive on the margins, so to speak, of the great *usina* plantations. One study carried out in Pernambuco a few years ago estimated that sixty *usina* corporations owned or controlled 57 percent of all the sugar-cane-producing lands of the state; about 19 percent of the land was in the hands of *fornecedores*, operators who sell their cane to *usinas*, and only 24 percent of the land was in the hands of the old-type mills.[13] The process of elimination of the small family plantation in the sugar industry has gone even further in São Paulo, which is now Brazil's most important sugar-producing state. Likewise, coffee plantations in São Paulo and Paraná states are often veritable factories in the field similar in many respects to the sugar *usina* plantations.

[13] See De Carli, cited in T. L. Smith, *Brazil: People and Institutions*, pp. 439–40.

As T. Lynn Smith has said, "For the laboring classes the coffee fazenda or the sugar usina frequently constitutes a little world—if it did not lack political functions it would rank as a community." [14] The central settlement of these large estates is a large village or even a town. It may contain from 500 to 2,000 people. There is a chapel, a school, a clinic (sometimes even a hospital), often a recreation club with a soccer field, a company store selling a wide variety of products, and sometimes even a cinema. On such usina-type plantations, housing is furnished by the management and is better and more permanent than on the engenho-type plantations. There is generally electricity and often a water-supply system that brings water to the workers' homes. The inhabitants are the managers, the technicians, the office workers, the barber, and others who provide services, as well as the factory and field workers. The latter have been described in Chapter 3 as the rural proletariat. Their relations with the corporation management are generally impersonal, and they no longer constitute a well-knit and cooperative little neighborhood of the engenho type. In fact, usina neighborhoods are often as heterogenous as the Brazilian small town.

T. Lynn Smith visited a coffee plantation of this type near Ribeirão Preto in São Paulo some years ago. In his excellent chapter "Leaves from My Diary" it is vividly described.[15] It was not a large estate compared to some others, but it consisted of 1,800 hectares (about 4,500 acres). Only 400 hectares were planted in coffee (360,000 trees). A thousand head of cattle were kept on the fazenda and provided manure to fertilize the trees. Eight hundred people lived on the estate, and their

[14] T. L. Smith, Brazil: People and Institutions, p. 510.
[15] Ibid., pp. 67–71.

homes extended "for nearly a mile along one side of the valley." The *fazenda* had a railroad station, a store, and a slaughter house in addition to the offices and drying floors for coffee. The workers' houses were three-room structures of masonry with tile roofs and floors. There was electricity and a water system. Each family was assigned a certain number of trees. A man and his wife alone could care for 4,000 and they were paid 350 milreis[16] per thousand trees. Each family paid a small amount for cooperative medical service, and the state supported a school on the premises. There was a chapel where services were held once a month. Many Brazilian small towns are more poorly serviced than this São Paulo coffee plantation, which was not as large and did not provide as many services as some others.

THE NEIGHBORHOOD AND THE TOWN

The Brazilian rural community consists of the village or town nucleus and a series of tributary neighborhoods of various types. A single community may contain several types of neighborhoods, and in some communities a single variety may predominate. In the Amazon community which I called Itá and which I studied some years ago, there were only peasant neighborhoods tributary to the town which was a municipal seat. But there were peasant neighborhoods of rubber collectors who seldom planted gardens, and there were neighborhoods of peasant farmers who derived their cash income from the sale of manioc flour.[17] In Vila Recôncavo, described by Hutchinson, there were a wide variety of neighborhoods—the *engenho-*

---

[16] Unit of currency prevailing in Brazil when Smith wrote. It was then worth 5 cents. In 1942 it was replaced by the *cruzeiro*.
[17] Wagley, *Amazon Town*.

type plantation described above, an *usina* neighborhood, a neighborhood of small peasant cultivators, and near the town a neighborhood of peasant fishermen.[18] Each Brazilian community might be analyzed in terms of the types of neighborhoods which are tributary to the village or town nucleus.

In a community dominated by monocultural plantation neighborhoods, either of the *engenho* or *usina* type, the rural population visits the town less frequently than in communities dominated by peasant neighborhoods. The whole community is dominated by the landed gentry who may live on their lands or in distant cities. Festivals are celebrated on the plantation rather than in the town. Political affairs are led by the landowners and not by the town upper class; thus, characteristically, these communities are less affected by political strife and competition. Unlike the peasant, the rural worker tends to shop in plantation stores rather than in the town. The town nucleus of the community becomes merely an administrative and political center, while the actual power lies with the landowners of the rural neighborhoods or with the executives and administrators of the large plantations.

Communities in which peasant-type neighborhoods predominate differ in many ways from those containing plantations. As stated earlier in describing the peasant-type neighborhood, the small town tends to be the focus of community life for cultivators, fishermen, rubber collectors, and others who have something to sell. The small town is their market and the place that attracts them for necessary religious, civil, and even social functions. Peasant-town communities are also somehow less progressive than plantation-town communities. Peasants

[18] H. W. Hutchinson, *Village and Plantation Life in Northeastern Brazil*. The name Vila Recôncavo is fictitious.

live in scattered neighborhoods which often lack schools, and children cannot go to school in the town because their families are poor and cannot spare them from work in the fields. Illiteracy is therefore very high, sometimes as high as 80 percent. In such communities, the priest, if there is one, lives in the town, and thus peasant religion is often unorthodox and filled with old folk concepts. While the monocultural plantation neighborhood is perforce tied to the outside world, since the product must be exported, the peasant neighborhood tends to be isolated and lacks adequate communication with the outside world. Thus the peasant-town and plantation-town types of rural Brazilian communities provide further variety on the complex national scene.

The urban community

An ever-increasing number of Brazilians live in urban communities; the population of cities, both large and small, is growing faster than that of the countryside and small towns. Not only are the great metropolitan centers growing with surprising rapidity, but so are middle-sized cities such as Campina Grande in Paraíba (126,000 people), Campinas in São Paulo (185,000), Corumbá in Mato Grosso (39,000), Anápolis in Goiás (52,000), and a hundred other urban communities in North and South Brazil. Some of these hardly existed twenty or thirty years ago. In fact, the time may soon come when the majority of Brazilians will live in urban communities with populations ranging from 25,000 to 100,000. But the great cities of Brazil are also growing at a fantastic rate. There are at least ten cities with over 250,000 inhabitants: São Paulo (3,300,000), Rio de Janeiro (3,300,000), Recife (789,000), Salvador (639, ooo), Pôrto Alegre (626,000), Belo Horizonte (663,000), Fortaleza (471,000), Belém (381,000), Curitiba (351,000), and Santos (263,000).[19] Most of these cities are old, but they have grown rapidly in recent years. In 1900, São Paulo had only 240,000 people. In the same year, Rio de Janeiro had 500,000, and, at that time, Belo Horizonte had just been built. The time may not be too far off when the majority of Brazilian people will be urbanites.

It is difficult to describe these Brazilian urban communities, whether middle-sized or metropolitan, for like all cities they are highly complex and the range of their ways of life is infinite. Some of the details of city life in Brazil have been described in a previous chapter, but something may be added here. Brazilian cities differ in many respects from North American and northern European cities; they are comparable in some respects to the Mediterranean cities. In New World terms, many are old —older than New York and other North American cities. They therefore have districts of narrow, winding streets, sometimes too narrow for a modern automobile. They have quaint *praças* or squares adorned with small churches; in some cities, such as Recife and Salvador, these churches are sixteenth- and seventeenth-century works of art. Since the early Portuguese colonization took place along the coast, most of the big cities are ports; there are white, palm-lined beaches near or even within the cities themselves. Few cities of the world can boast beaches such as Iracema in Fortaleza (Ceará), Boa Viagem in Recife (Pernambuco), Piatan or Itapoan in Salvador (Bahia), Copacabana or Ipanema in Rio de Janeiro (Guanabara), or Guarujá in Santos (São Paulo). Some of these cities, particularly Rio

---

[19] All figures are for 1960 and for the urban zone only; all of these cities continue to grow rapidly and by now have larger populations.

de Janeiro and Salvador, are already world-renowned for their natural beauty.

Brazilian cities differ profoundly in many ways from their North American counterparts. The difference in ecology and city plan is striking. Some of the newer cities and some new parts of older cities follow a quadrangular block plan similar

Bahia, upper and lower city

to that of North American cities, but in most Brazilian cities the streets seem to have followed old footpaths and the contours of the terrain. More than in North American cities, people speak of living in a particular district or *bairro*—in Laranjeiras or Copacabana in Rio de Janeiro, in Graça or Brotas in Salvador. There are upper-class and aristocratic *bairros* in most Brazilian cities, just as there are middle-class and lower-class districts. Surprising to the North American, however, is the mixture of fine homes and huts, of rich and poor, of well-paved streets and dirt paths, in almost every residential district. As cities expanded, pockets of unoccupied lots were left in less favorable spots. The shanty towns of the major cities have already been described. Furthermore, except in new cities and in very recent times, there were few zoning laws. As a result, commerce, residence, industry, stables, and food gardens are mixed in confusing array. Many people still keep chickens in their backyards near the heart of Rio de Janeiro. In the elite district of Barra where I lived in Salvador in 1962, I could often see from the veranda of our modern apartment horses, goats, and even pigs wandering down the street.

The settlement pattern of most Brazilian cities also differs from its North American counterpart in respect to the suburbs. Brazilian friends were always amazed when I told them that I lived in a suburb of New York. In Brazil the suburbs are lower-class areas, even for a professor. Transportation is inefficient and slow in Brazilian cities, and the suburbs are farther out in terms of time than they are in our big cities. Furthermore, Brazilian urbanites want to live near the center of things, for the shopping center and other urban facilities have not yet reached the suburbs. It is traditional for men in business and government to go home for lunch each day, and this would be impossible if they lived in a distant suburb. Difficulties of transportation, and the growing availability of lunchrooms and restaurants have reduced the number of people who return to their homes for lunch at mid-day; but still, even in Rio de Janeiro and São Paulo, the flow of people morning and evening between office and home puts a heavy burden on the already inadequate transportation system. So it is best to live near the center of town, and the suburbs are filled with lower-class housing.

Brazilian cities are old, but most of the urban services were installed between the turn of the century and World War I. It was at about this time that São Paulo became a modern urban center. During the years 1902 to 1906, Rio de Janeiro was almost remodeled, streets were broadened and new avenues opened. The first stretch of Rio's magnificent Avenida Beira Mar (Bay Shore Drive) was completed. "Electric lights and tree planting impressed a classic straightness of line on the old colonial plan." [20] In this period, water and sewer systems were built and concessions were granted to foreign companies to exploit them. After World War I, however, little was added despite the phenomenal growth of most cities. Even where there has been some effort to expand basic city services, the increase in population and demand has been far greater. Thus in the 1960s most Brazilian cities lag woefully in the basic services of a modern metropolis—water, sewers, garbage disposal, and in some cases electricity. Modern apartments in Rio de Janeiro are periodically without any water at all. Elevators in Recife suddenly stop functioning, not for lack of electric power, for Recife is connected to the Paulo Afonso hydroelectric system, but evidently because of the antiquated distribution system. As described earlier, telephones are inefficient to the point of hardly functioning at all in some Brazilian cities. Sewers serve but a portion of the city, and thus septic tanks are found in the heart of town. Garbage collection is sporadic, and dogs, even human scavengers, scatter scraps about the streets.

The situation in one Brazilian city, namely, Aracaju, the capital of the small state of Sergipe, illustrates the plight of

---

[20] José Artur Rios, "The Cities of Brazil," in Smith and Marchant, eds., *Brazil: Portrait of Half a Continent*, p. 205.

many Brazilian urban centers. In 1962, Aracaju was 107 years old and had about 116,000 people. It is a port and was built over swampland, and thus it has always had a mosquito and drainage problem. A sewer system was built in 1914, but it has hardly been expanded since. In 1962, this sewer system served only 10.6 percent of the population; only about half of the balance of residents had septic tanks. The city does not have a garbage disposal plant; it is estimated that 170 cubic meters of garbage are dumped per day in the outlying parts of the city. In the suburbs there are 300 pig sties of considerable size and 50 stables which add to the city's filth. Aracaju is in the poor state of Sergipe in northeastern Brazil. Although the Alliance for Progress offered some aid, it seemed unlikely that the municipality could ever raise the balance needed to improve public facilities.[21] Cities in the South are richer than Aracaju, and the more recently constructed centers such as Belo Horizonte, Goiânia, and Brasília have more up-to-date services; but throughout Brazil, in middle-sized and large cities, the level of public services is inadequate and even dangerous to the health of the people.

Brazilian urban communities maintain a level of public order that is amazing to the outsider in view of the apparent lack of police power. Tabloid-type newspapers in Rio de Janeiro and São Paulo report burglaries, murders, suicides, and juvenile delinquency with fanfare and gory detail; newspapers in other cities also like to report crime and scandal. The police are notably inefficient and few in number; in one Brazilian city, when a friend of mine attempted to report an accident involving his automobile, he was told by the officer in charge of the traffic department that there had been no accidents in the

[21] Report in the weekly news magazine *Visão*, July 27, 1962.

city that day. The matter rested there. When my wallet was stolen in a reputable hotel in Rio de Janeiro, the management did not think it worth-while to call the police. Yet one feels more at ease walking in dark streets in a Brazilian city than in its North American or European counterpart. Beggars will stop a pedestrian, and one sees homeless children, migrants, and cripples sleeping on benches. One has heard stories of assaults and muggings. Still one feels safe.

Perhaps this feeling of safety derives from my own innocence as an outsider. After living in Brazil for many years, I doubt that this is so, despite the many warnings of my Brazilian friends as to the dangers of their cities. I do not think every Brazilian urbanite is as safe as every other. It is the upper-class group that is relatively safe. The marked class lines of Brazilian society operate even today in the large cities. In a center of 500,000 or more people, one constantly meets friends in the street. I have yet to walk the length of the Avenida Rio Branco in Rio de Janeiro without stopping at least once to chat with a friend or acquaintance. Brazilian cities seem small in relation to their population figures. This is so because only a small segment of the population participates fully in urban life. The great masses of people are unable to make full use of the urban world. In line with this class system, individuals are recognized as upper class, or at least non-lower-class, by their clothes, their bearing, their speech, and their attitude toward the person encountered. Criminals are generally (though not invariably), lower-class people. They still have feelings of respect for the upper-class person—or the foreigner who looks like one. They are delighted to pick his pocket or burglar his room, but they would be almost embarrassed to "hold him up"—a personal confrontation. Besides, a crime against a person of high status generally leads to police action, while a crime against a *popular* may be simply recorded on the police blotter and forgotten. A person of status may, and generally does, have friends; he or she will put pressure on the police. The mistake of a personal encounter with a person of status can lead to trouble for the lower-class criminal. Thus for a minority of the population Brazilian cities have a peaceful appearance. The great cities are changing—gang warfare has appeared in São Paulo and Rio de Janeiro. In time, even urban crime will become impersonal.

Finally, it must be said that Brazilians are profoundly urban in their hopes. There is not a person in the nation who does not hope to visit Rio de Janeiro, São Paulo, or Brasília. Statistically, Brazilians are mainly rural, but in their aspirations they seek the city. They are interested in Paris, New York, and Rome, and they hope to visit these cities also. They like *movimento*, "progress," and the vivacity of urban life. Brazilians will continue to move, when they can, from the country to the town and from the town to the city.

❧ 5 ❧ FAMILY AND EDUCATION

THE family and the system of education are fundamental institutions which guarantee the continuity of any human society. It is in the family that most human beings begin their education in an informal manner and where most of any human culture is learned. And, in complex societies such as Brazil, it is in the school that people normally acquire the literate tradition and become fully functioning members of the nation. Both the family and the school are important in creating unity in the Brazilian nation, although neither institution actually reaches a large part of the Brazilian people. Both institutions function as "ideal patterns" toward which many Brazilians aspire and which many do not experience. There are many Brazilians without family or kinsmen and many who never attend a school, yet these two related institutions are basic in making people Brazilians. This is one of the many contradictions of Brazil.

The family

There seems to be unanimous agreement among students of Brazilian social history that the family has been in the past the most important single institution of Brazilian society. In the course of Brazilian history, important families have dominated the economic, political, and even religious life of various regions and of the nation. In his inimitable fashion, the Brazilian social historian Gilberto Freyre makes this point in his modern classic, *The Masters and the Slaves*:

> The family and not the individual, much less the State or any commercial company, was from the sixteenth century the great colonizing factor in Brazil, the productive unit, the capital that cleared the land, founded plantations, purchased slaves, oxen, implements; and in politics it was the social force that set itself up as the most powerful colonial aristocracy in the Americas. Over it the King of Portugal may be said, practically, to have reigned without ruling. The representatives in the municipal council, the political expression of these families, quickly limited the power of the kings and later that of imperialism itself, or, better, the economic parasitism that sought to extend its absorbing tentacles from the Kingdom to the colonies.[1]

While in other Latin American cultures familism has been an important aspect of social life, in Brazil there has been almost a cult of the family.

There is no doubt as to the historical importance of the family in Brazil on the part of most students of Brazilian society and culture, but there does seem to be some confusion as to exactly what social unit has played this role—the nuclear family (man, wife, and children), the joint family headed by a patriarch, or an even larger group of relatives. In Brazil, the term family is used to cover all three of these groups. This may well be related to a certain vagueness in Brazilian Portuguese, for when a Brazilian speaks of *minha família* (my family) as often as not he means a large extension of kinsmen rather than merely his wife and children.

It is obviously not the limited nuclear family that has dominated politics, economics, and religion. This role has been

---

[1] Freyre, *The Masters and the Slaves*, pp. 26–27.

assigned to the patriarchal family, the larger group consisting of the patriarch, his wife, sons and daughters, often the latter's spouses and children, sometimes his younger brothers, and even, during plantation days, his slaves. There is no doubt that this patriarchal structure did characterize the traditional Brazilian family, yet as one examines the structure of families who have been and in many cases still are important, it becomes clear that they consisted of a unit larger than the patriarchal family. The Vilas Boas, Tourinhos, Junqueira Ayres, and Calmons of Bahia, the Prados and Penteados of São Paulo, the Oliveira Castros, Alberto de Farias, and Pereira Passos of Rio de Janeiro, and the colonial Wanderleys and Cavalcantis of Pernambuco (mentioned so frequently by Freyre), although they carry the names of ancestral patriarchs, actually form large webs of kinship which are bilateral (i.e., which extend both on the father's and the mother's side) and extend far beyond any patriarchal nucleus. The unit might be described technically as a "kindred," but Brazilians have sometimes used the term *parentela* (kinship group) or even "clan" to describe these large groups. It is this *parentela*, and not the nuclear family or even the patriarchal family, that was traditionally the most important single institution in Brazil.

What, exactly, was the Brazilian *parentela?* In a few words, it consisted of all recognized relatives on both one's mother's and one's father's side, along with the kinsmen of one's spouse. A first cousin was called *primo irmão* (literally, "brother cousin"), and the term *primo* (cousin) was widely applied to very distant relatives. Often the terms for uncle and aunt were similarly applied. In the past, the middle and upper classes seldom moved from one part of the country to another, and even today such movement is far less frequent in Brazil than in the United States. Thus, one generally continued to live in the city, town, or rural zone near one's kinsmen. The number of people one might consider kin was limited only by genealogical memory, willingness to claim kinship with others, and willingness of others to recognize distant kinship bonds. Upper-class Brazilians are traditionally interested in genealogy. Thus, the *parentela* of an upper-class Brazilian, even today and in an urban setting, may often include literally hundreds of people.

In reality, however, the Brazilian *parentela* was not merely a bilateral extension of relatives as described above. On more careful analysis, there was another structuring principle which gave rise to what might be called ancestor-oriented families. By this I mean family groups that are descended either through the father or through the mother from a well-known personage —from a *donatário* (recipient of a land grant) of the sixteenth century, a rich *senhor de engenho* (plantation owner) of the seventeenth- and eighteenth-century sugar boom, a "coffee baron" of the nineteenth century, or a "nobleman of the empire" who was granted his title by the Emperor for his public service or simply for his wealth. Other ancestor-oriented families date from the early republic (late nineteenth and early twentieth centuries) and descend from a statesman or a diplomat of fame. Still other ancestor-oriented families are derived from twentieth-century capitalists who may even have been immigrants. Such groups have been known by the surname of the original patriach from whom they were descended. Members of such groups often carried on the "tradition" of the ancestral founder, and became known predominantly as politicians, diplomats, scientists, or professionals. Generally, such ancestor-oriented families were more limited than the larger *parentela.* There was a tendency for those individuals not carrying the illustrious name to lose their connection with the ancestor-oriented group (but not with the broader range of kinsmen).

Crucial to the traditional Brazilian *parentela*, and especially to its ancestor-oriented segments, was the system of name transmission. Surnames were the public symbols of membership in a *parentela* or in an important ancestor-oriented family. Unlike the Spanish system of name transmission, which has been retained in most Spanish-American countries, the mother's name was not appended to that of the father [i.e., José Aguirre (father's surname) y Sanchez (mother's surname)]. At least theoretically, a Brazilian also adopted both his father's and mother's name, but, unlike the Spanish custom, the mother's paternal name was inserted between the given name and the father's paternal name. Thus the son of João Mendes Campos and his wife Marieta Prado Almeida Campos would be called João Almeida Campos. In reality, however, it was expected that this rather theoretical system would be manipulated to indicate ties with important ancestors and *parentelas*, or simply to honor a particular side of the family or a specific individual. In fact, if there was any ideal pattern relating to the transmission of names, it was that a person should select the names of his parents or grandparents which carried the most prestige. Thus, in the imaginary nuclear family given as an example above, the son João Almeida Campos might well have as siblings Marieta Prado Campos, José Mendes Campos, and even Antônio Prado Almeida Campos.[2] Sometimes even the given

[2] Antônio Candido gives the following example taken from the *Nobiliarquia Paulistana Histórica e Geneológica* (2d ed., Rio de Janeiro, Instituto Histórico e Geográfico Brasileiro, 1926), I, 164: "From the marriage, in the 17th century, of Tomé de Lara e Almeida with Dona Maria de

name of a man of prestige might be adopted as a surname; thus, Artur Ribeiro might have children and grandchildren called Maria Artur Ribeiro, José Artur Ribeiro, and so on. "The name," writes one Brazilian sociologist in discussing the *parentela*, "expressed less the tie of filial relationship than participation in a vast kinship system." [3] Thus, certain well-known surnames, a few of which have been mentioned earlier, became symbols of large and important *parentelas*, and in each region of the country the interlocking of *parentelas* (and ancestor-oriented families) was indicated by the constant recurrence of famous surnames in the upper class.

In addition to those related by consanguinity or by marriage, the traditional Brazilian *parentela* also included "a periphery not always well delineated, made up of the slaves and *agregados*, Indians, Negroes, or mixed bloods, in which were included the concubines of the chief and his illegitimate children." [4] Often the illegitimate children of men from respectable families were brought into the *parentela* and were raised by a kinsman of the father; in many cases they were even adopted by the father's legitimate wife, who "accepted the children of her husband, especially if they were born before their marriage." [5] There was also the widespread custom of taking *filhos de criação* (adopted children) into the family. These were not necessarily illegitimate kinsmen, but children from the lower classes taken into upper-class homes partly as servants and partly

---

Almeida Pimentel (the pair having one name in common), there were born: Fernando Paes de Barros, Antonio de Almeida Lara, José Pompeu Ordonho, Lucrécia Pedroso de Barros, Maria de Almeida Lara, Sebastiana de Almeida, Branca de Almeida, Inácia de Almeida, Luzia Leme, and Maria de Almeida Lara Pimentel." Cited in Candido, "The Brazilian Family," in Smith and Marchant, eds., *Brazil: Portrait of Half a Continent*, p. 299n.

[3] *Ibid.*, p. 299.
[4] *Ibid.*, p. 294.
[5] *Ibid.*, p. 301.

as members of the family. Furthermore, people of the lower strata who were slaves, tenants, or employees felt associated, often vicariously, with the kinsmen of their *patrão*. In many cases this relationship between lower-class people and upper-class families continued for generations. Domestics were often the children of another generation of domestics (or even slaves) in the same family. In particular, there seems to have been a pattern of a continued familylike relationship with the children's nurse. In one contemporary case, a group of cousins have cooperated, each contributing a monthly sum, toward the retirement of an old Negro woman who was their childhood nurse. Tia Joana (as we may call her) visits their homes regularly, helps in their homes when babies are born, attends birthday parties and other family affairs, and regularly carries news (and gossip) from one household to another. She is an intimate and important member of the family.

The traditional *parentela* was also extended by means of the well-known *compadrio* system. Traditionally, in Brazil as in other Latin cultures, the sponsorship of a child at baptism sets up an important relationship not only between the *afilhado* (child) and the *padrinho* and *madrinha* (godparents), but also between the latter and the parents of the child, who call each other by the reciprocal terms *comadre* and *compadre*. Traditionally, these were relationships of mutual aid and support as strong as those of consanguinity. The godparent was expected to take the place of a parent in case of need and to aid the godchild on any occasion. Likewise, the godchild held his godparents in the highest respect and would seek their blessing on every possible occasion. The relationship between *comadres* and *compadres* was not only one of mutual aid and support, but was also subject to the rules of incest. In addition to baptism, an individual in Brazil might normally expect to acquire another godparent at Confirmation, and two more at marriage. And, at least in northern Brazil, there were the *compadres, comadres, afilhados, padrinhos,* and *madrinhas de fogueira* (godfather, etc., "of the fire") acquired by mutual consent on St. John's Eve simply by reciting a verse and jumping over the ritual fire together. Any individual might, therefore, expect in the normal course of life to extend his pseudo-kinship ties to at least ten individuals in this way.

This system of *compadrio* was traditionally used in Brazil in two ways. On the one hand, it might be used to reinforce and strengthen already existing kinship ties. Thus, it was traditional for an older sibling to be made the godparent of a younger brother or sister; or, more commonly, an uncle and aunt, or perhaps a distant cousin and his spouse, were invited to serve in this capacity. On the other hand, it was just as traditional to use the *compadrio* system as a mechanism for bringing outsiders into the family circle. Members of the upper class thus related themselves and their progeny to upper-class individuals of other *parentelas.* More important, members of the lower class invited individuals of large and powerful upper-class families to serve as godparents to their children, thus linking themselves and the godchild in a pseudokin relation to such groups. In his history of the city of Salvador, Thales de Azevedo describes these patterns clearly:

The Christian institution of *compadrio* not only wove strong ties of spiritual kinship among families of the same category but also among families on different [social] levels, and in this way secured for many poor, black, illegitimate and rejected children the protection of rich or prestige-laden *padrinhos* who were concerned with their health, nutrition, education, and future occupation—

padrinhos who often gave their own surname to their favorite god-children, who sometimes made them their heirs, who arranged marriages and employment, and who raised them in the midst of their own children.[6]

The system of *compadrio* was so important in traditional Brazilian society that the term *compadrismo* came to be synonymous with a system of political protection.

Finally, in discussing the traditional Brazilian *parentela*, the point must be made that it was not a corporate group, although segments of it, united under a strong patriarch, sometimes held *latifúndios* in common and engaged in bitter feuds with one another over generations.[7] The traditional authority of the patriarch was practically unlimited, and cases of men ordering their sons or daughters to be put to death are cited by historians.[8] But generally such landholding groups and such patriarch-led families were only segments of the larger *parentela*. Sometimes there seems to have been a sort of family council of the oldest males in a kinship group which provided a rather vague kind of leadership. However, in general, the *parentela* was an amorphous and interlocking web of kinsmen rather than a well-defined, corporate social group.

In addition to the ideal patterns which people held as to how the traditional *parentela* ought to be organized, there were

[6] Azevedo, *Povoamento da cidade do Salvador*, p. 171.

[7] Costa Pinto, in *Lutas de famílias no Brasil*, studies the famous feud between the Pires and the Camargos which began about 1640. Individuals of various other names participated. The feud began as a fight between two patriarchal families and extended to their *parentelas*.

[8] Antônio Candido cites the cases of a patriarch who "executed a daughter who waved a handkerchief to one whom he thought to be her lover" and of another who ordered his retainers to kill his illegitimate son for making off with the father's mistress ("The Brazilian Family," in Smith and Marchant, eds., *Brazil: Portrait of Half a Continent*, p. 295). Gilberto Freyre cites similar cases (*The Masters and the Slaves*, pp. 418 ff.).

of course a series of ideal patterns which stated how an individual ought to act as a member of the kinship group. These ideal patterns of behavior influenced how and whom a Brazilian married, how his children were brought up, how he carried out his economic and professional life, with whom he associated in his normal round of social life, and even his political activities and viewpoints. Perhaps more than any other Brazilian institution these ideal patterns provided points of reference throughout an individual's life.

Fundamental among the ideal patterns associated with kinship were those relating to the bringing-up of children. As in most societies, the care of small children was primarily the task of the nuclear family, and it was this more restricted group which had the most important influence on the early development of the child. Yet, in Brazil, particularly among members of large and traditional *parentelas*, the scope of a child's world during his early years was to a large extent limited to the kinship circle. This group might almost be said to have been as important as the nuclear family in the education of the child. On plantations, in provincial cities, and in small towns, children were surrounded by affectionate uncles, aunts, grandparents, and godparents, with whom they might spend almost as much time as with their own parents. The primary task of caring for children was left to domestics, who were themselves often on the periphery of the *parentela*. The child's playmates, at least in early years, were generally cousins or the children of domestics and employees of the family. So close was the relationship of first cousins that they came to be considered almost brothers and sisters, as the term *primo irmão* implies. It was thought that one's children ought to play with children of relatives and with children of friends rather than with "unknown" schoolmates and children of the neighborhood, for one could be sure of the social and moral background of these kinsmen and near-kinsmen. As children grew older, the preference for association with kinsmen continued.

The importance of kinship in the formation of the individual personality is shown by the widely held Brazilian belief that there are well-defined family characteristics, at least among ancestor-oriented families. In speaking about the past, Gilberto Freyre points to specific families known for their "alcoholic degeneracy," "tendency to lie," "horror of paying their debts," and "love of a fight." He speaks of others who were known as "weak minded" and as "traditional misers or sharpers in business." "In the words of the people," he writes, "there is not a Wanderley who does not drink, an Albuquerque who does not lie, a Cavalcanti who does not owe. Nor a Sousa Leão or a Carneiro da Cunha who does not like a Negro woman." [9] Other families were known for their "love of luxury," "ability as scientists," and "astuteness in politics," to mention but three well-known cases. There was, of course, confusion in the public mind between genetically determined and learned behavior as the basis for these supposed family characteristics. Often they were attributed to the frequency of cousin marriage, but it was also recognized that they were the result of family tradition and the early acquisition of personality traits within the family circle.

Kinship also played an important role in ideal patterns of marriage. In the days of the old rural gentry, marriage was very often almost a contract between families, or, almost as often, between members of the same *parentela*. Marriages between *primos irmãos* occurred frequently, as well as between

[9] Freyre, *The Masters and the Slaves*, p. 268 and note.

distant cousins.[10] Obviously, such marriages were often economically motivated, serving to retain wealth within the
parentela. It would seem that they were also socially motivated,
based upon the desire to keep the family from being tainted by
those who might have Negro ancestry. But, in addition, it may
be that cousin marriage was often an outcome of the social
relations and intimacy allowed to young people within the
parentela. In a society which restricted the activities of young
women and which looked with suspicion upon the attentions
of unmarried males, social relations between young men and
women who were not related were highly circumspect. At
least cousins might meet freely in family gatherings, and
parents felt secure in allowing their daughters the company
of male cousins, of whose background and moral qualities they
were fully aware. Thus, it is not surprising that romantic at-
tachments frequently blossomed between kinsmen.[11] Since most
upper-class families within any given region of the country were
interrelated, many marriages, even when not between cousins,
were between individuals who could trace some distant relation-

[10] An analysis of sixty-two marriages covering seven generations (1780–
1900) of one "family" in the municipality of Vassouras (Rio de Janeiro
state) "reveals thirty-six unions between participants not recognizably
related, twenty among first cousins, three involving uncles and nieces,
and one between an aunt and nephew" (Stein, *Vassouras*, p. 154). There
was considerable concern in the late nineteenth century over the possible
biological consequences of frequent consanguineous marriages (Freyre,
The Masters and the Slaves, p. 267).

[11] A story told me by a well-known Brazilian novelist of her own
northeastern "family" illustrates with some exaggeration the pattern of
marriage within the same kinship group. According to the story, when
she was almost twenty years old, she once heard her parents in a rather
violent argument during which her father spoke harshly and in violent
language to her mother. The mother, shocked and angry, exclaimed to
her husband of over twenty years, "What right have you to say things
like that to me! You are not even my relative!" (*O senhor nem é meu
parente!*)

ship. On the other hand, marriages sometimes took place between a young lady of a large and powerful family and an unusually ambitious and socially mobile man. In such cases, it was the groom who adhered to his wife's *parentela*, ignoring as far as possible his inferior origins.

Members of traditional *parentelas* were tied to one another by a series of social obligations. These obligations were strong in the case of closely related kinsmen such as parents, siblings, grandparents, uncles and aunts, nephews and nieces, and first cousins, but they included in somewhat attenuated form all members of a *parentela*. For example, one was supposed to remember a kinsman's birthday (some people kept notebooks for the purpose, but others seemed to have phenomenal memories for such facts). On one's own birthday, one expected to receive visitors, most of whom were relatives. Even on the birthday of a small child, there would be a reunion of mothers and children who were served ice cream and a variety of typical Brazilian cakes and sweets. Toward the end of the afternoon, they might be joined by fathers and other male relatives. A child's birthday party became an event in which both children and adults (domestics included) participated. Similarly, one was expected to attend weddings, wedding anniversary celebrations, graduation exercises, funerals, Masses for the dead, and other family rituals and celebrations. If an individual had some 200 kinsmen in the community, as did many middle- and upper-class Brazilians, it should be readily apparent that most of his social life was filled with family affairs.

Kinship has traditionally dominated Brazilian economic life. As many Brazilian writers have pointed out, many of the important families or clans originated as the owners of sugar and

coffee plantations or vast cattle ranches. In the early days of
Brazilian history, the so-called large patriarchal families were an
integral part of an essentially agricultural, rural, semifeudal,
economic regime which depended upon slaves for labor. But,
in time, the influence of large *parentelas* spread from the agricultural regions into the cities. Practically all Brazilian commercial and industrial enterprises were once family-owned and
administered. Furthermore, a man's role as a member of a
kinship circle influenced his daily performance of business activities. In the world of business and professional life it was
expected that kinsmen would constantly call upon one another
for favors and support. A businessman would call upon a cousin
or *compadre* to seek his help in speeding up the issuance of an
export license or to clear a legal document more quickly
through a government bureau. Or, lacking a kinsman to perform a particular service, he would make use of the broader
aspects of the *parentela*. He would seek out a cousin of a
compadre or a friend of a cousin who might be able to help
in the particular instance. Such small favors were to be repaid
in kind. Likewise, one might select one's lawyer and one's
physician from among one's kin. The mechanics of business
and bureaucracy were made palatable and smooth by using
personal relations stemming in one way or another from kinship ties.

Kinship also had important functions in politics. In fact,
at the beginning of the century, state politics were spoken of
as oligarchies dominated by one or two large *parentelas*. In
each state certain well-known *parentelas* or ancestor-oriented
families dominated local political parties, which were but reflections of family interests. The families who were politically
dominant in the state depended upon local political leaders in

the small towns and rural zones whose power, in turn, depended upon their own *parentela*. Both state and local political leaders sought votes among the middle and lower classes, not so much on the basis of political or public issues as on the basis of personal loyalties to themselves and their families. Even national politics operated in terms of coalitions between large regional *parentelas*.

In keeping with the important role of kinship in political life, it is not strange that nepotism was rife in Brazilian government service. It was rather expected that when a man was appointed or elected to office he would find positions for numerous relatives. This is an "evil" of which Brazilians have long complained and yet in which they have fully participated. Nepotism reflected both a man's obligation to his kinsmen and his dependence upon them. And, in a sense, nepotism was not always evoked simply to advance the interests of kinsmen. A man in an important office sought assistants and employees of whose abilities, honesty, and loyalty he could be assured. It thus seemed logical for him to look for such people among his relatives—the people he knew best. Thus nepotism was not necessarily looked upon as an evil but simply as the most efficient way of surrounding oneself with people of known qualifications.

Up to this point, I have consciously treated the Brazilian *parentela* as if it were a thing of the past. Some students of Brazilian society as well as many Brazilians will argue that this is so. The drastic social, economic, and political changes in Brazilian society during the last decades would seem to mitigate against the continuation of such a way of life. Furthermore, the majority of Brazilians have never had a large *parentela*. It was an institution of the small elite in which the lower classes of the city and the rural zone participated only marginally. Yet it is my thesis that this institution persists today, as in the past, and that its study is essential to an understanding of modern Brazil. The *parentela* continues today, although in modified form, and it helps us understand the nation's unity. As one well-known student of Brazilian culture has written of contemporary Brazil:

There is probably not a single major institution in Brazil which is not to a considerable extent controlled or deflected by family interests. It is true that in areas of heavy foreign immigration the position of the family oligarchies was not strong enough to prevent the rise of a new economic and political elite, *but it also is true that the new elite has adopted the same patterns of familism and nepotism which characterized the traditional power structure.*[12]

And, as a very astute Brazilian writer states succinctly, "The patriarchal system still impregnates the minds of Brazilians, even when they are no longer able to live it out."[13]

A series of interviews (unfortunately the author does not state how many or among what socioeconomic groups) undertaken in the city of São Paulo, perhaps the most urbanized locale in all Brazil, showed that people "were able to distinguish between 30 and 500 relatives, a considerable part of whom lived in the same city."[14] And, in the city of Salvador, one of Brazil's most conservative societies, one member of an important and traditional family was able to name 290 relatives (53 of whom were deceased) and give their precise

---

[12] Willems, "The Structure of the Brazilian Family," *Social Forces,* XXXI (1953), 345. The italics are my own.

[13] Tavares de Sá, *The Brazilians: People of Tomorrow,* p. 10.

[14] Willems, "The Structure of the Brazilian Family," *Social Forces,* XXXI (1953), 343

genealogical relationship from memory, without recourse to the aid of other people or of documents.[15]

My own interviews and my experience among the middle and upper classes in Rio de Janeiro, Salvador, and other localities indicate that people of the middle and upper classes have 100 or 200 kinsmen with whom they maintain relations, while people related to wealthy and traditional families often have many more. Crowded urban conditions have dispersed these kinsmen throughout the city, but constant telephone conversations, frequent visiting, and many family gatherings at weddings and baptisms keep these large groups in intimate and continuous contact. There is also a trend, which is often noted but as yet unstudied, for kinsmen to purchase co-operative apartments in the same building, thus bringing, as it were, part of a *parentela* under the same roof. Particularly in the less industrialized and more conservative cities of northern Brazil, *parentelas* continue to be very large and are the focus of social life for the upper class.

To a large extent, the new Brazil has brought to an end the political power of family oligarchies on the national scene,[16] although in small communities and rural zones kinship still dominates politics. Today, with mass communication and political campaigns appealing to the large urban populations, political issues cannot be decided between *parentelas*. Yet certain upper-class families such as the Melo Francos, originally from Minas Gerais, are still leaders in politics. Despite the creation of federal and state civil service commissions and the

---

[15] C. J. A. Hutchinson, "Notas preliminares ao estudo da família no Brasil," *Anais da II Reunião Brasileira de Antropologia* (1957), 268.

[16] This is not strictly true. Governor Brizzola of Rio Grande do Sul is the brother-in-law of President Goulart; members of the ancestor-oriented family of Getúlio Vargas are found throughout the government.

use of competitive examinations for public positions, nepotism still plays an important role in the recruitment and advancement of personnel in any Brazilian government organization. The persistence of nepotism, according to one Brazilian, "is a carry-over from the days when the head of the family felt responsible for finding work for all his male relatives that would keep them at hand. Today when a man reaches high office, as often as not he embarks upon the distribution of well-paid public jobs among members of his family, close and distant." [17]

Large and important *parentelas* and ancestor-oriented families still dominate Brazilian economic life. In writing about contemporary Brazil, Tavares de Sá notes: "This economic solidarity of the family group accounts for the very large number of corporations, commercial enterprises, and industries whose stock is controlled entirely by different branches of one family." [18] An American economist writing about Brazil only a few years ago (i.e., 1949) says: "The power of the oligopolists and the duopolists is enhanced by the strong ties which exist among a few great families that are strong in business and politics." [19] This same writer mentions the names of such families as the Matarazzos, Crespis, Fontes, Klabins, and Lodis, some of whom are recent immigrants who would presumably have but few kinsmen. But, as I have said, the members of this new upper class have adapted easily to the ideal patterns of Brazil. They have intermarried with traditional Brazilian families and have already established their own ancestor-oriented families. A study of the society columns of the newspapers of Rio de Janeiro and

[17] Tavares de Sá, *The Brazilians: People of Tomorrow*, p. 11.
[18] *Ibid.*, p. 10.
[19] Henry William Spiegel, *The Brazilian Economy*, p. 228.

São Paulo indicates the rapid increase of non-Luso-Brazilian names in high society and the frequency of intermarriage of this new upper class with the older family lines.

The other social segments of the large metropolitan centers of Brazil do not share, in practice, this emphasis upon kinship, although it stands before them as a model of the desirable form of Brazilian behavior. Members of the emerging middle class are often recent migrants from provincial cities and small towns. They frequently help their kinsmen migrate to the metropolitan centers, and they maintain contact with their kinsmen at home. They sometimes have many relatives and *compadres* in the big city, and these may have middle-range positions in government and commerce where they are exceedingly useful to kinsmen and even to mere acquaintances in their home town or state. The lower-class groups in the big cities suffer most from the lack of kinsmen. When they come from not too distant small towns and rural zones, they may be accompanied by relatives or compatriots. But they often come from very far away—from the Northeast to Rio de Janeiro or São Paulo. Many of them are illiterate, or at least unaccustomed to writing, and thus lose contact with their relatives at home. It is this segment of the Brazilian society, more than any other, that would seem to lack the support of a *parentela*, or for that matter of the personal relations which Brazilians prize so much. As I have pointed out earlier, they are thus highly vulnerable to the charismatic approach of leaders who stress paternalism.

The *parentela* is still very important among the local elite of the small Brazilian town. Evidence from the many studies of small communities shows that kinship groups control the economic, political, and social life of most localities. The evidence is too extensive to cite here, but such writers as Borges Costa[20] and Maynard Araujo[21] describe the large families or *parentelas* of small communities in the arid Northeast; Harris reports on those of a community in the Eastern Highlands,[22] Willems on the coastal mountains of São Paulo,[23] and Hutchinson on the Recôncavo region of Bahia.[24] Such groups were also important in the small Amazonian community which I studied in 1948.[25] It must also be noted that peasants, plantation workers, and lower-class groups in small towns have not shared historically in the institution of the *parentela*; but in most cases they have formed the periphery of large families, being attached either economically or socially to these important groups. These provincial and small-town *parentelas* are hardly as extensive as those of the larger cities, but they control the local scene. Furthermore, they often have kinship connections with important families in the state capital. The web of kinship in Brazil, even today, cuts across class barriers and extends from the small towns into the cities. Curiously, kinship unites social classes and people from disparate communities.

The image of the traditional *parentela* persists in Brazil as an ideal pattern for people of various classes in the cities, the towns, and even the countryside. The persistence of familism has acted as a block to the formation of national political parties, the creation of an impersonal bureaucratic system of gov-

[20] Borges Costa, "Relações de família em Cerrado e Retiro," *Sociologia*, XVII (1955), 132–46.
[21] Maynard Araujo, "A família numa comunidade alagoana" *Sociologia*, XVII (1955), 113–31.
[22] Harris, *Town and Country in Brazil*, pp. 148–49.
[23] Willems, *Cunha: tradição e transição em uma cultura rural do Brasil*, pp. 56–57, 77.
[24] H. W. Hutchinson, *Village and Plantation Life in Northeastern Brazil*, pp. 127 ff.
[25] Wagley, *Amazon Town*, p. 148 f.

ernment, and the development of economic enterprises that would enlist wide public participation. The relative absence in Brazil of such organizations as parent-teachers associations, garden clubs, and civic clubs is related to the preference of Brazilians to associate with kinsmen. Brazilians used to be first members of a family, then of a region, and finally of their nation; now I would say that they are Brazilians first, but they never forget their family connections.

Education

The formal educational system of Brazil would seem to be a weak institution in which to seek a basis for national unity. Almost 50 percent of the Brazilian people are illiterate, and almost the same percentage of school-age children are not attending school. The growth of educational facilities cannot keep pace with the rapid expansion of the population. In fact, there is a danger that Brazil may become an "India of South America"—a country filled with illiterates yet boasting an elite with a great literate tradition. The formal educational system remains out of reach for many Brazilians, and offers a program of study beyond the grasp of most teachers and their pupils. Weak as the educational system may be, however, it is the principal mechanism carrying on the literate Great Tradition mentioned earlier in this book, namely, the written codes of law, historical records, philosophy, theology, science, literature, and other aspects of the European tradition in Brazil.

Brazilian educators who wish to revolutionize their country by educational means are confronted with monumental barriers deriving from the past. The Brazilian educational system is oriented toward the upper class. It is theoretical and encyclopedic in orientation, with little emphasis upon what we might call empirical and pragmatic problems. A person educated according to the official curriculum from primary school through the university would be among the better trained people of the world, with a general and technical background unparalleled in most Western countries. In reality, however, the Brazilian educational system from primary to university level consists of a series of "ideal patterns"—concepts projected by the society and held in esteem by all, but realized by only a small fragment of the population. In other words, much of the Brazilian educational system exists only on paper. However, it is a uniform and standardized system from one end of the country to the other. It is a unifying force in Brazil despite the fact that it reaches such a small percentage of the people.

The Brazilian heritage of colonialism, slavery, and latifundia was not conducive to providing an educational system for the mass of the people. The mercantile policy of Portugal was perhaps even more strict than that of other European powers: it denied the Brazilian colony even the printing press and any form of university education. Unlike the Spanish who early established some form of university in their American colonies, there was no form of university in Brazil during the colonial period. It was not until 1808, the date of the arrival of the Portuguese Royal Family, that there was a legal printing press in Brazil and that interest in Brazilian education began to develop. In 1810, Dom João VI established a national public library, a medical school (Bahia), a law school (São Paulo), the Botanical Gardens and the Military Academy (Rio de Janeiro); in 1812, a laboratory of chemistry was founded. Throughout the colonial period, what primary and secondary education did exist was mainly in the hands of the Church.

When the Jesuits were expelled from Brazil in 1759, several institutions were thus abandoned. There were a few professional schools, but there was no organized university.

The educational situation in Brazil improved during the empire, but it would be an exaggeration to say, as did one patriotic Brazilian educator, that there was a "burst of renovated effort." During the empire, Brazil remained a plantation slavocracy; education was available only for a small elite. As early as 1827, a law was passed which allowed the provinces to establish public elementary education. In 1837, the Colégio Pedro II, named after the twelve-year-old emperor, was founded in Rio de Janeiro as the model institution of secondary education for the entire country. Soon afterward, a few high-level secondary schools appeared in Minas Gerais, São Paulo, and the northern provinces. However, in 1871, when Brazil had about 10 million people, only about 150,000 were receiving an elementary education and less than 10,000 a secondary education. This education was so "personal" that at the end of the century Emperor Pedro II could attend the academy carrying his name and give oral examinations to some of the students. In 1872, illiteracy was estimated at 80 percent, and this was probably an optimistic figure.

The early republic maintained the same educational policy, namely, the education of a small elite. But, even before the establishment of the republic, a commission under the great Rui Barbosa called attention in 1882 to the poor status of education in Brazil as compared with other parts of the world.[26] The early republic did take some steps to remedy the situation. There was a short-lived Federal Ministry of Education under Benjamin Constant. Primary education was declared to be free,

[26] T. L. Smith, *Brazil: People and Institutions*, p. 547.

gratuitous, and secular; yet, at the same time, the republican government made elementary education the responsibility of the poverty-stricken provinces. In São Paulo, for example, Marcia Browne of Boston (now a historical figure in Brazilian education) came on contract to establish a model primary school. It was in this period that the Protestant missionary schools, such as São Paulo's Mackenzie College, were founded. Some progress seems to have been made in this first decade of the republic, for, in 1900, according to Anisio Teixeira, about 35 percent of the population above the age of fifteen were literate.[27]

The growth of education from 1900 to the 1930s, when Vargas' dictatorship began, was steady but terribly slow. During the decade before Vargas came to power, there was a strong interest, especially among Brazilian intellectuals, in educational problems. In this period, the Association of Brazilian Educators (ABE) was established, and many of its members were profoundly influenced by the educational theories of John Dewey. A series of important steps were taken during this period. The first organized university was founded in 1922,[28] namely, the University of Rio de Janeiro. In 1930, the Ministry of Education and Health was reestablished. In the next decade, a series of commissions, institutes, and new faculties were formed, including the faculties of philosophy which correspond roughly to our liberal arts colleges but which aimed above all at train-

[27] Teixeira, *Educação não é privilégio*, p. 28.
[28] This date is questionable. A friend of mine has a diploma dated 1922 from the University of Rio de Janeiro which later became the University of Brazil. This "university" was, however, only a loosely organized group of independent faculties. Most sources credit the University of São Paulo as being the first organized university, with a Faculty of Philosophy, Science, and Letters established in 1933 as the central and unifying faculty. The argument depends upon what constitutes a university; in any case the Brazilian university is a very recent phenomenon.

ing secondary school teachers. Prior to 1930, there had not been a single educational institution for the preparation of secondary school teachers. The later years of the Vargas regime were hardly favorable to the development of education in Brazil. Many of the leaders of education and most of the young trained educators in the Ministry of Education were transferred to other services. Under the dictatorship, education was a tenuous career plagued by politics and the danger of being called a Socialist or a Communist.

Brazil began its modern educational life only in 1946 with the reestablishment of its democracy. In the last fifteen years or so, there has been a tremendous effort to improve the educational situation of the country. But Brazil has its past to overcome—in 1946 over 50 percent of the people were illiterate, there was a physical shortage of schools, a lack of trained personnel, and, perhaps most difficult to repair, an antiquated system of education out of keeping with modern needs. Faced with these initial disadvantages, Brazilians have, in addition, hardly been able to keep up with the rapid population growth and the changing nature of Brazilian society.

What is formal Brazilian education like? The bare framework of the Brazilian school system is the same throughout the country, although there are vast differences in local abilities to carry out the program. At seven years of age, a child enters a four-year elementary school. Theoretically, after completing the fourth grade successfully, he may enter the secondary level. But, in fact, to do so, the student must pass entrance examinations. Generally, to be prepared to pass these examinations, an extra year of elementary school is needed. This fifth year, called *admissão* (admission year), has been added formally to many elementary schools, particularly by many public schools which prepare students for the secondary level.

The secondary level of education is divided into two levels —the *ginásio*, which is roughly equivalent to our junior high school but has four years or grades, and the *colégio*, roughly similar to our senior high school, with three years. In the *colégio* the student has the choice of two curricula: the *clássico*, which emphasizes Greek, Latin, modern languages, and the humanities, and the *científico*, which focuses upon the sciences, mathematics, modern languages, and the like. In addition to these academic secondary schools, there are also a series of vocational schools roughly on the secondary level. From elementary school a student may enter a school of commerce, of industrial apprenticeship and training, of agriculture, or a normal school. The latter trains elementary school teachers and is on a level which allows its graduates to enter a faculty of higher education if they wish to do so. The schools of commerce, industry, and agriculture are aimed at preparing technicians and skilled labor and they do not usually lead to higher education.[29]

In the regular academic career, the next step after graduation from the *colégio* is directly into one of the faculties of higher education such as law, medicine, engineering, dentistry, agronomy, industrial chemistry, or philosophy. The courses in the professional schools vary in length: medicine takes six years, engineering and law five, agronomy and industrial chemistry four. The faculty of philosophy also offers a four-year course. There are few electives; rather, a student elects a curriculum sequence of fixed courses, for example in physics or

[29] In 1955 a "law of equivalence" provided the opportunity for a student to switch from the vocational to the academic curriculum by special examination.

geography and history. In the fourth year the student may continue in his special field and graduate with the *bacharel* degree, or follow a special course emphasizing education and teaching to become a *licenciado* and thus be qualified for secondary school teaching.

On the basis of sheer growth in the number of primary schools, students enrolled, and teachers employed, it would appear on the surface that Brazil has effected an educational revolution in the last generation. In 1933, there were in the entire country only 27,770 primary schools with a little over 2 million students. By 1959, the number of schools had almost increased fourfold and there were over 7 million students.[30] Yet the remarkable progress in elementary education in Brazil must be set against the exceedingly low baseline of the educational situation in the 1930s and against the fact that the population has almost doubled in the last two decades. Furthermore, Brazil's rapidly expanding population is a young population with a large proportion of school-age children. Thus, despite the rapid expansion of elementary education, only about half the school-age population (i.e., between seven and fourteen years of age) is attending school.

There is a great disequilibrium between the various regions of the country with regard to primary school enrollment. Of over 7,000,000 children in primary school in Brazil, only 8.5 percent were found in the northwestern states (Amazonas,

---

[30] In this chapter statistics are generally taken from the *Anuário estatístico do Brasil* (1961) and from the *Sinopse retrospectiva do ensino no Brasil, 1871–1954* (1956); both are published by the Instituto Brasileiro de Geografia e Estatística, Rio de Janeiro. Data derived from other sources are duly indicated. I have also used *CAPES Bulletins* (Rio de Janeiro) for data. CAPES (Campanha Nacional de Aperfeiçoamento de Pessoal de Nível Superior) is a specialized agency created to stimulate higher education. Its monthly bulletin is a rich source of information on Brazilian education.

Pará, Maranhão, Mato Grosso, Rio Branco, and the territories of Amapá, Rio Branco, and Rondônia), 20 percent in the northeastern states (Piauí, Ceará, Rio Grande do Norte, Paraíba, Pernambuco, Alagoas, Sergipe, and Bahia), and 71.5 percent in the southern states.[31] This disequilibrium is even more marked in relation to the numbers who finished the four-year primary course. Of 558,944 who finished in 1959, only 26,868 came from the northwestern states and 42,997 from the north-eastern states. The rest were found in the South. A much smaller percentage of children are enrolled in school in the North than in the South; this is a result, of course, of the comparative backwardness of the northern region.

There has been a relatively rapid expansion of elementary schooling in the rural zones of Brazil during the last ten years or so; but, despite the overwhelming rural population of the country and the growth in the number of rural schools, the great majority of elementary school children are found in the cities. Many rural schools, especially in the North, provide only two grades. Distances are so great and transportation so difficult that attendance is low. Although a typical rural school may have forty or fifty students registered, the average attendance may be only twenty or twenty-five.

The main problem is not only to make schools available in the rural zones, but to provide the physical and economic conditions for the children to make full use of these facilities. As in so many underdeveloped countries, children are often forced to miss school because their labor is needed at home. But, in

[31] This grouping of states into northwest, northeast, and south was used by CAPES for a special survey. It does not correspond to the five regions used by the Brazilian census or to the cultural regions described in Chapter 2 of this book. But the North-South contrast is made strikingly in this CAPES survey.

addition, the trip to school may involve long distances by horse, canoe, or foot. I shall never forget the disgust of a small boy aged nine whom I met in Paraná state. After walking about five miles to school the boy had found that the teacher had taken the day off to receive her pay check in the city. It happened often, he said. According to his own estimate he missed school once a week.

In the large metropolitan cities, such as Rio de Janeiro and São Paulo, there is also a shortage of schools. Now it is common for a single elementary school to have two or three shifts. Although the law states that all parents who seek to enroll their children may do so, long lines of mothers have been reported waiting with their children to register them in elementary school. The problem of providing elementary schooling for Brazilians of school age is, moreover, multiplied by the rigidity of the educational system, the pedagogical methods, and the prevailing philosophy of education. It is clear that too much is expected of a Brazilian first-grader. There is some variation in the curriculum from state to state, but in one southern state the child in the first grade is expected to learn to read, count and write numbers to 1,000, perform addition, subtraction, division, and multiplication of simple numbers, learn to find one-half, one-quarter, or one-fifth of any number up to fifty, and learn the first twelve Roman numerals, as well as to acquire a notion of other subjects such as Brazilian history.[32] Few states are so exacting, but all are rigid and have theoretically very demanding curricula.

Teaching methods vary widely from the most modern techniques in the model school to utter dependence upon rote, which is the most usual method. This is made more difficult

[32] Cited in T. L. Smith, *Brazil: People and Institutions*, pp. 557–59.

by the fact that many of the teachers coming from the middle class have little or no understanding of their pupils who come from lower-class districts, city *favelas*, and isolated rural zones. Many first-year pupils come from illiterate families; they can hardly count on family help and background to help them along. Despite these problems which individual students may have, the rules of promotion are strictly applied.

The result is a wasteful repetition of grades by a large percentage of Brazilian elementary school children. In 1960, 53 percent of the children in elementary school throughout Brazil were attending the first grade, 21 percent the second grade, 15 percent the third grade, and only 9 percent the fourth and fifth grades. To some extent, this results from the fact that not all rural schools offer the third and fourth year. But more important in bringing about the diminishing enrollment is the fact that such a large percentage of children are failed and made to repeat their grade. For example, it has been estimated that some 25 percent of the children in elementary school in the state of São Paulo in 1957 failed to pass and were made to repeat their grade. This is said to have cost the state about 750 million cruzeiros and to have blocked some 100,000 openings in the São Paulo elementary schools.[33]

Since the schools are filled with repeaters, there is not enough room for the new crop of seven-year-olds. After failing once or twice under such rigid standards, the child from a poor family loses interest. The family, hard pressed to support the child, frequently removes him from school. Anisio Teixeira has shown that less than about 10 percent of Brazilian children complete the four years of elementary school.[34] The INEP

[33] *CAPES Bulletin*, No. 73 (1958), 10.
[34] Teixeira, *Educação não é privilégio*, pp. 34 ff.

(National Institute for Pedagogical Studies), under his direction, is urging the states to modify their teaching systems and their rigid qualifications for passing from one grade to another. Several experiments in various states, including one in the city of Pôrto Alegre in Rio Grande do Sul, are now allowing children to advance by age rather than by achievement. This is being done in an effort to remove the crush of numbers in the lower grades. As presently constituted, even the Brazilian elementary school reinforces the old closed class system of Brazil, maintaining an elite and making it difficult for those of lowly origin to move up in the society.

Yet, theoretically, there is equality of opportunity, at least on the elementary level. Elementary education in Brazil is generally publicly financed. In 1959, of 93,080 schools, 37,280 were maintained by state governments, 46,288 by municipal governments, and 403 by the federal government. Only 9,109 were maintained by private organizations. It is quite clear that the elementary school system acts as a filter, making it impossible for the majority of the Brazilians to have the necessary qualifications for secondary education in any form. Secondary education has been in the past, at least, reserved for the elite. Until as late as 1933, only 417 schools in all of Brazil offered regular academic secondary education of any kind, and only 66,420 students were regularly enrolled in them. Most of these schools were maintained by private and religious organizations; the states generally had one secondary school in their capital, and the federal government maintained only the famous Pedro II as a model secondary school in the nation's capital. By 1960, however, academic secondary education had expanded almost ten times in terms of the number of schools, and there were almost a million students.

This would seem to be a veritable revolution, but once again Brazilian education has not overcome its heritage or the problem of a rapidly expanding population. In his excellent study of Brazilian secondary education, Jaime Abreu estimates that only 6 percent of the population between the ages of twelve and eighteen were in academic secondary school in 1954. While most of those who complete elementary school seem to enroll in some form of secondary school, the filtering process begins anew. Thus, in 1954, there were 168,009 students in the first year of the *ginásio* but less than half that number in the fourth year. The filter works again between the *ginásio* and the *colégio*, for there were in that year only 35,559 students in the first year of the *colégio*, and again half that number in the last year.[35] The number of students at all levels has increased appreciably since that time, but it is still quite clear that only a very small percentage of Brazilians acquire the qualifications for higher education in any form.

Moreover, advanced secondary education is not as yet generally available. About three-fourths of all academic secondary schools in Brazil in 1960 offered only the *ginásio* course. While the majority of elementary schools are supported either by state or municipal funds, by far the majority of secondary schools are private, being maintained by religious orders or private owners. Of 1,850 *ginásios* reported in 1955, 1,395 were private. A more recent set of statistics (1961) shows that a little more than one-third of all *ginásios* (now numbering 3,027) are absolutely free of cost and are maintained by the public coffers; while the other two-thirds charge tuition, almost all now have some openings, free of tuition, provided by state subsidies or by the schools themselves. It is also clear that

[35] Abreu, *A educação secundária no Brasil*, pp. 10 ff.

secondary education is generally costly and that an economic barrier remains between those who are able to take advantage of the still limited facilities and those who are not.

In addition, the problem of the location of the secondary schools plagues the Brazilian student. Well over 50 percent of all the secondary schools are found in the states of Minas Gerais, Rio de Janeiro, São Paulo, and Guanabara, that is, in the most urbanized region of the country. Even in these states, most of the secondary schools are situated in the capitals and in the larger cities and towns. Most of Brazil, especially in the smaller towns and rural zones, is still practically without any form of education beyond the basic instruction offered in the elementary schools. Since the majority of Brazilians are still rural, this means that most Brazilians do not have secondary education available unless they send their children to a larger town or a city where there is a *ginásio* and/or *colégio*.

As previously described, the growing middle class with its desire for secondary education, places heavy pressure on Brazilian society to expand education rapidly on this level. Expansion of secondary education, however, is made difficult by the lack of trained teachers and the nature of the secondary school curriculum. Without going into details, it can be said that ideally the curriculum of both the *ginásio* and the *colégio* is far beyond the ability of most teachers and of the majority of students. The curriculum is based fundamentally upon the French *lycée* and is obviously aimed at training an elite for higher education.[36] The basis of the accreditation of secondary

[36] "The obligatory curriculum—during the four years of the first cycle or *ginásio*—includes Portuguese, Latin, French, English, mathematics, general history, world geography, history of Brazil, geography of Brazil, natural sciences, drawing, manual training, home economics, and choral singing" (*Ibid.*, p. 38). This was modified in 1961 by new laws to be discussed later.

schools and the program they should teach is the model school Pedro II in Rio de Janeiro, where both teachers and students are a highly select group. Theoretically, all of the secondary schools throughout the country and in the most diverse regions and communities should follow a uniform program established by the Ministry of Education and Culture. In the average secondary school, however, teachers are drawn from among professionals who have other occupations, and very frequently they teach in several schools during the same day. Seldom are they able to complete the program set for them by the requirements of any course within a year. Many schools cannot even offer the obligatory courses. Brazilian educators seem to agree that the stilted and highly academic program of their secondary schools is totally out of keeping with contemporary Brazilian society; it derives from a time in the recent past when only a very few attended secondary schools and is hardly adjusted to mass education on the secondary level.

Several model schools have been established in various states to seek new directions in secondary education. A bilateral agreement was signed by Brazil and the United States to establish a model high school in Rio de Janeiro. Teachers for this school were being trained in the United States, but, unfortunately, this project has not to date become a reality. There is considerable ferment and much awareness of the need for a system of secondary education adjusted to modern Brazilian life, but to actually achieve this ideal calls for much more than a few model schools. Secondary education must be modified radically; schools must be made available in the less developed parts of the country and to the people who cannot pay.

The regular secondary sequence is only one of several educational careers which might be selected by the elementary school graduate. There are several other secondary sequences, as indicated earlier, which aim to prepare a student for a specific occupation or set of skills, namely, schools of commerce, education (normal schools), industry, and agriculture. On the surface, it might seem that Brazil is admirably equipped to train the skilled workers and teachers that its expanding economy needs so badly. Again, the aristocratic tradition stands in the way. So strong is the value placed upon literacy and scholastic education that only a relatively small percentage of secondary students attend these schools as compared to those of the regular academic sequence. The number of students enrolled in each of these schools is directly related to the prestige granted to the occupations involved.

Next to the regular academic secondary schools, courses in commercial education and training draw the largest number of Brazilian secondary students. Since such schools prepare the student for white-collar occupations, they act as important agencies of social mobility. There are two levels or "cycles" in the commercial sequence as recognized by the Ministry of Education and Culture and established by law. The first four years which are roughly equivalent to the *ginásio*, called the Basic Course, train people for general work in offices and commerce. The second cycle, called the Technical Course, corresponding somewhat to the *colégio*, calls for specialization in commercial administration, bookkeeping, or secretarial work.

Almost all of the commercial schools in Brazil are privately managed. All are "inspected" by state and federal authorities, and their curriculum must conform to government standards. Some of them are maintained by SENAC (National Service of Commercial Apprenticeship), which is an organization of the National Federation of Commerce cooperating with the federal government. Large commercial enterprises pay for the education of a certain number of apprentices in the skills needed in running their business. SENAC schools have a good reputation, but most privately run commercial schools operate under the most haphazard circumstances with part-time teachers, poor installations, and students who arrive tired from their jobs.

The normal school system in Brazil attracts the middle class. Since primary school teaching is an acceptable occupation for women, and since by far the majority of normal schools are public (or managed by religious organizations), middle-class families are anxious to send their daughters to such schools. They provide a prestige occupation for a young lady hoping for marriage, and "insurance" in case of an unfortunate marriage.

There are two kinds of normal schools: those which train teaching assistants (*regentes de ensino*) can be entered directly from elementary school. Graduation qualifies a person to teach in rural schools, most of which are located in distant zones. In the more advanced central and southern states, these low-level normal schools have been supplanted by those of the second type. The more advanced normal schools prepare the student for the title of *professor primário*. Graduates of such normal schools not only have a full license to teach in primary schools, but they may also enter a faculty of higher education. Some of these high-level normal schools, such as the Institute of Education in Rio de Janeiro and its namesake in São Paulo, are among the best educational institutions in Brazil.

Admission to such high-level normal schools is much sought after. They have their own *ginásio* courses leading to the specialized three- or four-year training, and they are free. In

February of 1957, it was reported that over 5,000 candidates had taken the entrance examinations to compete for the ninety openings on the *colégio* level of the Institute of Education in Rio de Janeiro.

In 1961, over 70,000 young women were studying in normal schools in Brazil.[37] At this rate, it would seem that Brazil would soon be able to have all of its elementary schools staffed with trained teachers. However, this will probably not be the case. First, the expansion of elementary schooling calls for more and more teachers, and 5,000 to 8,000 new teachers are needed each year to maintain the status quo. Second, a large number of normal school graduates never exercise their profession, and many more teach only for two or three years before abandoning their career for marriage. Third, most trained teachers, girls of middle-class families, are unwilling to take teaching positions in small towns and isolated rural areas. In São Paulo, Rio de Janeiro, and other cities there may even be a surplus of normal school graduates competing for positions, but in most northern and western states, such as Ceará, Rio Grande do Norte, Pará and Mato Grosso, teachers with a normal school education are in the minority. They are very rare in the distant rural areas of those states.

Despite the recent surge of industrialization in Brazil, the expansion of industrial education seems to have lagged. From 1947 to 1957, according to one set of figures, industrial education grew only 3 percent in terms of the number of students matriculated, as against 114 percent growth in regular academic secondary schools, 65 percent in commercial courses, and 197 percent in normal schools.[38] An important group of these in

[37] There were also 2,400 male students.
[38] *CAPES Bulletin*, No. 64 (1958).

dustrial training schools is maintained by SENAI (National Service of Industrial Apprenticeship), an organization of the National Confederation of Industries. By law, all larger industrial enterprises are required to matriculate in a SENAI school a number of apprentices varying from 5 percent to 20 percent of the total number of skilled workmen employed. SENAI schools now offer training in more than forty different trades.[39] Some of the SENAI schools are models of their kind. The young apprentices attend school while working in a factory, and they receive a salary while they alternately work and study. Despite the recent expansion of SENAI and the real interest of the Brazilian government in industrial training, this branch of education has not expanded as rapidly as the more academic schools. Whenever families of the lower class are able to maintain their children in school, they want them trained for a white-collar occupation. Until skilled workmen receive higher wages than they do at present, and until the stigma of any form of manual labor disappears, it will be difficult to attract socially and economically mobile Brazilians into industrial training.

Brazil also maintains vocational schools on the secondary level in different parts of the country to train plantation foremen and to provide technical training in agriculture and animal husbandry for small farmers. These schools should not be confused with the faculties of agronomy or agriculture, which are schools of higher education. Rather, they are aimed at improving and educating those who work directly in agricultural production. It might seem that in an essentially rural country, which derives so much of its national income from cash crops, such schools would be much sought after. This is hardly the case. In 1961, there were only about 6,500 students enrolled in

[39] *Ibid.*, No. 69 (1958).

these schools of agriculture. Some agricultural schools go begging for students. Commercial agriculture has not seen fit, as has industry, to attempt to train skilled workmen.

The miserable condition of the small farmer makes it difficult for him to send his sons to school. Furthermore, the farmer sees so little future potential in farming as a career that he can hardly urge his son to study for that occupation. There is little incentive toward agriculture as an occupation, except perhaps in the South where the European tradition of family farms was established. Even the sons of prosperous farmers and plantation owners tend to take academic courses and migrate to large towns and cities. The traditional Brazilian attitude toward the land is that it is to be exploited and left behind. It is not regarded as an investment that will produce for generations.

Despite the fact that such a small percentage of Brazilian students acquire the prerequisites, there has been a terrific demand for higher education in the last decade. As a response, there has been an expansion of faculties and schools of higher education to a point that makes many thoughtful Brazilian educators fearful of the consequences. Higher education in Brazil is full of paradoxes and dilemmas, some of which are faced by most South American nations, and by the United States. These revolve around the problem of providing higher education for a larger and larger mass of people while still attempting to make the university a center for advanced research and teaching.

It must be remembered in discussing Brazilian higher education that it is a recent development. Although there were isolated faculties of higher education dating back to the nineteenth century, the first organized Brazilian university is no more than forty years old. Even today, the Brazilian university organization is loosely knit as compared to that of the United States. Furthermore, it must be remembered that the first faculty of philosophy, corresponding roughly to our liberal arts college, was first introduced in Brazil in 1933. Now there are thirty-seven universities in Brazil. In addition, there are numerous isolated faculties, schools, and programs of higher education scattered through the entire country.

The most numerous courses of advanced study are philosophy, science, and letters, engineering, economics, law, nursing, dentistry, music, medicine, social work, and pharmacy, in that order. In addition, there are schools of public administration, industrial chemistry, agronomy, library service, journalism, veterinary medicine, architecture, physical education, public health, art, and numerous other specialized fields. Almost the full range of technical, scientific, and professional schools found in the United States are present in modern Brazil. The number of students enrolled in these institutions shows that, as in all of Latin America, law is still the most sought-after profession in Brazil; that there are almost as many students of music as agronomy; that there are many times more students of medicine than nursing; and that faculties of philosophy, which train secondary school teachers, are now second in enrollment. These numbers reflect some of the fundamental Brazilian values previously discussed.[40]

Many of these schools and faculties were established during the last fifteen years. In the last few years, well over a hundred faculties of philosophy have been founded; in São Paulo state, where there were but two faculties of philosophy eight years ago, there are now at least nine—the new ones have been founded in the cities of the interior. Similarly, new faculties of

[40] *CAPES Bulletin*, No. 60 (1957).

medicine, pharmacy, dentistry, and engineering have been established in São Paulo state within the last decade. This growth of institutions of higher learning is not limited to São Paulo, and there is a tendency to expand existing institutions.

However, despite the number of new institutions and the fact that so few Brazilians graduate from the *colégio*, it is difficult to obtain admission to these faculties and schools of higher education. Once one has filtered through the elementary and secondary schools, there is no longer an economic barrier, for most institutions of higher learning are public and absolutely free, and even those which are private, such as Catholic universities and Mackenzie College, have exceedingly low fees. The difficulty occurs with the entrance examination (the so-called *vestibular*) and the way it is administered. Following graduation from the *colégio*, candidates must take entrance examinations for whichever school or faculty they wish to enter. On the basis of statistics, it would seem that Brazilian institutions are very selective. In 1957 CAPES carried out a survey among 358 schools of higher education as to the number of candidates for admission, the number of openings in the first year of their course, the number who passed the entrance examination, and the number admitted. The survey showed that in eighteen medical schools, there were only 1,175 openings and 7,883 candidates. Only 1,015 of these candidates passed the entrance examination. Likewise, in the seventeen engineering schools covered by the survey, there were 5,751 candidates but only 1,124 passed the entrance examination. There was also a large percentage of failures in other branches of higher education covered by the survey, e.g. agronomy, architecture, art, law, nursing, and philosophy. In twenty-three faculties of philosophy included in the survey, there were 5,119 openings;

4,017 candidates appeared, and 2,114 passed the entrance examination.

What does this mean? On an over-all basis, it seems to indicate that there are several times more candidates than places available for them in Brazilian institutions of higher learning. Yet it also seems to mean that so many fail the entrance examination that many places which are available go begging. Does this mean that Brazilian secondary schools do a poor job of preparing students for advanced study—a situation not unheard of elsewhere? This seems to be partially the case. Officially, the secondary school curriculum in Brazil is broader and stronger in basic subjects (i.e., mathematics, science, languages, etc.) than that in the United States. The fact is that this curriculum is realized and fully presented to the student in only a small minority of Brazilian secondary schools, mainly in the model institutions such as Pedro II. In the many privately organized secondary schools, with their harried teachers who sometimes work in two or three schools, and who are not too well trained, the official curriculum is but an ideal goal, and never completed.

Still, the onus for the apparently poor showing of the secondary school graduates in these entrance examinations cannot be placed entirely on their secondary schools. To some extent, it rests on the way in which these examinations are administered. In fact, it is known, and it is shown by statistics, that those faculties which draw the largest number of candidates (i.e., law, medicine, and engineering) make use of entrance examinations not so much to test the ability of the student, but rather as a manner of weeding out candidates so that the numbers accepted are about the same as the number of openings. Furthermore, it must be realized that in Brazil an entrance examination passed for one university or school permits entrance only into that particular school; there are no national entrance examinations. Thus, if there are 300 openings in a faculty or school, 300 candidates arbitrarily pass the entrance examination, and the rest are failed.

Examinations in the medical schools of Rio de Janeiro and São Paulo are made extremely difficult, expecting that a large number will fail. This is not just hearsay, but it is substantiated by the previously mentioned data referring to medical schools (1,175 openings and 1,015 passed, leaving just enough room for those who would have to repeat the first year). The situation is similar in engineering; fewer candidates pass the entrance examinations than the number of openings that are available in a particular engineering school, but the competition for such places is intense; thus the examinations are a method of selection and not simply a way of cutting back candidates. In nursing, which is a proselytizing profession in Brazil, thirteen schools reported 278 openings in 1957, but there were only 261 candidates and only 172 passed the entrance examinations. These nursing schools enrolled 221 students for the first-year curriculum, thus 57 openings were left unfilled for lack of qualified students. There has been a real effort, with the help of foreign-trained technicians, to develop the nursing profession, and I am sure that if the candidates were up to par they would not have been refused. The same was true of agronomy, where 134 openings remained unfilled in the eight schools covered by the CAPES survey. In addition, there were unfilled openings ostensibly because of lack of candidates who passed the entrance examinations in public administration, art, economics, pharmacy, philosophy, and veterinary medicine.

Then why all the effort and enthusiasm to expand the facilities of higher education? It is understandable that there should be an effort to expand facilities and create new schools of medicine and engineering. It is even understandable that new schools of law should be founded in response to the tremendous demand for admission, although it is well known that most graduates of law schools never practice law. They go to law school for the valued title and diploma which will help them in business, civil service, or politics. But it is hard to understand the explosive expansion of the faculties of philosophy. There is obviously a national need for more secondary school teachers, but the present faculties of this type are not filled to capacity, and still each year new ones are created. Perhaps this expansion can best be understood on a regional and local basis.

Brazilians do not have a tradition of sending their children away to the university, nor do most of them have the finances to do so. Furthermore, the faculties of Rio de Janeiro, São Paulo, and the other capitals are crowded, and the students from small towns and from the North have little chance of admission there. There is a desire, in fact a local patriotic fervor, to have faculties of higher education in the various states, in Pará, Amazonas, Goiás and Mato Grosso, to mention a few isolated states where there are struggling faculties. And even in São Paulo state, as described above, the towns and small cities, such as Assis, São José do Rio Prêto, Araraquara, and Piracicaba, want faculties at home. There is already a reaction among Brazilian educators against this rapid expansion of higher education. There is no doubt that Brazil needs to train a larger percentage of its people on an advanced level. Still, haphazard growth of facilities could be equally wanting in terms of quality.

The curriculum of all these schools, faculties, and universities is subject to supervision and control by the federal government which grants them recognition. In 1950, a group of universities and faculties throughout the country were federalized, that is, directly subjected to federal control, and maintained by federal funds. If one remembers that most federal funds designated for education are spent on higher education, then it is understandable that federalization should be important to provincial universities which had been limping along, mainly on state or private funds. Overnight, for example, the salaries of many professors in such universities as those of Bahia, Pernambuco, and Ceará were doubled or even tripled as their pay was raised to federal standards.

Federalization of these universities and faculties also had its drawbacks. At present, all of them are obligated to offer the courses listed in the official regulations, following the pattern of the University of Brazil in Rio de Janeiro. This has led many of them to offer courses entirely outside the realm of necessity or the local potential. One example will suffice, although I am certain that parallel cases could be found in other fields. Under pressure from São Paulo, where there was a well-known professor specializing in the Tupí language, a chair of Tupí languages and Brazilian ethnology was created in the official curriculum of the faculty of philosophy. Once created, however, this chair was opened in a series of provincial faculties. Of course, professors were appointed and competitions were held for this new position. It was filled in most cases by default; it is now held by a few scholarly M.D.'s and curious amateurs in anthropology. Now that these chairs have been filled, even though by people without tenure, it will be years before they can be turned over to adequately trained ethnologists.

In December of 1961, after some twelve years of often heated discussion between educators and legislators, a wide sweeping set of laws governing education on all levels, known as the Lei de Diretrizes e Bases (Law of Directives and Bases), were enacted. These laws amend and extend the educational provisions of the 1946 constitution. Their aim is to adapt the Brazilian school system to regional conditions and, in the words of a well-known Brazilian educator, "to adapt the school to the conditions of a democratic and rapidly developing Brazil." According to these new laws, each state is given the right to formulate its own educational system, limited only by the minimum requirements set by federal law and by the supervision of the Federal Council of Education. The latter is a supervising body, appointed by the president, composed of well-known educators from throughout the nation. The federal government retains the right to require of the states only certain minimum conditions such as a set number of school days per year and a basic curriculum, especially on the professional level. The new laws allow universities and professional schools to adopt their own rules and regulations, subject only to review by the Federal Council. It is hoped in Brazil that these laws will allow decentralization and reduce the rigidity of the educational system without losing the positive values of national unity.

The primary school has been extended to six years. Graduation from the sixth grade of the primary school allows the student to enter the second year of the ginásio, which in the future will be reduced from a four-year to a three-year sequence. The colégio will remain a three-year course. With six years of primary schooling, three years of middle school similar to our junior high school, and three years of high school similar to our senior high school, the Brazilian educational system more nearly approximates our own.

These new educational laws attempt also to modify the curriculum. Only five subjects are made obligatory, to be taken at different levels each year in the secondary schools, namely, Portuguese, mathematics, history, science, and drawing. The other subjects to be studied are established by the state or the school, or may be opted by the student. No more than seven subjects, however, may be taken during any one year; in the past a student in a secondary school might have taken eleven or twelve subjects during any one academic year. Furthermore, greater equivalence is established between vocational and academic secondary schools, allowing greater freedom of transfer from a vocational to an academic course of study. The vocational schools now offer the upper sequence (i.e., *colégio*) of secondary education. The last year of the *colégio* now offers considerable freedom to the student, allowing those who aim at continuing in the university to prepare for entrance examinations and allowing those in terminal years to take vocational subjects.

The new laws also stipulate how federal funds for education will be distributed. The federal government will contribute 12 percent of all income received from taxes to education. This total sum will be divided into four parts: 1.2 percent of all taxes collected for the support of the Ministry of Education and Culture, 3.6 percent for federal aid to primary education, 3.6 percent for federal aid to secondary education, and 3.6 percent for higher education. The new educational laws attempt to correct the educational imbalance between regions by an ingenious method of distribution of federal funds. Thirty percent of the funds available as federal aid to the states will be granted to the states in proportion to the size of their population; thus, of the parcel, the states with the largest populations receive the largest share. The remaining 70 percent, however, is to be distributed to the states in amounts inversely proportional to the level of their per capita income; thus, the poorer states will receive the largest amounts.

There is great enthusiasm among most Brazilian educators for these new laws which they feel will allow them to create a more flexible educational system. It is too soon, however, to judge the full implications and the effect of these laws upon the functioning educational system of Brazil. After all, the educational systems adopted by the individual states may be almost as rigid as those in force before the new laws appeared. Brazilians, like most Latin Americans, are legalistically inclined. They attempt to solve problems by elaborate, often brilliantly conceived laws and edicts. Brazilian labor laws are said to be models of their kind, yet the condition of the laboring class in Brazil does not seem materially improved by them. Whether or not the Lei de Diretrizes e Bases of 1961 will truly modify Brazilian education remains to be seen.

❦ 6 ❦ RELIGION

AND THE STATE

TWO other nationwide institutions have been fundamental in providing Brazil with national unity, namely, the Catholic Church and the national State in its various forms. Both the Church and the State are at once the basis for and the result of national unity. Had Brazil not had religious unity of a sort and a religious tolerance based upon common understanding which allowed differences in regional and class manifestations of religion, Brazil might not have achieved its unity of national culture. Similarly, the relative stability of the Brazilian State during the colonial period, during the empire, and during the republic allowed governmental institutions to extend into, but often not profoundly influence, the most isolated areas of the nation. This relative stability of the State also allowed Brazil to maintain and even to extend its frontiers, sometimes at the expense of its neighbors. One cannot understand modern Brazil without a picture of these institutions.

Religion

Brazil should be thought of as a "Catholic culture," so deep are the roots of Catholicism in the national way of life. In terms of the size of the population formally adhering to Cathol-

icism, Brazil has been called "the most Catholic nation of
our times." There are more Catholics in Brazil than in any
other country in the modern world, and Catholicism is intimately related to the whole history of Brazil—its colonization,
the occupation of its territory, and the establishment of its
fundamental institutions. By far the majority of Brazilians
profess Catholicism; well over 90 percent are Catholics. On the
surface it would seem that the Church provides Brazil with a
strong unifying force, and to a certain extent it does. But, in
fact, Brazilian Catholicism has a rather unique national quality
and a rather special social role; it coexists with other forms of
religion, some of which are peripheral to Catholicism and others
frankly antagonistic to it.

A large proportion of Brazilians are Catholics by tradition
rather than by strong faith. What else would one be? To be a
Brazilian is to be a Catholic. Women tend to be more actively
religious: attending Mass, going to confession, receiving Communion, and seeing to it that their children receive the sacra-
ments and get some religious training. Many men, on the other
hand, never go to Mass (unless it is in memory of a deceased
friend or relative), and many have not gone to confession since
just before their marriage. Many men are anticlerical, fond of
anecdotes which cast doubts on the priest's vow of chastity and
of the proverbial Brazilian joke that a priest brings bad luck as
a traveling companion. Yet such men are Catholics; they are
baptized, married, and hope to be buried as Catholics.

This nominal and traditional form of Catholicism results to
some extent from the fact that Catholics are a majority. Like
Protestants in the United States, they tend to be relaxed in
their principles and in following the dogma and ritual of their
Church. This form of Catholicism, however, is also an historical

heritage. As one well-known Brazilian Catholic lay leader (also a social anthropologist) has written, "Brazilian Catholicism inherited from Portuguese culture a certain softness, tolerance and malleability which an exalted, turbulent and hard Spanish religious character did not know." [1] Furthermore, in the history

Church of Our Lady of the Rosary in Salvador

of Brazil, the Church has been subordinated to two important institutions, namely, the family and the State.

The early missionaries, especially the Jesuits, fought the colonists with some success for control of the aboriginal peoples; however, the Jesuits were expelled in 1661 and 1687, and

[1] Azevedo, "Catholicism in Brazil: A Personal Evaluation," *Thought*, XXVIII (1953), 257.

definitely in 1759. During the colonial period, Catholicism tended to be a family affair. Gilberto Freyre has described the familial Catholicism of the sugar plantations. The padre was often one of the sons of the patriarch. He officiated in a private chapel attached to the *casa grande*. This so-called private Catholicism "penetrated even into the cities of the littoral and into the Church itself." [2] The priests were more traditionally motivated than religiously inclined. They sometimes had a female companion and children; they were tolerant of slavery, African and medieval superstition, and the customs of the time. "Custom also required that the [upper-class] young girls who did not marry should shut themselves up in convents, but these convents were no mystic cloisters. There they made preserves and candies, received visitors, gossiped, and acted in comedies." [3]

During the empire, the Church was protected by the State. Catholicism was the official religion, but this seems to have meant in fact that the Church was subordinated to the State. One pastoral letter of the time speaks of "this protection which smothers us." The emperor intervened on occasion in the appointment of bishops. He closed the novitiates of some religious orders. Many Brazilian Catholics and many important priests in the hierarchy were Freemasons. When the bishops of Bahia and Pará excluded Freemasons from religious brotherhoods, they became the object of violent campaigns by liberal newspapers. Rather than support the bishops, the emperor had them arrested, tried, and condemned to four years of forced labor. Clearly, the Church was not a dominant force during the colonial and imperial periods. But individual priests such as

[2] Roger Bastide, "Religion and Church in Brazil," in Smith and Marchant, eds., *Brazil: Portrait of Half a Continent*, p. 336.
[3] *Ibid.*

Padre Feijó (the regent for Pedro II) were important. Sometimes their local power led the Brazilian clergy to suggest the formation of a Brazilian Catholic Church separated from Rome, but in the end Rome was victorious, and the Brazilian clergy was brought closer into line with orthodox behavior.

Today, Church and State are theoretically separated in Brazil according to the constitution. By law, there is complete freedom of religious belief and activity. It must be said that religious tolerance is practiced in Brazil, perhaps to a greater extent than in any other Latin American republic. However, the relationship between the Church and the Government is close; this is not for legal or ideological reasons, but simply because Brazilians are so traditionally Catholic. Important Catholic holidays tend to be public holidays. When a new public building (a school, health center, city hall, etc.) is inaugurated, the bishop is called upon to bless the building. Religious statues stand in the offices of Catholic officials and in the public rooms of government buildings. Church social welfare and educational institutions (including seminaries for the training of priests and projects for the reconstruction of churches) receive financial support from federal and state governments.

There are Catholic political parties, but none of them has wide or popular support. Nevertheless, the Church is considered a political power; Brazilians have been unable to push through a law legalizing divorce (it was tried in 1945 and again in 1952) against its opposition. Yet the candidate for vice-president (João Café Filho, who later served as president) ran on a platform favoring such a law and was elected despite the fact that he was vetoed by the Church. The Church is "official" because Brazilians are Catholics, but it is not an overriding power.

The lack of strength of the Brazilian Church is reflected in its present organization. The Brazilian Church has been honored, perhaps because of the large number of Catholics, by the appointment of three Brazilian cardinals. But, at the lower level, the Church is understaffed. In 1947, there were only 6,383 priests in all of Brazil, responsible for some 3,038 parishes (about one priest for every 7,000 or 8,000 people); but this hardly describes the situation. The majority of these priests (like physicians and dentists) are found in the cities. Many of them belong to teaching orders and are thus occupied. In the prosperous diocese of Ilhéus in Bahia, for example, each priest was responsible for 23,000 people and several parishes. In some parts of northern Brazil, padres are in charge of two or three parishes which include thirty or more communities. While in 1950 the United States had 44,000 priests for 30,000,-000 Catholics. Brazil had little more than 6,000 priests for more than 50,000,000 Catholics. Even England and India have a higher ratio of priests.[4] The situation is not improving, especially in the northern regions of the country. "In the principal archdiocese of the north, whose central seminary prepares priests for other dioceses, only 176 priests were ordained between 1907 and 1951, an average of four a year."[5]

Brazilians rarely seek out the Church as a career. In fact, since the end of the nineteenth century, Brazil has depended on other countries (and missionary orders such as the Dominicans, the Salesians, the Franciscans, and now the Maryknoll

[4] Azevedo, "Catholicism in Brazil: A Personal Evaluation," *Thought*, XXVIII (1953), 264.
[5] *Ibid.*, p. 265.

Fathers) to furnish them with priests. In 1947, almost half the priests in Brazil were foreigners—Germans, Italians, Spaniards, Frenchmen, Dutchmen, Poles, Portuguese, and others. Since then a group of North American priests has arrived. It is in keeping with the spirit of Catholicism in Brazil that Brazilian men, as they say, "have no vocation for the Church."

While the clergy has been weak, there has been a strong force in Brazilian Catholicism, namely, the religious lay brotherhood or *irmandade*. From the earliest days of the colonial period, these religious brotherhoods have been important. They arose both in the rural zones and in the cities. Some of them were limited to the white plantation aristocracy, some to mulattoes, and others to Negro freedmen and slaves. Sometimes, in rural zones such as the Amazonian community of Itá, the officers of religious brotherhoods provided leadership and formal organization for neighborhoods and even for communities. Such brotherhoods provided their members with a form of social security, with burial, and with Masses after death. In the cities, some of these brotherhoods became exceedingly wealthy, inheriting land and money from their members. They established hospitals (often the Santa Casa or public hospital of a city originated as a brotherhood hospital), retreat houses for women, and other institutions, and built beautiful churches.

Such lay brotherhoods sometimes came to be more powerful than the clergy, and the Church saw them as a competitive force. In one rural region of the North with which I am well acquainted, the parish priest set out systematically to undermine the local brotherhoods because he believed that they represented unorthodox religious beliefs and practices and because they had a greater hold on the people than the Church itself. A few years ago, the Church threatened all the members of a brotherhood in a large southern city with excommunication, mainly, it seems, because of disagreement over property held by the organization.

Furthermore, in Brazil the parish priest does not have a strong prestige position in the local community. He often does exert considerable influence over the women in his parish, but his influence is negligible among the men, who sometimes resent his power over their wives and daughters. Furthermore, the parish priests have heavy economic burdens. They are forced to support themselves on the "receipt of alms" (fees) for baptisms, marriages, and Masses. Sometimes, when officiating in several communities, such alms may provide a relatively good income. In a series of communities studied by anthropologists, the padre (when there was one) was among the more prosperous local citizens. Yet his insistence upon charging for his services was irritating to the people involved, and, more important, was sometimes an economic hardship to those of the lower economic echelons. Many priests, in their struggle to make a living, do not limit themselves to Church services, but have been known to enter business, farming, and politics. Their mundane activities do not strengthen their position as spiritual leaders in the eyes of the people. In general, the local priest is not a strong leader in his community.

Perhaps as a result of the lack of religious supervision and leadership, the form of Catholicism practiced among most Brazilian peasants and people of isolated small towns is more closely akin to the Catholicism of the seventeenth century than to that of the twentieth. It has been called *catolicismo de bairro* (neighborhood Catholicism). It includes many beliefs and practices long since forgotten in the large cities. This "folk Catholicism" is most spectacular when manifested in the

shrines and pilgrimages so characteristic of rural Brazil. There
are numerous important shrines all over the country to which
people travel, literally by the thousands, on the occasion of
the annual festival of the saint. There is Nossa Senhora da
Aparecida, near Guaratinguetá in São Paulo state, the chapel
of Nosso Senhor do Bonfim in Salvador, Bahia, the so-called
Círio of Belém, Pará, where the day of the Virgin of Nazareth
is celebrated, and many others. One of the most spectacular
rural shrines is that of Bom Jesús da Lapa on the São Francisco River in Bahia. Each year, 20,000 or 30,000 people go
there for the annual day of celebration. Some travel 400 or
500 miles on foot, to fulfill a vow or seek supernatural help.

The weakness of the Church's position in Brazil, however,
can easily be overemphasized. In many ways, the Church is
influential and strong, often exerting a critical influence on
public policy. As noted previously, the Church has twice been
able to stave off laws legalizing divorce. The hierarchy of the
Church has been critical of the ideas and policies of "liberal"
educators and has from time to time stymied their planned re-
forms. The high officials of the Church have been said to influence appointments to public office and even election nomi-
nations. There is also, it seems, a new social consciousness in
the Brazilian Church, as indicated by the efforts at rural social
welfare undertaken by the Bishop of Manaus in Amazonas,
the campaign of Bishop Elder Câmara to resettle the inhabitants of the Rio de Janeiro shanty towns, and the concern with
social problems of recent eucharistic congresses. There are also
intellectual Catholic lay leaders such as Hamilton Nogueira, a
former senator, Alceu Amoroso Lima, a writer and professor
who writes in the press under the name of Tristão de Athayde,
Thales de Azevedo, an anthropologist and professor, and many

others. Furthermore, the Catholic Church has become active in recent years in higher education; the new Catholic University in Rio de Janeiro is a notable instance of this trend.

Some of these new social, educational, and religious activities of the Church obviously result from recent Brazilian religious trends. They represent a recognition that the old and traditional forms of religion which have become fused with Catholicism do not make for fervent orthodox Catholics. Obviously, orthodox Catholicism has not satisfied the level of religious fervor of the Brazilian people. The frustrations of their present economic and social situation lead them to seek religious satisfactions which orthodox Catholicism does not provide.

One of the non-Catholic forms of religion which Brazilians follow is not a recent development—the traditional African fetish cults brought to Brazil by slaves and reinterpreted in the New World now flourish in nearly all large Brazilian cities. Although these cults derive ultimately from Africa, they are now fused thoroughly with Catholicism and it is somewhat unfair to call them non-Catholic, since most of their adepts insist that they are fervent Catholics. The cults are called by a variety of names—*candomblê* in Bahia, *xangô* in Recife, *macumba* in Rio de Janeiro, and *batuque* in Belém. They run a wide spectrum from cult groups highly traditional and proud of the purity of their African ritual and ideology, to cults which are mixed with spiritualism and which are African only in the rhythm of the drums and other ritualistic details. The most traditionally African of these cults derive from Yoruba and Dahomey (West African kingdoms important in the slave trade). They are highly formal, ritualistic, and complex in their ceremonial and religious ideologies. Their songs are sung in the

Yoruban language, called *nagô* in Brazil, and their deities have the same names as those worshipped even today in Africa. Less traditionally African are cults which can be shown to have originated among the Bantu-speaking peoples of the Congo River Basin and Angola; their ceremonial is less elaborate, the organization of the cult is less complex, and the deities carry Bantu names. Most of the cults in Rio de Janeiro (the *macumbas*) are of this type. Still less traditionally African are the cults called *caboclo*; they have incorporated American Indian practices and deities and they are most apt to have acquired traits of spiritualism.

The most traditionally African of these cults are strongest in Salvador (Bahia). Some of them have a remarkable stability; Gantois, Engenho Velho, Opo Afonjá, and several other cults have been known as on-going organizations for over a hundred years, and they certainly existed earlier. Each cult has a *terreiro* (literally, its land or place) where its temple or headquarters is situated. At the *terreiro*, there is a large central building where the public ceremonies are held. This is sometimes a converted mansion house and sometimes a large *barracão* or shed constructed for this special purpose. Nearby are smaller structures where the altars of the gods are kept and where the leaders and a few novices may live. These cults follow a precise ceremonial calendar. Each deity has its sacred days on which it must be propitiated by ceremonials. The ceremonials follow a strict and complex ritualistic pattern. Each deity has a symbol (the symbol of Xangô is an ax), a set of colors, a set of songs, a way of dancing, a characteristic garb worn by the individuals who represent it, and preferred foods which are offered at its altar.

The divinities of these cults of African origin, the so-called *orixás,* are recognizable African gods generally of Yoruban or Dahomeyan origin, but each is identified with a Catholic saint. Xangô, a god of lightning and thunder, is equated with St. Jerome (young Xangô) and sometimes with St. Peter (old Xangô). Ogun, a god of the hunt in the Yoruban pantheon, is St. Anthony in Bahia and St. George in other parts of Brazil. To members of these cults, St. Anne is the same as Nanã, the "mother of all *orixás.*" Just as there are a multitude of Christian saints, there are numerous West African gods, each with its own special characteristics.

Furthermore, the organization of these cults is formal and elaborate. The leader is known as the *pai de santo* or *mãe de santo* (father or mother in sainthood). It should be noted that the most famous leaders have been women, such as Aninha and Menininha in Bahia. Under these leaders, there are a series of officials, such as the "little mother" (*iya kererê* in Yoruban) the *sidagá* who cares for Exu, the deity who is the messenger of the gods, and the *iya bassê* who cooks the foods offered to the gods. These, and others, are women. But the drummers are men, and there are a number of male sponsors known as *ogan.* Politicians often serve in this latter capacity, for by backing such cults they gain a close relationship with the people and thus garner many votes. Such cults have been accused in Brazil of holding religious orgies. The fact is that the more traditionally African cults are as formal and proper as a Catholic Mass. Male and female spectators are seated on opposite sides of the room. Smoking is prohibited, and people are as quiet and orderly as they would be in church. It is true that people are possessed by their gods, but even this is done in an orderly and correct manner. It may be true that some of the *caboclo-*type cults and some of the unstable *ma-*

cumba (i.e., Bantu-spiritualist) cults provide some rather wild performances, but they are analogous to some of the wild revivalistic Protestant cults in the United States as compared to the traditional African cults.

At one time African fetish cults were confined largely to the Northeast Coast, which had the largest Negro population. Now, as mentioned earlier, they have proliferated up and down the coast of Brazil. They are reported as far south as Rio Grande do Sul and as far north as Amazonas. Once very discrete in Rio de Janeiro, they may be found today in any district of the city and in the suburbs. Nowadays, some of the most famous leaders of the African cults of Bahia reside in Rio, where their income is higher and where they can enjoy the attractions of the great city. Their major temples are still in Salvador, but they have "branches" in Rio de Janeiro. Nowadays, one can see candles and offerings of a syncretic nature almost any night on fashionable Copacabana Beach in honor of Yemanjá, a goddess of water. Furthermore, there are innumerable pseudo-African fetish cults in São Paulo, Rio de Janeiro, and other large cities which practice a watered-down version of the traditional ceremonies. This form of religion is a growing phenomenon. It is thoroughly mixed with spiritualism which, in its own right, offers a religious outlet to many Brazilians.

Spiritualism, long present in Brazil, seems to have grown rapidly in importance during the last decade or so. In 1940, some 463,400 people identified themselves to the census takers as spiritualists, and by 1950 their numbers had grown to 824,000. Today, there are probably well over a million of them. The various cults are grouped into a federation and maintain centers or temples mainly in the urban zones. Actually, spiritualists are not a homogeneous group following a dogma. As Roger Bastide points out, they are in a sense stratified. At the top are the intellectual middle- and upper-class spiritualists who are preoccupied with extrasensory perception. In the middle are those who follow the spiritualism of Alan Kardec; their meetings include the reading of the gospel according to Kardec, prayer and the confession of sins, and finally possession of the mediums around the table by the spirits of the dead. Such seances are similar to those that take place in New York or Paris, although there are Brazilian overtones. At the bottom of the ladder of the spiritualist hierarchy are centers where spiritualism is thoroughly mixed with African and American Indian concepts. African gods and American Indian spirits possess the mediums along with the spirits of the dead. Herbal remedies are dispensed and magical formulas are used. Thus, this "lower spiritualism" fades into a form of African fetishism, while all forms of spiritualism, as well as the African cults, are thoroughly fused with Catholicism.[6]

Fanatical religious movements of the type led in the past by Antônio Conselheiro and Padre Cícero in the arid Northeast continue to appear from time to time in modern Brazil. Such movements are seldom more than purely local in scope and of passing importance, but they indicate the capacity of frustrated rural Brazilians to resort to a form of religion not provided by their traditional Catholicism. Recently, a religious movement developed in the arid *sertão* which was a direct continuation of the fanaticism of Antônio Conselheiro and Padre Cícero. It took the form of a collective community called Santa Brigida, situated near the town of Jeremoabo in north-

[6] See Roger Bastide, "Religion and Church in Brazil," in Smith and Marchant, eds., *Brazil: Portrait of Half a Continent*, pp. 353–54.

ern Bahia. It was led by a mystic who claimed to be the re-incarnation of both Padre Cícero and Antônio Conselheiro. He demanded of his followers rigid adherence to Catholicism, hard work, and abstinence from alcohol and tobacco. Several years ago, his followers numbered some 2,000 or more. They seem to be a peaceful, hard-working group, and they are pro-tected by local politicians despite the official opposition of the Church.

Not so peaceful was the movement (it was really only an incident) that broke out in Catulê, a small settlement of sub-sistence farmers in the Malacacheta *município* of Minas Gerais during Easter Week of 1955. There, according to Carlo Castaldi, an anthropologist who interviewed many of the participants, four children accused of being possessed by the devil were sacrificed by the leaders of the community. The people of Catulê, formerly rural Catholics but lacking all Church super-vision, had become converted to Adventism (so-called *ad-ventismo de promessa*). Living as they did in isolation and without any teacher or leader in their new religion, they were subject to the religious interpretations of the two leading men in the small village. One of these leaders claimed to have seen the devil in the form of a cat issuing forth from the body of a small girl. The horrible incidents of Easter Week ended with the arrival of the state police who killed the two leaders and placed the adults of the community in jail.[7]

The events of Catulê were reminiscent of what happened over a century ago at Pedra Bonita in central Pernambuco. There a group of fanatics sacrificed thirty children, twelve men, eleven women, and fourteen dogs by throwing them from high rocky cliffs in the belief that the "New Jerusalem" would ap-

[7] See Castaldi, "O demônio no Catulê," *Anhembi*, XXI–XXIII (1956).

pear. Isolation, poverty (the people of Catulê were squatters), lack of education, and other frustrations have in the past, and can still today, lead to the appearance in Brazil of what sociologists and anthropologists have termed "messianic movements," especially in remote rural zones. In the cities, people resort to cults of African origin or to some form of spiritualism. It is curious that the relief of this frustration so seldom takes a political form. It does not seem to have been expressed in a class struggle or as yet in the growth of communism among the rural masses. Yet these same people when they are transferred to the cities and when they become politically aware are fair game for charismatic leaders.

Reaction to the relatively weak control of the Church over the Brazilian people has taken still another form, namely, a complete break with Catholicism and conversion to Protestantism. Although Brazil is still overwhelmingly Catholic, Protestantism is growing rapidly. It is now significant in total numerical strength, if not in the percentage of Protestants in the population. In 1900, there were from 40,000 to 45,000 Protestants in all of Brazil, mainly among the German colonists in the South. By 1940, over one million people were listed in the census as Protestants; by 1950, this number had expanded to 1,741,000, and today the number continues to increase. They belong to a number of Protestant sects including Episcopalians, Evangelicals, Methodists, Lutherans, Presbyterians, Baptists, and Seventh-Day Adventists.

At first the Protestant sects were identified with foreign influence, either with colonists who were Protestant by tradition or with Protestant missionaries. In the last decade or so, however, Protestantism has, in a sense, been nationalized. Nowadays, the ministers of most churches, except in the interior frontier zones where foreign missionaries are at work, are Brazilians. Many of the Protestant churches are now separated from their mother churches abroad (e.g., there are two Brazilian Presbyterian churches). Today in Brazil there is no intense anti-Protestant feeling among Brazilian Catholics like that reported for certain sections of Mexico and Colombia. Catholic clergymen and leaders talk about the challenge of Protestantism, and at least one archbishop publicly denounced the "U.S. State Department as responsible for the facilities conceded to North American Protestant pastors to go to Brazil to 'break the religious unity of the country.'" [8] But, in general, even Catholic leaders merely acknowledge the rise in Protestantism as a result of the weakness of their own Church and call for a strengthening of Catholicism.

In terms of the masses of Brazilians, Protestants are considered "strange, a little mad, and exaggerated in their faith and worship." [9] They are thought of as perhaps more moral than others; Protestants do not generally drink alcohol or smoke, and they are known to have a stable and worthy family life. They are known to attend worship regularly, not only on Sundays but also for prayer meetings during the week, and they contribute financially to their churches.

The masses of Brazilians also know something of the Protestant educational contribution to Brazil. By stressing the reading of the Bible, Protestants naturally have given importance to literacy and thus to further instruction. They have also wanted to prove their social usefulness to the country. In Brazil they have founded a series of well-known schools to

[8] Azevedo, "Catholicism in Brazil: A Personal Evaluation," *Thought*, XXVIII (1953), 272.
[9] Roger Bastide, "Religion and Church in Brazil," in Smith and Marchant, eds., *Brazil: Portrait of Half a Continent*, p. 352.

which Brazilians, both Protestant and Catholic, send their youth. Such schools as Colégio Bennett (a school for girls in Rio de Janeiro), the Agricultural College at Lavras in Minas Gerais, and Mackenzie College in São Paulo (which was first a school of commerce and then added an engineering faculty) had Protestant missionary beginnings. Some of them continue to have some foreign support, but they are now rather thoroughly nationalized.

Finally, something must be said regarding the role of Protestantism in the process of social mobility and in the formation of the Brazilian middle class. Although I do not have the necessary statistics to prove my hypothesis, it seems to me, and to other observers of Brazilian society, that conversion to Protestantism is generally a result and concomitant of social mobility. There are Protestants, especially Episcopalians and Methodists, among the conservative bourgeoisie of Brazil; other sects, namely, Baptists and Pentecostals, seem to attract people of mixed racial ancestry and lower-class origin. It is my impression that the majority of Brazilian Protestants are found in the middle class, and many of them have worked their way up from lowly beginnings.

The particular tone of Brazilian Protestantism is conducive to social mobility. It stresses hard work, abstention from drinking, gambling, and extramarital sex, and a high level of general morality. As Brazilians say, if people live in this manner, they are less likely to get into debt. It was pointed out earlier that Protestantism stresses education for oneself and one's children. As people improve their economic and educational status, they move up, even though slightly, in Brazilian society. Such people sometimes break their kinship ties, and many of them migrate to other towns or to cities. They look down upon spiritualists, African fetish cults, the folk beliefs of Brazilian Catholicism, and even what they consider to be the lack of faith of more orthodox Catholics. Once they have broken with their kinsmen, they can break with the Catholic Church. Then, the strong in-group feeling of local Protestant churches, and even of the various sects, provides them with a new, highly personalized social milieu in which their new values and achievements are given prestige. It may be that Max Weber's hypothesis of the connection between the Protestant ethic and the formation of the middle class is being borne out today in Brazil.

Brazil is far less homogeneous in religion than the statistics seem to indicate. On the surface, the country is Catholic. But, in fact, there are important differences between regions and between socioeconomic classes. Protestantism is, of course, stronger in the South with its many European immigrants; but it is also strong in Goiás and Mato Grosso in the frontier region of Brazil. It is less evident in the traditional region of the Northeast from Maranhão to Bahia. The syncretism of American Indian beliefs with Catholicism is strongest in the Amazon; African elements and cults are fused with Catholicism along the Northeast Coast. The members of the upper class are what might be called relaxed Catholics, although the fervent lay leaders of Catholicism come from this segment of society. The middle class follows a traditional form of Catholicism, and some of its members are now Protestants. The lower class in the cities turns increasingly to spiritualism and cults of African origin. The rural peasants follow a folk Catholicism which includes many practices and beliefs inherited from the past and at odds with the contemporary Church. It is clear that orthodox Catholicism is but one of Brazil's many forms of

religious experience. Yet Catholicism permeates Brazilian national culture, not so much as an active religious system but
as a way of life—a fundamental national institution.

The state

Brazil has experienced most of the Western forms of state
organization except communism. It was a colony from 1500 to
1821, and a constitutional monarchy from 1822 to 1889. As a
republic it has passed through a variety of stages. The early
republic was formally a democracy but was in fact ruled by a
small oligarchy. Then, from 1930 until 1945, Brazil experienced
a dictatorship under Getúlio Vargas, who in his constitution
of 1937 set up a form of government patterned somewhat after
the Italian corporate state. In 1946, Brazil returned to a democratic form of government, this time with wider suffrage and
greater participation by the mass of the people. In 1961, after
the resignation of President Jânio Quadros, it amended its constitution to establish a parliamentary form of government with
powers lodged in a prime minister. In 1963, after a plebiscite,
it returned to the presidential system. Brazil has had five constitutions: the Imperial Constitution (1824), the Constitution
of the Early Republic (1891), the first Vargas Constitution
(1934), the New State (*Estado Novo*) Constitution (1937),
and finally, the Constitution of 1946. In addition, there have
been amendments. It seems strange that these shifting political
forms, reminiscent of Alice in Wonderland, should have provided unity for a nation; yet, they have done so.

Curiously, Brazil has had more political stability and continuity and a less turbulent and violent political career than
most South American nations. There were a series of local but

sometimes bloody wars which broke out in the years just after independence from Portugal, such as the Cabanagem of Pará and Amazonas, the Cabanada of Pernambuco, the Sabinada of Bahia, and the Guerra dos Farrapos (Ragamuffins' War) of Rio Grande do Sul. Yet there was no nationwide war for independence. The abolition of slavery, the overthrow of the empire and establishment of the republic, the coup when Vargas took over as a dictator, the attempted secession of São Paulo state in 1932, Vargas' ultimate removal, the crisis of 1954 ending with his suicide, the unexpected resignation of President Quadros in 1961, and other political crises have been met peacefully and with little or no bloodshed. There seems to have always been a system of checks and balances in Brazilian society which allowed for adaptation to new forms of government. The same leaders have often adapted themselves to new roles in shifting situations. This may be explained in part by the passivity of the mass of the people, which of course may be transformed any day, but it must also be credited to the adaptability of the Brazilian elite. The essentially peaceful history of Brazilian political life is perhaps unparalleled in the Americas, and it has provided a continuity of state organization, however weak, which has given unity to the nation.

What is the formal structure of the Brazilian state? It follows broadly that of the United States of America (the proper name for Brazil is the United States of Brazil), but it reflects the influence of Portugal and France. As in the United States, the federal government has executive, legislative, and judicial branches. At the head of the executive are the president and vice-president, who are elected nationally by direct vote for terms of five years. The president appoints his ministers, each of whom is the head of a large bureaucratic organization. There are ministries of education and culture, health, finance, labor, agriculture, justice, foreign affairs, interior, mines and energy, navy, air force, and army. The DASP (Department of Public Service), roughly equivalent to our Civil Service Commission, theoretically controls appointments and examinations to all civil service appointments, as well as salary levels within these ministries and other federal agencies. In 1958, there were approximately 240,000 federal employees, not counting the personnel of the three armed forces.

The Brazilian civil servant has more rights and privileges than his counterpart in the United States. Many of these rights are stated specifically in the 1946 constitution. For example, it is stated that women employees who become pregnant have a right to time off both before and after delivery. Tenure is next to absolute for a federal employee; even if he gives up his position, he may sue for reinstatement. Individuals move easily from one position to another and from one ministry to another, "on loan" and "on requisition." Thus, a man may hold a permanent position as a public health officer in the Ministry of Health, but he may also be serving "on loan" in the Ministry of Education as the executive of an important new program—at a higher salary, of course. The federal bureaucracy of Brazil has, especially since the time of Vargas, reached rather monolithic proportions, and there are strong and well-entrenched interests at work.

Similarly, the body of personnel of the three armed forces is an important part of the national state. Of the three, the army is traditionally the most democratic; its ranks are formed to a large extent by draftees and young men serving their regular term of military service. The officers are traditionally socially mobile individuals drawn from the middle class. They are highly nationalistic, sometimes inclined to the political right or left, but always patriotic. The army is thus a focus of political and social ferment. In courses at the Escola Superior de Guerra, analogous to our War College, both officers and civilians study and discuss the national problems of Brazil. The Military Club publishes a journal which reflects the current trends of political opinion in the country. The air force tends to be less ultranationalistic. Its officials tend to be more youthful, and many were trained in the United States. They are no less interested, however, in Brazilian problems. The navy is by tradition rather aristocratic, and in fact perhaps less powerful than either the air force or the army. In any case, the three armed forces provide a stabilizing influence on Brazilian political life. In an atomic age, the primary function of the Brazilian armed forces would seem to be that of providing Brazil with an internal police force. They have often intervened in civilian political life, but to date they have limited themselves to providing a stable situation for continued civilian rule. For better or for worse, the armed forces have been an important factor in national unity.

Since the time of Vargas, the federal government has steadily increased its power throughout the nation. There are nine federal universities, and some of the state and private universities have federal subsidies. The *reitor* (rector or president) of a federal university is nominated by the president of Brazil from a panel of candidates selected by the faculty (themselves, of course, federal employees). The *reitor*, or to be exact the *magnífico reitor* as he is called, of a federal university in a northern state may have funds at his disposal almost as large as those of the state governor. Then there are the federal development programs which have proliferated in Brazil, such as the São Francisco Valley Commission, the SUDENE (Northeastern Development Commission), SPVEA (Amazon Development Commission), CAPES (Campaign for the Development of Higher Education), SESP (Special Public Health Service), and DNOCS (National Department of Works Against Drought). There are so many of these federal, extraministerial agencies that a special dictionary has been published to translate the "alphabet soup" into titles. Each of these agencies implies an expenditure of federal funds and increased power for the federal government.

In addition, the federal government, particularly the executive branch, controls a multitude of semigovernmental agencies and "mixed companies," most of which arose under the Vargas regime. They take a variety of forms. There are mixed companies where the stock is shared between the public and the federal government. Such companies control and run railroads, shipping lines, port authorities, hydroelectric plants, and even iron mills. The Central Brasil and the São Paulo railway systems are controlled by the federal government. The giant steel mill at Volta Redonda is a mixed private-government enterprise. Another type of semigovernmental agency has to do with economic control and cartelization. For almost every major product (sugar, salt, coffee, and maté), there is an "Institute." These institutes, at least theoretically, further the development of trade in a specific product, and they attempt to control prices, set quotas of production, and establish standards. Then, too, there are federal banks. The Bank of Brazil is similar in many ways to our Federal Reserve, but it also governs foreign exchange and other aspects of economic life. The Bank for Economic Development and the Bank of the Northeast make loans locally for development projects, and administrate funds from foreign loans granted to the federal government. Finally, there are a number of social security agencies which are semigovernmental. Unlike the United States, Brazil has several social security systems—one for industry, one for commercial employees, and so forth. They are similar to private insurance companies in the United States, but are controlled by the federal government. These semigovernmental agencies of all types control and spend enormous sums. They are manned by personnel who although outside the federal civil service have strong guarantees of job tenure and are in fact but an extension of the enlarged federal civil service. In the absence of a strong and active formation of private capital, the federal government of Brazil has penetrated into many realms of economic life which are in the United States considered private.

The federal legislative system is bicameral, as in the United States. There is a Senate and a House of Deputies analogous to our Congress. There are three senators for every state, and they serve for a term of eight years. As in the United States, the vice-president presides over the Senate and may cast the deciding vote. The number of deputies representing each state or territory is proportional to its population. Each state is granted one deputy for every 120,000 inhabitants, up to a limit of 20 deputies; thereafter, one deputy is elected for every 250,000 people. The minimum number of deputies per state has been set at seven. The federal territories are guaranteed the right of electing one deputy each, since their population is so sparse. These elaborate regulations are obviously aimed at preventing domination by such highly populous states as São Paulo and Minas Gerais, and giving some voice to the smaller or less highly populated states like Sergipe and Amazonas. Each deputy serves a term of four years. In the House of Deputies, there is a chairman and there are leaders of the majority and minority, but, as we shall see later, the presence of a series of political parties and some strange coalitions make for complexities in the legislative process.

The Brazilian legislative system parallels closely that of the United States, but there are some basic differences. In Brazil, residence in a state is not a requisite to candidacy for office. A candidate may run for office in several states, or in a state where he does not reside. In 1946, for example, Getúlio Vargas ran and was elected senator in several states. He accepted the office in his native state of Rio Grande do Sul. In 1962, to cite another example, the governor of Bahia, Juracy Magalhães, was an unsuccessful candidate for senator in the state of Guanabara. The Brazilian system of elections for deputies also differs from that of the United States. There are no congressional districts. Deputies represent states as a whole, although they may favor those parts of a state from which the majority of their electors come. In an election, there is always a long list of candidates for deputy in each state; votes are counted on a statewide basis for each candidate. Those candidates having the most votes are elected, in accordance with the quota of representatives allotted to each state. Thus, if a state has seven deputies, the seven men who receive the highest number of votes are elected.

In the same way, the judicial branch of the Brazilian government seems to resemble our own but is actually markedly different. There are five sets of courts. The Supremo Tribunal Federal is roughly analogous to our Supreme Court, but it has never had the same decisive force in the Brazilian government. Brazil has a Tribunal Federal de Recursos which oversees the expenditure of federal funds, a Tribunal Militar which considers military cases, a Tribunal Eleitoral which deals with and supervises elections, and a Tribunal do Trabalho which handles cases concerned with labor. Court procedure and law generally follow the Napoleonic Code. It is strange, however, that a people so concerned with legalism should place so little emphasis upon the courts.

The government of each Brazilian state is to a large extent a replica of the federal system. The government is elected by direct vote for a term of four years. Most states have but one legislative body, a local House of Deputies, but some also have a Senate. The states have *Secretarias* which are analogous to federal ministries and which deal with education, health, agriculture, and other fields. Sometimes they also have civil service commissions analogous to the federal DASP. Often one finds specialized agencies such as the Cacao Institute of Bahia, and these agencies frequently have economic planning commissions.

Although the powers of the federal government overshadow those of the states, the latter retain a large residue of power. Each state has its own constitution and its own laws, but these are severely limited by the federal code. Education, both primary and secondary, is a state function, although the federal government supervises it and influences it strongly through subsidies. The federal constitution theoretically guarantees the autonomy of the states, and allows intervention only to maintain national unity and the exercise of certain rights established by the federal constitution. There is, in fact, considerable overlap and even conflict between federal and state powers. The Brazilian states enter into agreements with federal agencies and even with agencies of foreign governments to carry out specific projects. In 1962, the small state of Paraíba entered into a direct agreement with the U.S. Administration for International Development (Alliance for Progress), bypassing the federal authorities. Not too long before that, the government of Minas Gerais had reached a triangular agreement for an educational program with the Brazilian Ministry of Education and the U.S. Institute of Inter-American Affairs. There are members of Brazilian federal agencies, however, who maintain that such agreements are the exclusive prerogative of the federal authorities. At least to the nonlegal mind, the division of authority in Brazil between the federal and state governments is something of a no-man's land.

On the same level as the Brazilian states are the federal territories, which are, however, administered directly by the federal government. Acre, the oldest of these territories, on the frontier with Bolivia, became a state in 1962. The three remaining territories, Rondônia, Amapá, and Rio Branco, were carved out of various states over the last twenty years. With the creation of these federal territories, Brazil has sought to guarantee its boundaries in sparsely inhabited areas and to develop its distant frontiers. The governor of a territory is appointed by the president. The civil servants working in such areas are federal employees who are paid higher salaries than the states could afford and who, in addition, often receive "hardship" allowances. Because these territories are directly dependent upon the central government, federal funds can be poured into them. Since there is no local legislature, the governor acts with considerable freedom. Success in the development of these territories has been uneven, depending as it does upon the flow of federal funds, the dynamism of the governor, and local potentialities. Most successful in recent years has been the territory of Amapá, bordering on French

Guiana and formerly a part of the state of Pará. It has had several energetic governors since it was created in 1943. It has rich deposits of manganese as well as other minerals. Its capital, Macapá, has grown into a modern tropical city on the Amazon River. Communications have improved within the territory and with the outside world. In 1962, it was estimated that royalties on its ore exports yielded $40 million, which were being invested in hydroelectric plants to stimulate industrial growth. Ultimately, such territories may be reincorporated into the states of which they were once a part, or become, like Acre, Brazilian states.

Earlier in this book, the basic local unit of government, the *município*, was described briefly in discussing Brazilian communities. Most *municípios* are divided into *distritos de paz*, usually referred to as *distritos*. Although the *município* is a territorial division similar to the North American county, the term is often translated as municipality. This can cause misunderstanding as to the nature of the *município*. First, unlike the county seat in the United States, the *sede* (seat) of a *município* never has a corporate existence apart from the surrounding rural zone and the other towns and villages within the countylike area. No city, town, or village has a corporate existence apart from the *município* in which it is situated. This is important because the total income of the territorial unit and all its facilities are at the command of both the townspeople and the rural inhabitants.

Each *município* has a mayor called a *prefeito*, as well as a varying number of town councilmen called *vereadores* who are elected by direct vote for a term of four years. In addition, there is a *município* bureaucracy. In one very small and isolated *município* in the southern part of Bahia state, with a total

population of 5,000 people, there were 29 official employees
aside from the mayor and his councilmen. These ranged from
the *município* secretary and treasurer to the dogcatcher and
street cleaner. In this relatively poor *município*, about two-thirds
of the funds available come from the federal government, for
the Constitution of 1946 states that poor *municípios* are to be
subsidized.[10] In more prosperous and populous *municípios*, the
number of public servants would be much larger in production
to the population. The city of Rio de Janeiro spent for a time
(i.e., *ca.* 1953) more than 90 percent of its total revenue on
salaries. Some idea of the comparative strength of federal, state,
and *município* governments can be obtained from the percentage of the national revenue they expend: in 1950, the
federal government spent approximately 50 percent of the total
revenue, the state governments 39 percent, and the *municípios*
about 11 percent. By now, the percentage expended by the
federal authorities has certainly increased. It should be obvious
why most Brazilians learn to expect all social welfare, education, public health, and other programs to originate outside
the local community, either in the state or federal government.
In many ways, the *município* is the weakest link in the governmental system. Yet it is important in politics, for that is where
people vote and follow their political leaders.

Such is the formal political structure of the Brazilian state.
However, the Brazilian political system cannot be explained
in terms of its legal and constitutional structure alone. There
is also the "game" of Brazilian politics and the great divergence
between laws and their application. Brazil guarantees universal
suffrage to all Brazilians over eighteen years of age, except to
those who cannot read and write. One need only be able to

[10] Harris, *Town and Country in Brazil*, pp. 179 ff.

sign one's name to be allowed to vote, but even this restriction eliminates more than half of the voting-age population. This means that a large portion of the rural population cannot vote, and that most of the people in urban slums are eliminated. Despite the tremendous growth of the electorate in Brazil from 1930 to the present, only a small minority actually participate in the Brazilian democracy. In his excellent book on Brazil, *Os dois Brasis,* Jacques Lambert points out the similarity of the prerequisite of literacy to the various tests required of North American Negroes before they can vote in our South, and the early Russian constitutions which equated two votes from urban areas with five votes from rural areas.[11] All three of these systems guarantee that a minority will control the vote. Formally, Brazil looks like a representative democracy similar in many respects to that of the United States, but in fact it is not. This is why Lambert is able to say: "But, even when the presidential regime functions normally and constitutional legality is respected, the institutions inspired by the United States work in such a different way and produce such unexpected results that North American observers cannot believe they are honestly carried out and become indignant at the duplicity of the officials." [12]

This lack of active participation in the political scene by the large mass of Brazilians is the basis for the phenomenon of *coronelismo,* the domination of local politics by local leaders who control their electorate through traditional paternalistic favors, sometimes by outright purchase of the vote, and sometimes by intimidation with armed force. The *coronel* is largely a thing of the past in the southern and central states, but has

[11] Lambert, *Os dois Brasis,* p. 266 f.
[12] *Ibid.,* p. 249.

by no means disappeared in the more archaic North and West. There, and sporadically even in the South, certain families, or *parentelas* as we have called them, dominate the local political scene. Even in the more advanced areas, *coronelismo* has often been replaced by bossism or by political machines dominated by individual political leaders. To a large extent, the Brazilian political process involves a series of deals between individuals and small groups. A local leader pledges to deliver his electorate to a state leader, who in turn reaches an understanding with a national leader or group.

The contemporary system of political parties in Brazil has little historical depth. Before Vargas, political parties, political campaigns, and political issues were mainly regional. Communications between one region and another were so poor that political campaigns could hardly be national in scope; it would have taken a candidate for president literally months to visit and appeal directly to the electorate in various parts of the country. There were three loci of political power: the traditional North where Bahia and Pernambuco were the leading states, the populous central states where São Paulo and Minas Gerais held the most power, and the extreme South, centering upon the state of Rio Grande do Sul. In fact, it has been said that there was an unwritten covenant by which São Paulo and Minas Gerais were expected to furnish the president of Brazil on a rotating basis. Political parties, therefore, were generally statewide or at best regional in scope.

Brazil has not yet experienced a social and political revolution similar to that of Mexico, for example, which, although it provided only a one-party system, did provide a continuing ideology. During the Vargas regime, however, Brazil did go through a series of economic, social, and administrative changes which profoundly modified the political milieu. In a sense, Vargas wiped the slate clean in politics. From 1934 until 1946, voting was suspended and so was, to a large extent, all political activity. Brazilians who came of age during this period did not vote until 1946. Vargas, among other things, was a paternalistic and charismatic leader who directed his appeal to the growing urban working classes. His government promulgated labor codes, and established minimum wages and government-controlled labor unions. He was known by several affectionate nicknames such as O Velhinho (the Old Man), Pai dos Pobres (Father of the Poor), or just by his first name. Speaking personally, or in a prerecorded broadcast, he addressed himself each evening to the Trabalhadores do Brasil (Workers of Brazil) in a warm and protective voice. His followers never formed as strong a political party as did the Argentine *peronistas.* In the Brazilian tradition, Vargas was a highly personal figure representing a reaction against oligarchy and political chicanery, but he did not leave behind a set of enduring revolutionary symbols, like the agrarian reform, nationalization of the petroleum industry, and Indianism of Mexico.

With the end of the Vargas dictatorship in 1945, political parties and political alliances quickly appeared on the Brazilian scene. Some of them derived from the pre-1930 state and regional parties, some represented new political forces, and at least one represented the Vargas regime. The latter, called Partido Trabalhista Brasileiro (Brazilian Labor Party) or PTB, had an initial advantage, since the labor unions were administered by government officials appointed by Vargas and could act as party organizers. The other major party to appear in 1946 was the UDN (National Democratic Union). It was formed by the rather traditional and conservative critics of the

Vargas regime. When the well-known communist leader Luís Carlos Prestes was released from prison in 1946, he quickly organized the PCB (Brazilian Communist Party), which was national in scope and sufficiently powerful to seat him in the senate and to elect fifteen deputies. In 1948, the Communist Party was declared illegal. Since then it has continued underground, and there are rumors that it has split into several factions. Other parties dating from the pre-Vargas period reappeared. The PSP (Social Progressive Party) was organized around the figure of Adhemar de Barros, who was twice elected governor of São Paulo and was once an unsuccessful candidate for president. A series of other parties such as the PST (Social Labor Party), PDC (Democratic Christian Party), PSN (National Socialist Party), and PRP (Progressive Republican Party) have had regional and even national influence during the last decade.

None of these parties are truly national in scope. In fact, even the most important parties, which are theoretically organized on a national basis, actually operate on a regional or statewide basis. In different regions of the country, the same party may represent different sectors of the electorate. Roger Bastide has this to say about one of the two most powerful national parties:

In the North and in Minas Gerais, the National Democratic Union . . . represents the middle class in their struggle against the oligarchy; in Rio de Janeiro, it is the party of the "petite bourgeoisie," who feel challenged by the communists; in São Paulo, it is the party of the planters against the industrialists. The program of the party, however, does not vary from place to place.[13]

Furthermore, parties form different alliances and coalitions in

[13] Bastide, *Brasil: terra de contrastes*, p. 244 f.

different parts of the country. Candidates are often the candidates of several parties. For example, in 1958, a candidate to the federal senate in the state of Rio de Janeiro was supported by the Brazilian Labor Party, the National Democratic Union, and the Social Progressive Party. The conclusion is inevitable. There are not as yet any national political parties with well-established programs. Political life is dominated by personalities —by "Jango" (João Goulart), "Jânio" (Jânio Quadros), "Juscelino" (Juscelino Kubitschek), and others too numerous to mention—with regional and even national influence.

Brazil has long been legally and structurally a national state with all the apparatus of a modern Western nation. It has developed the institutions, traditions, symbols and myths of a nation. But, even in the second half of the twentieth century, many of the national institutions are not living realities to a large proportion of its people. Brazilians place high value on family loyalty, but the great mass of people have few relatives since they have left their native communities or come from poor and broken homes. Brazil has an educational system theoretically available to all, but in fact closed to many. Apparently, it is a nation with religious homogeneity, but in fact a variety of religious forms exist side by side. Brazil is a representative democracy with universal suffrage, but in fact a large segment of the population is disfranchised by illiteracy. Alongside the patriotic nationalists of Brazil, there are Brazilians in the deep interior who do not even know that they live in a nation called Brazil. It may be said that Brazil needs to extend full citizenship to all Brazilians. Yet these national institutions and traditions and the framework of the national state system provide Brazil with its unity as a nation.

❦ 7 ❦ IF I WERE A BRAZILIAN

IN seeking the unity of a society and national culture so complex as that of modern Brazil, I realize that certain things cannot be stated scientifically, with full substantiation. Much of the unity of Brazil comes from just being a Brazilian—from feeling and acting like a Brazilian. These implicit, almost intuitive, aspects of a culture are difficult to make explicit and to define, even for the native observer, although they are expressed every day in books, newspapers, and movies, and in the common understandings which the members of a culture share. Sometimes the foreign visitor who has come to know a people sees them with a freshness and objectivity which helps them understand themselves. Histories of Brazil are filled with references to the observations of foreign visitors—Maria Graham, Henry Koster, D. P. Kidder, James C. Fletcher, and other travelers who visited the country in the nineteenth century and earlier.

I have lived in Brazil for almost ten years out of the last twenty. I have learned the language, read novels, poetry, and the daily press, attended movies and the theater, gone to soccer games and rooted for my favorite team, lived in the deep interior, in small towns, and in the great cities. I feel at home in the Brazilian way of life; the culture of Brazil is one that I know intuitively, I like to think, almost as well as my own.

I have often daydreamed about what I might do or be if I

were a Brazilian. Sometimes I have thought that I would be a
revolutionary, attempting to break rapidly and drastically
through the lethargy of an archaic class system. Yet, if I were
a Brazilian, I would, of course, almost certainly want to be
of the upper class. I would not want to be one of the unfortunate 49 percent who cannot read or write, and I would want
to be one of the small minority who somehow achieve a university education. I would want to travel abroad to Europe, to
the United States, and perhaps even beyond the Iron Curtain
to compare my own country and society with that of others.
If my Brazilian friends will forgive me, I shall indulge this
fancy for a while and write subjectively, as if I were a Brazilian, seeking to describe the pros and cons, the strengths and
weaknesses, the unity and disunity of Brazilian society.

We Brazilians have suffered for a long time from what many
of us call a national inferiority complex. Our fathers and grandfathers looked toward France as a country of superior culture
and traveled there if they could afford it. They learned French
early and read French books throughout their lives. They valued
all things French—art, wine, and women. Until the last generation, we of the upper class depended almost entirely on foreign
things and ideas. Butter was often imported from Europe in
cans and our clothes were made of imported linens and wool-
ens. Of course, we attended the Brazilian theater, sang Brazilian carnival songs, and danced the samba; but these were not
valued so highly as visiting French players, a French crooner,
or the fox trot. Brazilian wines were commonly said to damage
the liver. There was a disdain for anything made or produced
in Brazil.

We must admit that some of this national feeling of inferiority derived from the fact that we are a racially mixed people. Gilberto Freyre, one of our outstanding intellectuals and writers, expressed this in the preface to the first Brazilian edition of *The Masters and the Slaves:*

Once upon a time, after three straight years of absence from my country, I caught sight of a group of Brazilian seamen—mulattoes and *cafusos*—crossing Brooklyn Bridge. I no longer remember whether they were from São Paulo or from Minas, but I know that they impressed me as being the caricatures of men, and there came to mind a phrase from a book on Brazil written by an American traveler: "the fearfully mongrel aspect of the population."

This anxiety about miscegenation was shared by many Brazilians; many of us suspected, or feared, that the theories of the racists of the early twentieth century might be correct and that we were doomed to be an inferior people. So, Itamarati (the Brazilian Foreign Office) and our navy limited their personnel to men of Caucasoid appearance; these would be the people who represented us abroad. We rationalized this action by saying that Brazilians of color would be uncomfortable living in the many foreign lands where racial prejudice was rife. As late as the Vargas regime, just before World War II, our Department of Propaganda sought to avoid the export of pictures of the Negro population of Bahia and to suppress Afro-American religious cults. There was a feeling that the Negroes of Brazil somehow detracted from the image of ourselves as a white, European people living in the New World.

Then, almost imperceptibly, the world of my generation in Brazil began to change. This change in perspective on the world and on Brazil had been in the making many years before World War II, but it was only after the war that it reached most Brazilians. As early as 1922, the Semana de Arte Moderna (Modern Art Week), a gathering of young writers and artists, had denounced the traditionalism of Brazilian arts and letters and called for a break with the fetish of European influence. Mário de Andrade, the leader of the Semana and of this movement, wrote a novel called Macunaíma—its Paul Bunyan-like hero is a Brazilian Indian who speaks in the Brazilian idiom as distinct from classical and European Portuguese. Supporting this movement either consciously or unconsciously, Brazilians began to produce works of art and literature of uncommon value which attracted some international attention. Cândido Portinari painted Brazilian scenes with a skill and imagination that gained him recognition as one of the important painters of this century. Heitor Villa-Lobos, working with Brazilian musical themes, gained international fame as a composer. In poetry, Manuel Bandeira, Augusto Frederico Schmidt, and Carlos Drummond de Andrade wrote about Brazil in the Brazilian language. The Brazilian novel flourished in the years before World War II, with José Américo, Graciliano Ramos, Rachel de Queiroz, José Lins do Rêgo, Viana Moog, Érico Veríssimo, Jorge Amado, and a dozen other novelists. In the social sciences, there was Arthur Ramos, who wrote about the Brazilian Negro, Gilberto Freyre, who was achieving international fame, and a younger group from the São Paulo School of Sociology and Politics which included Oracy Nogueira, Florestan Fernandes, and Darcy Ribeiro.

Brazilians began to discover themselves intellectually during the 1920s and 1930s, but it was not until after World War II that we began truly to view our country with real pride. Whatever the ills of the Vargas dictatorship, his regime made the federal government stronger than it had ever been before, overshadowing regional political machines and interests. Franklin D. Roosevelt's Good Neighbor Policy brought the United States into the Brazilian scene; many Brazilians of my generation studied English and looked to the United States for intellectual and political inspiration. Then, during the war, Brazil sent a force to fight in Italy alongside the North American GI's, and we felt that we had contributed positively to the defeat of Hitler. The return to democracy after 1945 brought a renewed interest in national welfare, and many Brazilians of my generation voted for the first time. It is true that the ex-dictator Getúlio Vargas was elected in 1950, but this was done through an honest and free election. Brazil began to take on an increasingly important role in the United Nations and its specialized agencies.

More important, perhaps, the end of World War II marked the beginning of the industrialization of Brazil. We ended the war with a dollar credit resulting from the purchase at controlled prices of our raw materials such as rubber, bauxite, quartz crystal, and mica. This credit was soon spent on heavy machinery and even luxury products sold to us at rapidly inflated postwar prices. This is when we first became irritated with the United States, but liberal loans from your country helped us for a time to expand our industry and develop our hydroelectric power. Industry boomed, especially in and around São Paulo. By 1950, Brazilian-made products were more numerous than imported ones, and as the years went by almost everything we needed or used came to be "Made in Brazil." Ready-made men's clothes became commonplace; we made automobiles and trucks, radios, refrigerators, washing machines, ladies' nylon hose, and a thousand other products which we had formerly imported. The hydroelectric plant at Paulo Afonso Falls was completed in its first stages and began to furnish power to the large cities of the Northeast, and other great hydroelectric projects such as Três Marias and Urubupunga were initiated. Air transportation was expanded and VARIG Airlines, noted for its efficiency and service, became one of the most extensive of all international air networks. Brazil changed rapidly before our very eyes.

Alongside those who felt that they must apologize for Brazil, we have always had many strong nationalists, almost blindly proud of our country. Even the apologists had a streak of stubborn nationalistic pride. One of my old aunts told me she was sure that Brazilians had more native intelligence than the French or Americans; she pointed out the case of Seu Antônio, an illiterate workman at the National Museum, who had become a rather skillful carpenter and mechanic. Could a Frenchman or an American have overcome such disadvantages? Quietly, Brazilians had harbored a national pride for centuries, but after World War II it appeared with new strength. Many of us became more articulately nationalistic, proud of our country and countrymen and jealous of those who would interfere with our national destiny.

This new nationalism took many forms. Sports became a matter of national interest. A Brazilian was Olympic champion in the hop-skip-and-jump in 1958. Maria Bueno was the Wimbledon female tennis champion in 1960. Above all, in 1958 and 1962, Brazil won the soccer championship of the world. Pelé, the young Brazilian Negro, became a star known wherever soccer is played, and he is a hero to Brazilian youths. In 1962, Garrincha and Amarildo, two brilliant soccer stars, were names on the lips of every Brazilian when we won the cup at Santiago, Chile. *Futebol* came to be a symbol of the na-

tion and of national unity. When our champions returned to
Brazil from Chile in 1962, they were received by the President.
We celebrated their victory by an impromptu carnival and a
holiday. Our soccer players are known around the world; they
play for Real Madrid, Rome, and other European teams, but
the most famous ones play in Rio and São Paulo, where they

*Pelé, the King of Soccer, at Stockholm where Brazil won the
world championship*

attract over a hundred thousand fans on a Sunday. Wherever
we are in the world, we Brazilians are interested in the *futebol*
scores, and in pulling for our favorite team.

National pride takes other forms. I suppose that North
Americans invented beauty contests; in any case, Miss Universe
is selected at Miami and Long Beach each year. But North
Americans hardly take these contests as seriously as we do in
Brazil. Each year there are local, then state, and finally national
contests to select Miss Brazil. The newspapers, magazines, and

newsreels give these contests full coverage, and Miss Brazil becomes a figure of national pride and renown. While Miss Brazil ranks among the most beautiful women in the world, not until 1963 was she selected as Miss Universe. The fact had never occurred to me before, but all our beauty queens are white and generally brunette, although some have had light-brown hair. We idealize the beautiful *mulata* in song and poetry, but for export we seem to send our Caucasoid beauties.

Our cinema has been generally crude and awkwardly produced, but recently one of our films, "Pagador de Promessas" (The Man Who Fulfilled His Vows), won a prize in Cannes, and the whole country vibrated with the news. Moreover, this film presented exactly those aspects of our national life which in the past were a source of embarrassment. It pictured the arid backlands and the religious fanaticism, the Afro-Brazilian cults of Bahia, the mulattoes and *pardos*, and the lower-class side of our national life. Our newspapers described in detail the new achievement in our cultural life which this film represented. In addition, there is *bossa nova*, the new form of jazz which our musicians and poets developed and which the North Americans discovered. It is a form of samba, quiet and smooth with poetic lyrics, and it gave Brazil considerable publicity in the United States. We no longer feel that we are an isolated country; we now have influences on the modern world.

Our new national pride is not really based only on these rather frivolous achievements. After all, in less than three years we built Brasília, a new city in a wilderness. We often discuss far into the night whether this effort and expense should have been undertaken, but most of us agree that Brasília stands as a symbol of national achievement, and we are proud of its international fame as a planned city. Nowadays we make excursions to Brasília by bus and plane. In addition to visiting the imposing new modern buildings, world-famous architecturally, we go see the simple wooden structure which Juscelino Kubitschek used as his presidential residence while Brasília was being built and which is now a museum. When we visit Brasília most of us see for the first time the great heartland of our vast country; it is not a jungle or wasteland filled with jaguars and wild Indians, as our fathers and grandfathers seemed to think. Nowadays, tourism in Brazil by Brazilians has become fashionable. People visit the colonial towns of Ouro Prêto and Congonhas do Campo in Minas Gerais, and Salvador with its many churches and its African cults; the more adventurous even go up the Amazon River as far as Manaus. Those of us who live in Rio de Janeiro and São Paulo complain about the accommodations along the road and in small towns, but for the first time we are on the road. Our interest has turned inward, toward the grandeur of our own country.

Thus we have in this generation overcome to a large extent the national inferiority complex from which we suffered so long. We believe in the strength and future of our own country. In fact we may have somewhat overdeveloped our nationalistic pride—"overcompensated," I think the psychologist might say—in our rejection of our former feeling of inferiority. One of our serious thinkers, for example, criticized our Brazilian sociologists for following European and North American theories and called for a Brazilian sociology. Some intellectual friends of mine argue that Brazilian secondary schools and universities are superior to those of Europe and the United States. In some of us national pride almost approaches fanaticism. Yet most of us really know that our country still has a long way to go before reaching the level of many other countries in science, industry, education, and material well-being. We can still learn from such countries, and, for all our sensitivities, we are a friendly and receptive people, eager to learn. By now, in any case, we are certain that we are not inferior in any way. Science makes it clear that there are no "inferior" races. We are praised abroad for our racial democracy and we try to live up to this image of ourselves. We see all around us daily proof of our ability to be creative in industry, science, the arts, and human relations.

This new Brazilian nationalism can be troublesome for us as well as for others. It provides ammunition for our extreme left, which makes use of it in anti-imperialistic and anti-American propaganda. Because we are so proud of our recent achievements, we are more vulnerable to any encroachment upon our rights and to exploitation from the outside. Most of us are honestly and strongly anti-imperialistic. We believe truly that "O Petróleo é Nosso" (The Petroleum Is Ours)—a slogan used to indicate that the oil industry should be exploited by Petrobrás, a government company, rather than by any of the great international combines. We would rather continue to spend most of our foreign exchange credit on petroleum than take the chance, as did Argentina, of falling into the hands of the giant foreign oil companies. We wonder, then, how much truth there is in the accusations that Standard Oil has tried to influence some of our politicians and some of our journalists so that it might secure concessions to explore and exploit Brazilian oil. We were suspicious of the reports of an American technician employed by Petrobrás who was pessimistic about the prospects for petroleum deposits in our country, and he was forced to resign his position.

Every day we see new products being "Made in Brazil," but often these products have foreign names and the companies that make them are Brazilian affiliates of foreign concerns. There is a little pamphlet called "One Day in the Life of Brasilino," by Paulo Guilherme Martins, which has gone through at least four editions and which makes this graphic for us. Brasilino, a typical Brazilian, believes strongly in Brazilian enterprise, but as he goes through the day he is shown to be paying dividends and royalties to foreign corporations. He brushes his teeth with a brush called TEK made by Johnson and Johnson of Brazil; he shaves with a blade called Gillette made by Gillette Safety Razor do Brasil; he uses a soap during his morning shower which is either Lever or Palmolive; he breakfasts with bread made of wheat (the result of a long-term loan from the United States) which was milled by an English-owned company; he leaves his apartment via an elevator made either by Otis of Brazil or by Schindler of Brazil; and he goes to work in his Volkswagen made by Volkswagen of Brazil. Thus Brasilino goes through his entire day using products made in Brazil, but by a foreign company. Recently the same idea has been used in a record called "The People Sings," played and sung by excellent musicians and issued by the National Union of Students. In this record, the average Brazilian uses Colgate dental cream, Gillette blades, and Esso gasoline; he drinks Coca Cola with rum or whiskey rather than Brazilian beer. He does not like the samba but thinks the "rock" (rock 'n' roll) is wonderful. We liberal and objective Brazilians are not overwhelmed by this rather obvious propaganda, but curiously it seems basically true.

Serious studies of the economy show the rapid penetration of foreign capital and the outward flow of profits in the form of dividends and royalties paid for the right to produce foreign-trade-marked products in Brazil. A recent study of our pharmaceutical industry showed that during the last ten years most Brazilian laboratories, of some of which we were justly proud, had been taken over by North American, English, Swiss, and French companies. Theoretically, at least 51 percent of the stock continues in Brazilian hands, according to our law, but there is some doubt that this is in fact true. With the appearance of those famous pharmaceutical companies on the Brazilian scene, we seem to have much to gain. They offer the Brazilian market the widest variety of modern medicines, we are assured of almost impeccable standards of production, our physicians no longer need to frantically cable London or New York for a new drug, and we take advantage of the continued research which these large firms continually support. But, many people argue, what will become of our own pharmacists and our own pharmaceutical industry? Our few research pharmacists have well-paid administrative positions with these foreign-dominated companies; they do not carry out research, for that is done more efficiently abroad in the home laboratories. According to the label, the medicines are made in Brazil, but many people say that this is not strictly so. Instead, the basic elements are imported separately and mixed and packaged according to a foreign formula and technique. So, our pharmaceutical industry becomes no more than a mixing and packaging organization. Then, as nationalists insist, each year we pay more and more royalties and dividends to foreign companies. As a Brazilian, I find the situation hard to swallow, yet I can see the material advantages of having the most modern medicines. Perhaps the new law which seeks to limit the amount of profits to be exported by any company with foreign investors to 10 percent of its capital will help. Many of my friends are doubtful, for there are many ways of estimating the value of the capital of the companies.

It is confusing to be a Brazilian, I can tell you. One hardly knows what to think. In the New York *Times* of December 8, 1962, I read with horror of the deteriorating financial situation of our nation (I read it much later because it takes a long time for the New York *Times* to reach my hands). As of December 31, 1962, we will have an external debt of about $2,735 million, of which some $1,300 million are owed to the United States. As of that date, the article says, we will have no gold in our reserves or foreign-exchange reserves to meet our foreign-exchange debts, which amount to over $100 million. The deficit in our national budget in 1963 might be as much as $1,600 million. When I translate these sums into cruzeiros my mathematical mind goes blank, for the cruzeiro was quoted on about the same day at $.0022. In the New York *Times* of the same date another article by Juan de Onís, perhaps the best newspaper correspondent ever assigned to Brazil, states that our deficit in the national budget approved by Congress will be 251 billion cruzeiros. Catastrophic inflation is said to be mainly to blame. Yet the New York *Times* points out that the Brazilian economy continues to grow at an average of more than 6 percent each year. A large portion of what we borrow goes to pay interest to the United States, Japan, and European countries. Can we continue to borrow on our future, or are we headed for economic and political disaster?

It is frustrating, too, to be a Brazilian. This book has given the facts about our educational system and the number of schools we have built since 1930. However, our illiteracy rate remains about the same. This book mentions several times the rapid growth of industry, the spread of transportation and development of communications throughout the country, and the large sums poured into our public services and hydroelectric plants. Several economists have described Brazil as being in the "take-off stage," meaning, we hope, that the material welfare of our population is about to be improved.

Somehow this phrase makes little sense to us who live day by day in Brazil. We are faced with the reality of other facts. Each year, for example, there are almost 2.5 million more Brazilians. They are, of course, Brazilian babies, because immigration to Brazil is negligible. Infants and small children are not producers, but they must be fed and educated. We middle-aged Brazilians must then work harder and longer to support this so-called unproductive youthful population. The answer for the man in the middle class is a *cabide de empregos* ("a hatstand of jobs," meaning two or three jobs), but this is only a personal answer to the problem. The problem of the nation is the mass of youths without adults to support them, and the lack of workers of productive age with skills that make possible such extra jobs. Brazilians are not lazy; a North American friend commented on how hard a professor works, teaching at several schools and holding down an administrative position as well. Young executives generally have several jobs, or work long hours from 8:00 A.M. to 7:00 P.M. and into the night. We rather envy our North American colleagues who teach in one school or who work full time for one company.

Our public education system is rigid, elite-oriented, and mechanical. Despite the drive for more schools by Anisio Teixeira and his group, there are not enough public schools and nearly all schools are crowded. I must send my children to private schools, and even these schools do not really give a satisfactory education. They announce a teaching program which they do not in fact fulfill. The teachers are half-trained and often teach in several schools. But I think my children are privileged, for they go to relatively good private schools. In comparison, I know how bad the schools are in small towns and rural zones, and I know of some private schools that are only money-making businesses.

Another frustration is that of living under rampant and increasing inflation. Twenty years ago I deposited 1,000 cruzeiros (which was $50 in your money at the time) in the name of my daughter at the Caixa Econômica (a federal savings bank). It has earned 8–12 percent interest, compounded annually, ever since; my daughter now has almost 3,000 cruzeiros in the Caixa Econômica, but it will hardly purchase a simple dress for her and is worth less than $5 in your money. Inflation is certainly not conducive to saving, at least through banks. Fortunately, we bought a cooperative apartment in Rio de Janeiro around 1945. I paid what seemed to be an exorbitant price for it at that time, but I got a ten-year mortgage; my monthly payments of 10,000 cruzeiros were hard to meet at first but they became extraordinarily small at the end, and now we own our apartment. It is said to be worth millions of cruzeiros, and it represents our only savings. Perhaps it is owning an apartment that makes it possible for us to live with inflation—I wonder what I would do if I had to pay from 60,000 to 80,000 cruzeiros a month or more for rent.

I never know what our family budget will be for any six-month period. How can I judge, since prices have doubled and even tripled over the last year or so? A sociologist came to my door the other day asking me to answer an elaborate questionnaire regarding my expenditures and my income. I could have helped him if we had taken this month alone as a basis for our estimates, but he insisted upon trying to make an estimate for a whole year. Now, I like such people and I enjoy being interviewed. He is a professor and an intelligent man, but his questionnaire, obviously influenced by some study carried out in a foreign country, made little sense to me. How on earth can I tell what I shall have to spend next month to maintain our present way of life? If prices go up, I shall have to make more money somehow. It is getting harder to buy "on time" because of the increasing inflation. Still, I buy on time whenever I can, and it is curious that advertisements for refrigerators, men's suits, air conditioners, and other expensive products state only the monthly payments and not the total price. Last year, my wife and I visited the United States for six weeks. My company paid my passage, but I bought my wife's ticket on the "travel now and pay later" plan. It is a shifting economy that we live in, and one must "roll with the punches," as you Americans say.

It is not only inflation that frustrates us. Sometimes there is a shortage of basic necessities. In July and August of 1962, for example, we lacked beans and rice and even sugar. COFAB (Comissão Federal de Abastecimento e Preços or Federal Commission on Distribution and Prices) set basic prices for these products. Inflation was at work. Wholesalers and retailers refused to sell at these set prices. COFAB forced them to sell some of their products; the result was long lines of people waiting for hours to buy a few pounds of rice or beans. Fortunately, our own income and personal relations are such that we were able to find these foods at a slightly higher price but on a personal basis (this is not quite a black market). Merchants were accused of withholding food and storing it up for higher prices. COFAB was accused of creating an artificial situation, with enough of these basic foods stocked in different parts of the country but being withheld because of COFAB prices. In the Northeast, there were scandals about the distribution of North American beans, maize, and powdered milk. The patience of our people gave out for a moment; near Rio de Janeiro, they burned grocery stores. The police intervened, several hundred people were hospitalized and almost a hundred died. Now and again, as I mentioned earlier, our people flare up—they burn a coach on an overcrowded or excessively slow suburban train, overturn a streetcar, or just go on strike. But services keep getting worse and food harder to find. I am continually amazed by the patience and peacefulness of our *povo*.

I learned much about your country and mine during my short visit to the United States. We visited New York, Washington, Chicago, Kansas City, and even Los Angeles and San Francisco. In New York we stayed at the Diplomat Hotel, which is a haven for Brazilians. It has a bar that serves Brazilian coffee. It is relatively inexpensive in your terms, but I could not even bear to translate such prices into cruzeiros. It would have killed my pleasure. At the Diplomat and elsewhere in New York, I heard my language spoken now and then. Now I speak English and so does my wife; we studied your language at the Instituto Brasil-Estados Unidos for four years, and before that we had English as a foreign language in school, beginning with the first year of the *ginásio*. We have a heavy accent, but we can speak and understand except when someone from Brooklyn or the Deep South speaks rapidly.

You North Americans speak English, which waiters, taxi drivers, tourist agents, and many other people speak around the world. In our country, hotel employees are hired just because they speak English. We study your language eagerly. In all of our big cities, there are binational centers called Brazil-United States Institutes, Centers, or Associations, which are supported mainly by Brazilian funds with some United States help, and where thousands of Brazilians are learning English. While a small, early twentieth-century elite knew French, now a veritable mass of Brazilians know at least some English. In contrast, I learned that many North Americans do not even know that we speak Portuguese. I understand that in one of your great universities elementary Portuguese attracts only fifteen or twenty students. Your government has found it necessary to declare Portuguese a crucial language, along with Arabic, Russian, Chinese, Urdu, and a few others. They have made available some very lucrative fellowships to study Brazilian Portuguese and Brazilian affairs, but few people apply.

This seems incredible to us. We are a nation of over 70 million just to the south of you. The Portuguese writer Eça de Queiroz once wrote that Portuguese was "a tomb of thought," meaning that whatever was written in our language was lost to the rest of the world; but nowadays we do not think it is so. Gilberto Freyre, Viana Moog, Érico Veríssimo, Jorge Amado, and other Brazilian writers have been translated into English. They write in a Brazilian Portuguese as distinct from European Portuguese as your language is from British English. We have our Thomas Wolfes, John dos Passos, William Faulkners, and John Steinbecks, but ours are called Jorge Amado, João Guimarães Rosa, Dalcídio Jurandir, and Mário Palmério. So, whenever I met an American who spoke Portuguese, I felt impressed and pleased—he was usually a businessman or a professor who had spent some time in my country. When I overheard Portuguese spoken in a restaurant or on Fifth Avenue, it was generally some fellow Brazilians. We felt equally pleased. If we could catch them in conversation, we asked, "Where do you come from?" and they would say Rio de Janeiro, São Paulo, Minas Gerais, or another place in Brazil. This always helped me place them. When I would ask, "May I know your name?" and they said Sousa Pereira or some other pair of surnames, this often allowed me to place them in their local society, for I am very expert at genealogies. But even if they came from Goiás and their names meant nothing to me (such people now travel abroad very frequently), the fact that they spoke my language on foreign shores gave me a feeling of belonging.

In the United States I had frank discussions with many friends. North Americans are an open people, really more like us than Europeans. If you meet an American away from home in New York or in Rio, he will pull out his wallet and show you pictures of his wife and children. We like that; we are a family-oriented people. North Americans like to talk, and they start conversations on trains, buses, and airplanes. They ask "Where are you from?" just as we do, but Brazil is all one place to them, even when they do know where it it. One of the first questions they want to discuss is, "What do Brazilians think of the United States?" This question should be evaded with some vague statement, for taken as a whole we Brazilians are quite ambivalent about the United States—we love it, we hate it, and we depend upon it.

Then, your North American friend will ask you about communism in Brazil. It is true that we have many people who are members of the *partido*, many of whom we know. Our friends in the *partido* are rather divided among themselves, and they are not very important in current politics. However, we do not define communists in the same terms as you; when Brazilians apply for a visa to visit your country, your State Department seems to consider as communists anyone who has signed all sorts of idealistic peace pleas and traveled to Russia, or who was once a left-wing student leader. This doesn't make much sense to us, for some of these people are exactly the ones who should visit your open, democratic society. Next, a North American friend will ask me, "What do the Brazilians think about Cuba?" *Ora bolas!* What should we think about an island in the Caribbean? We have enough to think about with half a continent of our own. All right, it is a big island, it is close to the United States, and it is a focus of communist influence in the Southern Hemisphere. Clearly, you cannot allow it to become a base from which offensive attacks might be made on the United States and South America, or a base for exporting propaganda.

I argued with my North American friends about Cuba. Some of their big companies lost a lot of money there. I asked them to think of the rest of Latin America. "Intervention" is a vague but sacred term to us. You are anxious to be fair with your Latin American neighbors and to respect their sovereignty. We feel strongly about national sovereignty, because we feel militarily weak and we fear encroachers. You North Americans must think about us and the other South American countries more than about Cuba. We represent the majority of the Latin American people. If you persist in talking about Cuba, then perhaps I might suggest that we all act like Guatemala and Cuba—"go left" and cause trouble for the United States, then we will get attention and economic help. The so-called Peasant Leagues of northeastern Brazil have rated more space in North American newspapers than in ours; they have caused near panic among your missions in Brazil. We may be naïve, but we worry less about such things than you seem to. After all, Julião is not in our opinion a very charismatic or intelligent leader, and the peasants are still passive. Why don't you send more technicians to northeastern Brazil who will move out of their offices into the backlands and get to know something more than the big coastal cities? Some of your technicians working for Point IV or the Alliance for Progress or AID, whatever it may be called by now, are good; they learn Portuguese, they travel into the backlands, they analyze our problems, and, just when they get to know something about Brazil, they are transferred to Asia or to the Middle East. Sometimes they become "almost Brazilian," and we suspect that they are removed because they come to think like us.

We Brazilians are very political. When we are not talking about soccer, we are discussing politics, endlessly speculating on the tortuous twists and turns of political figures and parties. We bring our friends the latest news of the most recent talks between Adhemar and Jango, the most recent activities of Governor Arrais of Pernambuco, what the Minister of War is supposed to have said to the President about Carlos Lacerda, the position of the UDN in São Paulo, the efforts of the PTB to block a bill in the Câmara (House of Deputies), and a thousand other facts and rumors about political affairs. When someone asks "O que há de novo?" (What's new?), as often as not he is asking for the latest political gossip. This is not just our favorite indoor sport, it is serious business. We are patriotic and want the best possible government for our country; but (as we often say to each other) look what we get, a bunch of dishonest demagogues whose astronomic expenditures in their campaigns make it a sure bet that they will recoup their finances when they win. We are highly critical of our politicians, as you can see, and rather cynical about their motivations. This is one reason for our close attention to politics, but not the only one.

Politics is very close to home for most upper- and middle-class Brazilians. Of course, I have a government job in addition to my private activities, and so do most of the people I know. If I did not have a position with the municipality, the state, or the federal government, then almost certainly my brother, sister, uncle, first cousin, or *compadre* would have. One of my first cousins has a high appointive office in the present government. I have never called upon him for a favor, but it gives me a feeling of security to know that I could, if and when I should need to. Each of us has a *panelinha* ("little pot")—a group of friends, associates, relatives, and supporters who are related to the political sources of power. When a minister resigns, a new governor takes office, or the leadership of a political party changes, we are directly affected. My first cousin who works for the Ministry of Labor does not get a needed promotion, and my sister-in-law who is anxious to get a teaching position in a public high school loses out.

This direct influence of politics on our personal and family lives extends right down into small communities. In the upper- and middle-class groups, we pride ourselves on knowing who's who—who their relatives are, who their friends are, and what obligations they have assumed. Our discussions of politics are not entirely objective and patriotic; as always in my country, there are personal and family affairs at stake. This is quite different from the United States, I understand; the people I met there had relatives working for the government, but a change in regime did not mean a loss of position or status for these relatives. Sometimes they even disagreed with their kinsmen about policies and politics. That is very fair, but it is an Anglo-Saxon luxury which seems rather cold to us. Now, though, you have a family, the Kennedys, who seem to act like Brazilians. They seem to be entrenching themselves in power—or do I again misunderstand the United States? We are a rather calculating people and we believe in the old expressions, such as "Believe in the Virgin and run" (Be idealistic but practical). Politics as well as economics are important to us.

Our politicians and statesmen have recently been attempting to formulate an independent foreign policy. We do not believe that this means a policy against the United States, although sometimes your newspapers and some of your senators and congressmen would seem to take it that way. It does mean, however, that you can no longer expect Brazil to automatically vote on your side in the United Nations, or to accept all your policies. It sometimes seems to us that you feel we are disloyal when we fail to see eye to eye with you and that you have paid well for our complete loyalty to your side by your generous foreign aid. That apparent attitude angers many of us, and we protest that we cannot be bought with your beans, wheat, maize, or powdered milk (which we feel you have to get rid of in some way to support your own economy) or with your millions of loan dollars. Sometimes our more hotheaded students paint signs of "Yankee Go Home" or even throw stones at your embassy and consulates. Our newspapers try to explain this by suggesting that they are egged on by a few agitators and communists, but in fact our students often reflect in an exaggerated way the feeling of the entire country.

Our statesmen are attempting to gain a strong voice on the international stage. They are fully aware that the United States

is the world power most able and most eager to help us. Furthermore, the perpetual crisis of Brazil sends them begging
to international banks. They are faced, however, with the same
problem that faces your statesmen. They must make statements and take positions which allow for the international
reality as well as the opinions of their constituents. We have
politicians such as Brizzola of Rio Grande do Sul who regularly rant against the United States and the Alliance for
Progress. They have an eye on the internal political scene—
on the extreme nationalists, the students, and the rather mild
left wing, but they would accept the support of the Communists if it would get them votes. Don't forget that we have
a democracy, with all the difficulties such a system involves.

Our new independent international policy is not just a re-
flection of our internal politics. After all, there are some hard
facts to be considered. We have to look for markets for our
products. We may have exhausted the North American market
with our coffee, cacao, iron ore, bauxite, and other riches of the
soil. You are good businessmen, "hard Yankees," on the
market, although you are "soft touches" on the social scene.
You set prices on many of your deals with us, and they are not
always favorable. We therefore look elsewhere to expand our
economy. Trade with other Latin American countries is still
small, although we have high hopes of selling them more
of our manufactured products. For the moment, our internal
market consumes almost everything we can manufacture, and
we are primarily exporters of raw materials. We look beyond
the Iron Curtain; we wonder whether Russians will ever drink
coffee—yet they might learn. Do Czechs like chocolate? We
have oranges to sell to France and Germany. Believe it or not,
we sold wine to France; it probably ended up in those modestly

priced French wines which I bought and drank in the United States. We have sent commercial missions around the world looking for new markets, but to date their success has been doubtful. We get trade and exchange agreements without too much profit to us. We are quite worried about the progress of the European Common Market. There is an agreement among the member countries granting favored treatment to their ex-colonies, which export to Europe exactly the products we have to offer. Does this mean the end of our European market for those products which bring us credits? We are thus anxious to maintain relations with Poland, Czechoslovakia, Bulgaria, Hungary, Yugoslavia, and the Soviet Union itself. You worry about our amicable relations with these countries. Why? For many years you maintained formal relations with the Soviet Union while we refused to do so.

You know little about us as yet. You had better take us more seriously, for we are certainly at present the most important South American nation and what we intend to do in our ambivalent and contradictory fashion is to become far more important. If you want to know us, then you must know us personally, because we are a most personal people. We try to be objective, but it is the individual who really interests us. Those of us who are close to the international scene often judge your ambassadors and other United States officials on a personal basis. Back in the 1940s, during the war, there was an American ambassador who "took to" Brazil. He learned Portuguese; he fired all the English-speaking servants at the embassy residence ("Whoever comes here should speak Portuguese," he is reported to have said). He invited Brazilian intellectuals of a wide variety of talents and political views on Sunday afternoons. There, in your embassy, was Portinari with his jeweled lapel ornament depicting the hammer and sickle. The ambassador's wife got to know Brazilian women of the upper class. She organized social welfare projects and she followed closely United States-Brazilian efforts in public health, nutrition, and other areas. They left after the war, but they did not cease to be our friends. We know that they understand Brazil. You have sent us other ambassadors, good and bad, some who were career officers and very careful about policy, and at least one who was a businessman whom we resented for his lack of knowledge of our country. Then, in 1962, you sent a professor. He is a man of knowledge and interested in us. We can forgive him for his faults, for we do not forget that the politicians are watching him. He, too, learned our language, and we do not forget that he is an intellectual and a man of good will. That is a type of North American that we like. He represents the kind of person that Franklin D. Roosevelt sent to us—an open-minded liberal. We are pleased that a man of his stature should become enamored of Brazil.

We are different in still other ways from you fellow Americans to the north of us. When I traveled to the United States, I noticed our different reactions to many social situations. First, there is the problem of etiquette with North Americans. They are a most friendly and overt people, but they do seem to be almost frightened of bodily contact. When you talk with Americans they stand back at a distance; we Brazilians get up close to each other when we talk, particularly when we get excited by an idea. Brazilian men shake hands often, almost every time they meet. It was difficult for me in the United States to give a handshake only when I was introduced. Then, too, Brazilian men offer each other an *abraço*, which can be a rather formal hand on the shoulder or a less informal bear hug with both arms. We have discovered that this custom embarrasses our American friends, but how do two American males show their friendship and affection? Our ladies have a habit of kissing each other on the cheek when they arrive and leave. We like to kiss a lady's hand, something we learned from Europe; often the wife of a good friend offers her cheek to be kissed lightly.

Many of our mannerisms are not too different from yours. We do have a hard time knowing who is upper, middle, and lower class in the United States, for everyone seems to act, dress, and talk alike. Because of our old-fashioned system of social classes, we cannot quite get accustomed to a man who drives a giant excavating machine, wears old work clothes while he works, and shaves only in the evening; but who earns a fabulous sum of money, dresses well after his work, has passable social manners, reads newspapers and discusses international affairs (often badly), and lives in style. This "type" does not fit into our social-class system, even now that it is changing so fast. We are rather confused about some people who come to see us and announce that they are university graduates. Some of them frankly lack any general "culture." They are engineers and lawyers with good technical training but no general knowledge of the world in which they live. Then, too, we learn that you have a larger percentage of people with a university education than we have of high school graduates.

Now and again we meet an American who, like our true elite and like many Europeans who come to visit us, impresses us with his general knowledge and comprehension. We feel that we are very *latino* and somewhat European. Yet, an Italian, Tulio Ascarelli, in a very thoughtful book on Brazil which was translated into Portuguese over ten years ago as *Apresentação do Brasil* (*Presentation of Brazil*), describes us very well: "An American country, yet fully participant in Latin culture, very young and yet old, Brazil finds itself between the United States and Europe, intermediary between one and the other. It is tied to the former by the direction of social change in its way of life, and to the latter by its cultural tradition. It is exactly in this position that it might find its own characteristic traits."[1] This is how many educated Brazilians view themselves.

There is another Brazilian trait that gives us a common national understanding and which you North Americans would understand if you understood our language, namely, a strange and objective sense of humor about ourselves. We are appalled by the seriousness with which most Spanish-Americans view themselves. They have a sense of "face" and dignity that works against them. We take life more lightly. We say that you can live in Brazil only with a sense of humor. A near best-seller in Brazil over a period of several years, *Brasil para principiantes* (Brazil for Beginners) by Peter Kellemen, an immigrant, pokes fun, which is not always gentle, at Brazil and Brazilians. He hits the right note, and we laugh with him at ourselves. It all begins when the Brazilian consul in Paris recommends that he declare himself as an agronomist rather than a physician (which he is) because the quota for agronomists is higher. He protests and is afraid, but then he understands.

I understood then that I was not being compelled into a dishonest act, but I did not as yet quite understand that I had just spoken with two representatives of a nation whose laws are re-interpreted,

[1] Ascarelli, *Apresentação do Brasil*, p. 204.

whose governmental regulations and instructions are decreed from the beginning with full awareness of how far they will be carried out, whose people are an important filter (in interpreting) laws, and whose public servants, small and big, create their own jurisprudence. Even if their jurisprudence does not agree with the original laws, it is granted general acceptance if it is stated with common sense.[2]

He learns to speak the two languages of Brazil, namely, Portuguese and the "secret code." The latter consists of the innuendoes, the patterns of behavior, and all of the other unspoken feelings that make one a Brazilian. On almost every page one finds charming observations: "The bee flies, although by every law of aerodynamics it should not even get off the ground. Brazil, in turn, is in full development, although this is absolutely impossible according to economic laws." Kellemen's book has gone through several editions in Brazil.

We also create and relate stories about ourselves each day, and we have traditional sayings that reveal our humorous self-criticism. "God is a Brazilian" indicates both some confidence in ourselves and a worry as to what would· happen to our country if He were not. We also say, in the same vein, "At night, God corrects the errors that Brazilians make during the day." We exchange sly political stories and jokes. Not too long ago, the hippopotamus in the São Paulo Zoo was elected to public office. Some citizens collected enough signatures to put him on the ballot. His opposition was rather weak, so theoretically he was elected. Since he could not speak Portuguese, he never took office, but he is a famous hippo. I could tell you story after story, for we, especially the *cariocas* of Rio de Janeiro, invent one every day, but not many of them can

[2] Kellemen, *Brasil para principiantes*, pp. 11–12.

be easily translated into your language. An old one concerns a politician of national prominence whose honesty was doubted. A bishop or archbishop had died, and our politician joined the line at the church to pay his respects to the corpse. The body lay with the jewels of office prominently displayed. As our politician knelt at the bier, the corpse moved slowly, covering the jewels with his hands. Our sly sense of humor extends into our music, our daily press, our literature, and our lives. It is an important factor of our national unity.

Now I must return to my proper role, which is that of a North American social anthropologist writing about Brazil. Despite my often dry analysis of Brazilian society, my criticisms and eulogies, I must confess that Brazil has provided me with the greatest experience of my life. I have traveled elsewhere, in France, Portugal, Africa, and all the other countries of Latin America, but Brazil became more than just another country to me. It became a second "homeland." For me, it is a country of great possibilities and potentials. It represents the future, not the past.

As a North American who grew up learning about the glories and excitements of the frontier, Brazil offered me the chance of actually seeing a living frontier. I saw the wildness of a vast heartland inhabited only by savage Indians and woodsmen. In a way, it was like living out an epoch in the history of my own country. I saw scenes analogous to those witnessed by Lewis and Clark. I got to know men who might have been Billy the Kid in real life, not on television. I walked in the streets of raw towns growing along a frontier that must have been similar in many ways to towns in early Texas, New

Mexico, Arizona, and other Western states. I saw the great cities of Brazil change from slow, rather isolated places to urban centers of dynamic urgency. I have looked in this book for the unity of the Brazilian people and for Brazil's unity as a nation. I have not fully answered my own query as to how Brazilians achieved and maintained their identity. But I did learn, at least for myself, that for all their diversity they are a people and form a nation distinct from all others.

A SELECTED BIBLIOGRAPHY

ON BRAZIL

Abreu, Jayme. A educação secundária no Brasil. Rio de Janeiro, 1955.

Agassiz, Louis. A Journey in Brazil. Boston and New York, 1896.

Amoroso Lima, Alceu. Voz de Minas. 2d ed. Rio de Janeiro, 1946.

Anuário estatístico do Brasil. Rio de Janeiro, 1961.

Araújo Lima. Amazônia: a terra e o homem. São Paulo, 1940.

Ascarelli, Tulio. Apresentação do Brasil. Translated from the 2d Italian edition, Sguardo sul Brasile, by Olinto de Castro. São Paulo, 1952.

Azevedo, Fernando. Brazilian Culture. Translated from the Portuguese, A cultura brasileira, by Rex Crawford. New York, 1950.

Azevedo, Thales de. Povoamento da cidade do Salvador. Bahia, 1949.

—— "Catholicism in Brazil," Thought, XXVIII (1953), 253–74, (Fordham University Quarterly.)

—— As elites de côr: um estudo de ascensão social. São Paulo, 1955. (French edition: Les Elites de couleur dans une ville brésilienne, Paris, 1953.)

—— "Classes sociais e grupos de prestígio na Bahia," Arquivos da Universidade da Bahia, V (1956), 81–90. (Faculdade de Filosofia.)

—— Gaúchos: fisionomia social do Rio Grande do Sul. 2d ed. Pôrto Alegre, 1958.

Baldus, Herbert. Bibliografia crítica da etnologia brasileira. São Paulo, 1954.

Bastide, Roger. Brasil: terra de contrastes. Translated from the French, Brésil: terre des contrastes, by Maria Isaura Pereira de Queiroz. São Paulo, 1959.

—— Les Religions africaines au Brésil. Paris, 1960.

Bastide, Roger, and Florestan Fernandes. Brancos e negros em São Paulo. 2d ed. São Paulo, 1959.

Bates, Henry Walter. The Naturalist on the River Amazon. London, 1864.

Bazin, Germain. L'Architecture religieuse baroque au Brésil. 2 vols. São Paulo, 1956–58.

Bezerra dos Santos, Lindalvo. "People and Scenes of Brazil," Revista Brasileira de Geografia (1945), 137–38. (Special edition for Fourth General Assembly of the Pan-American Geographical and Historical Institute, Rio de Janeiro.)

Borges Costa, Esdras. "Relações de família em Cerrado e Retiro," Sociologia, XVII (1955), 132–46.

Boxer, Charles. The Dutch in Brazil, 1624–1654. Oxford, 1957.

Brandão Lopes, Juarez Rubens. "Escôlha ocupacional e origem social de ginasianos em São Paulo," Educação e Ciências Sociais, I (1956), 43–62.

Brant, Alice. The Diary of "Helena Morley." Translated from the Portuguese, O diário de "Helena Morley," by Elizabeth Bishop. New York, 1957.

Buarque de Holanda, Sérgio. Raízes do Brasil. 3rd ed. Rio de Janeiro, 1956.

Burton, Sir Richard. Explorations of the Highlands of Brazil. London, 1869.

Callado, Antônio. Os industriais das sêcas e os Galileus de Pernambuco. Rio de Janeiro, 1960.

Callcott, Maria Graham. Journal of a Voyage to Brazil and Residence There During Part of the Years 1821, 1822, 1823. London, 1824.

Calmon, Pedro. Espírito da sociedade colonial. São Paulo, 1935.

Calogeras, João Pandiá. History of Brazil. Translated from the Portuguese, História do Brasil, by P. A. Martin. Chapel Hill, N.C., 1939.

Camacho, J. A. Brazil: An Interim Assessment. London, 1951.

CAPES Bulletin (Boletim Informativo da Campanha Nacional de Aperfeiçoamento de Pessoal de Nível Superior). Rio de Janeiro.

Cardoso, Fernando Henrique. "Os brancos e a ascenção social dos negros em Pôrto Alegre," Anhembi, XXXIX, No. 117 (1960), 585.

—— Capitalismo e escravidão. São Paulo, 1962.

Carneiro, Edison. O Quilombo dos Palmares, 1630–1695. São Paulo, 1947.

—— Candomblés da Bahia. Rio de Janeiro, 1948.

—— Antologia do negro brasileiro. Pôrto Alegre, 1950.

Carneiro, Leão A. Panorama sociologique du Brésil. Paris, 1953.

Carolina Maria de Jesus. Child of the Dark. Translated from the Portuguese, Quarto de Despejo, by David St. Clair. New York, 1962.

Castaldi, Carlo. "O demônio no Catulê," Anhembi, XXI (1956), 472–502, XXII (1956), 250–68, XXIII (1956), 477–82.

Castro, Josué de. The Geography of Hunger. Boston, 1952.

Costa Eduardo, Octavio da. The Negro in North Brazil: A Study in Acculturation. Monograph No. 16, American Ethnological Society. New York, 1940.

Costa, Sérgio Corrêa da. Every Inch a King: A Biography of Dom Pedro I, First Emperor of Brazil. New York, 1950.

Costa Pinto, Luís Augusto da. Lutas de famílias no Brasil. São Paulo, 1949.

—— Pesquisa sôbre o padrão de vida do comerciário no Distrito Federal (Rio de Janeiro). Rio de Janeiro, 1949.

—— O negro no Rio de Janeiro. São Paulo, 1952.

Cruz Costa, João. Contribuição à história das idéias no Brasil. Rio de Janeiro, 1959.

Cruz, Ernesto. Belém. Rio de Janeiro, 1945.

Delgado de Carvalho, Carlos. História diplomática do Brasil. São Paulo, 1959.

Denis, Pierre. Brazil. Translated from the French by Bernard Miall. London, 1941.

Diegues Junior, Manuel. Regiões culturais do Brasil. Rio de Janeiro, 1960.

Dominian, Helen G. Apostle of Brazil: The Biography of Padre José de Anchieta. New York, 1958.

Edmundo, Luís. Rio in the Time of the Viceroys. Translated from the Portuguese, O Rio de Janeiro no tempo dos viceréis, by Dorothea H. Momsen. Rio de Janeiro, 1936.

Ellison, Fred P. Brazil's New Novel: Four Northeastern Masters. Berkeley, 1954.

Estudos sôbre a composição da população do Brasil segundo a côr. Rio de Janeiro, IBGE, 1950.

Fernandes, Florestan. A organização social dos Tupinambá. São Paulo, 1949.

—— A função social da guerra na sociedade Tupinambá. São Paulo, 1952.

—— "Symposium etno-sociológica sôbre comunidades humanas no Brasil," in Proceedings of the XXXI International Congress of Americanists. São Paulo, 1955.

—— Mudanças sociais no Brasil. São Paulo, 1960.

Ferreira Filho, Cosme. Amazônia em novas dimensões. Conquista, 1960.

Fleming, Peter. Brazilian Adventure. New York, 1933.

Freyre, Gilberto. The Masters and the Slaves: A Study in the Development of Brazilian Civilization. Translated from the 4th edition of the Portuguese, Casa grande e senzala, by Samuel Putnam. New York, 1946.

—— "The Brazilian Melting Pot," The Atlantic Monthly (February, 1946). (Special issue on Brazil.)

—— Brazil: An Interpretation. New York, 1947.

—— Um brasileiro em terras portuguêsas. Rio de Janeiro, 1953.

—— O luso e o trópico. Lisbon, 1961.

—— The Mansions and the Shanties. Translated from the Portuguese, Sobrados e mucambos, by Harriet de Onís. New York, 1963.

Furtado, Celso. Formação econômica do Brasil. Rio de Janeiro, 1959. (Translation. The Economic Growth of Brazil. Berkeley, 1963.)

Galvão, Eduardo. Santos e visagens, um estudo da vida religiosa de Itá, Amazonas. São Paulo, 1955.

Geld, E. B. Stranger in the Valley. New York, 1957.

Gibson, Hugh. Rio. Garden City, N.Y., 1937.

Goldberg, Isaac. Brazilian Literature. New York, 1922.

Goodwin, Philip L. Brazil Builds: Architecture New and Old, 1652–1942. New York, 1943.

Graham, Robert B. C. A Brazilian Mystic. London, 1920.

Guerreiro Ramos. O problema nacional do Brasil. Rio de Janeiro, 1960.

Harding, Bertita. Southern Empire, Brazil. New York, 1948.

Haring, C. H. Empire in Brazil. Cambridge, Mass., 1958.

Harris, Marvin. Town and Country in Brazil. New York, 1956.

Hunnicutt, Benjamin H. Brazil Looks Forward. Rio de Janeiro, 1945.

Hutchinson, Bertram. Mobilidade e trabalho. Rio de Janeiro, 1960.

Hutchinson, Carmela Junqueira Ayres. "Notas preliminares ao estudo da família no Brasil," in Anais da II Reunião Brasileira de Antropologia. Bahia, 1957.

Hutchinson, Harry W. Village and Plantation Life in Northeastern Brazil. Seattle, 1957.

Ianni, Octavio. As metamorfoses do escravo: apogeu e crise da escravatura no Brasil meridional. São Paulo, 1962.

James, Preston. Brazil. New York, 1946.

—— Latin America. 3rd ed. New York, 1959.

Jobim, José. Brazil in the Making. New York, 1943.

Kellemen, Peter. Brasil para principiantes. Rio de Janeiro, 1961.

Koster, Henry. Travels in Brazil. London, 1816.

Lambert, Jacques. Os dois Brasís. Rio de Janeiro, 1959.

Landes, Ruth. The City of Women. New York, 1947.

Leal, Victor Nunes. Coronelismo, enxada e voto. Rio de Janeiro, 1948.

Leeds, Anthony. Economic Cycles in Brazil: The Persistence of a Total Culture Pattern; Cacao and Other Cases. Ph.D. thesis, Columbia University, 1957.

Lévi-Strauss, Claude. Tristes tropiques. English translation by John Russell. New York, 1961.

Lowenstein, Karl. Brazil under Vargas. New York, 1942.

Machado, José Bettencourt. Machado of Brazil: The Life and Times of Machado de Assis. New York, 1953.

Marchant, Alexander. From Barter to Slavery: The Economic Relations of Portuguese and Indians in the Settlement of Brazil, 1500–1580. Baltimore, 1942.

Mariani, Clemente, and Pinto de Aguiar. Diretrizes e bases da educação nacional. Salvador, 1959.

Martins, Paulo Guilherme. Um dia na vida do Brasilino. 4th ed. São Paulo, 1961.

Matthews, Kenneth. Brazilian Interior. London, 1956.

Maurois, André. Rio de Janeiro. Paris, 1953.

Maynard Araújo, Alceu. "A família numa comunidade alagoana," Sociologia, XVII (1955), 113–31.

Melo Neto, José Antonio Gonçalves de. Tempo de flamengos: influência da ocupação holandêsa na vida e na cultura do norte do Brasil. Rio de Janeiro, 1946.

Menezes, Djacir. O outro nordeste. Rio de Janeiro, 1937.

Métraux, Alfred. La Civilisation matérielle des tribus Tupi-Guarani. Paris, 1928.

—— La Religion des Tupinamba et ses rapports avec celle des autres tribus Tupi-Guarani. Paris, 1928.

Mindlin, Henrique F. Modern Architecture in Brazil. Rio de Janeiro, 1956.

Monbeig, Pierre. Pionniers et planteurs de l'état de S. Paulo. Paris, 1952.

—— Novos estudos de geografia humana brasileira. São Paulo, 1957.

Morazé, Charles. Les Trois Âges du Brésil: essai de politique. Paris, 1954.

Moreira, J. Roberto. Educação e desenvolvimento no Brasil. Rio de Janeiro, 1960.

Morse, Richard. From Community to Metropolis: A Biography of São Paulo, Brazil. Gainesville, Fla., 1958.

Müller, N. L. Sítios e sitiantes no estado de São Paulo. São Paulo, 1951.

Nash, Roy. The Conquest of Brazil. New York, 1926.

Nichols, Madeline Wallis. The Gaucho. Durham, N.C., 1942.

Nina Rodrigues. Os africanos no Brasil. São Paulo, 1932.

Nogueira, Oracy. "Skin Color and Social Class," in Plantation Systems of the New World. Washington, D.C., 1959.

Normano, J. F. Brazil: A Study of Economic Types. Chapel Hill, N.C., 1935.

Oliveira Viana, F. J. Populações meridionais do Brasil. 4th ed. São Paulo, 1935.

Oliveira, Franklin de. Revolução e contra-revolução no Brasil. Rio de Janeiro, 1962.

Pearse, Andrew. "Integração social das famílias de favelados," Educação e Ciências Sociais, II (1957).

Pierson, Donald. Negroes in Brazil. Chicago, 1942.

Pierson, Donald, and others. Cruz das Almas: A Brazilian Village. Washington, D.C., 1952.

Prado Junior, Caio. Formação do Brasil contemporâneo. São Paulo, 1942.

—— História econômica do Brasil. São Paulo, 1945.

Putnam, Samuel. Marvelous Journey: A Survey of Four Centuries of Brazilian Writing. New York, 1948.

Ramos, Arthur. O folklore negro no Brasil. Rio de Janeiro, 1935.

—— O negro brasileiro. São Paulo, 1940.

—— Introdução à antropologia brasileira. 2 vols. Rio de Janeiro, 1943.

—— Las poblaciones del Brasil. Mexico City, 1944.

Redfield, Robert. Peasant Society and Culture. Chicago, 1956.

Ribeiro, Darcy. A política indigenista brasileira. Rio de Janeiro, 1962.

Ribeiro, René. Cultos africanos do Recife: um estudo de ajustamento social. Recife, 1952.

Saint-Hilaire, Auguste de. Viagens pelas províncias do Rio de Janeiro e Minas Gerais (1822). 2 vols. São Paulo, 1932.

Schaden, Egon. Aspectos fundamentais da cultura Guarani. São Paulo, 1962.

Schurz, William Lytle. Brazil: The Infinite Country. New York, 1961.

Sinopse retrospectiva do ensino no Brasil, 1871–1954. Rio de Janeiro, IBGE, 1956.

Smith, Herbert T. Brazil: The Amazons and the Coast. New York, 1879.

Smith, T. Lynn. Brazil: People and Institutions. 2d ed. Baton Rouge, La., 1954.

Smith, T. Lynn, and Alexander Marchant, eds. Brazil: Portrait of Half a Continent. New York, 1951.

Southey, Robert. History of Brazil. 3 vols. London, 1817.

Spiegel, Henry William. The Brazilian Economy: Chronic Inflation and Sporadic Industrialization. Philadelphia, 1949.

Stein, Stanley. Vassouras: A Brazilian Coffee County, 1850–1900. Cambridge, Mass., 1957.

—— The Brazilian Cotton Manufacture; Textile Enterprise in an Underdeveloped Area, 1850–1950. Cambridge, Mass., 1957.

Steward, Julian, ed. Handbook of South American Indians. Washington, D.C., 1946–48. Vols. I and II.

Tavares de Sá, Hernane. The Brazilians: People of Tomorrow. New York, 1947.

Teixeira, Anisio. Educação não é privilégio. Rio de Janeiro, 1957.

Thornton, Sister Mary Crescentia. The Church and Freemasonry in Brazil, 1872–1875. Washington, D.C., 1948.

Unzer de Almeida, Vicente, and Antônio Mendes Sobrinho. Migração rural-urbana. São Paulo, 1952.

Veríssimo, Érico. Brazilian Literature: An Outline. New York, 1945.

Vianna Moog, C. Bandeirantes e pioneiros. Rio de Janeiro, 1955.

Wagley, Charles. "Brazil," in Ralph Linton, ed., Most of the World. New York, 1949.

—— Amazon Town: A Study of Man in the Tropics. New York, 1953.

—— "The Brazilian Revolution: Social Change Since 1930," in

Social Change in Latin America Today. New York, 1961.
Wagley, Charles, ed. Race and Class in Rural Brazil. Paris, 1952.
Wagley, Charles, and Eduardo Galvão. The Tenetehara Indians of Brazil. New York, 1949.
Wagley, Charles, and Marvin Harris. Minorities in the New World. New York, 1958.
Wallace, Alfred. A Narrative of Travels on the Amazon and the Rio Negro. London, 1853.
Willems, Emilio. "Some Aspects of Culture Conflict and Acculturation in Southern Rural Brazil," Rural Sociology, VII (1942), 375–85.
—— A assimilação dos alemães no Brasil. São Paulo, 1946.
—— Cunha: tradição e transição em uma cultura rural do Brasil. São Paulo, 1947.
—— "The Structure of the Brazilian Family," Social Forces, XXXI (1953), 339–345.
Williams, Mary W. Dom Pedro the Magnanimous, Second Emperor of Brazil. Chapel Hill, N.C., 1937.
Zimmerman, Ben. Monte Serrat. Unpublished.
Zweig, Stefan. Brazil: Land of the Future. New York, 1941.

Brazilian fiction

Amado, Jorge. Cacau. São Paulo, 1934.
—— Jubiabá. Rio de Janeiro, 1937.
—— The Violent Land. Translated from the Portuguese, Terras do sem fim, by Samuel Putnam. New York, 1945.
—— Gabriela, Clove and Cinnamon. Translated from the Portuguese, Gabriela, cravo e canela, by William L. Grossman and James L. Taylor. New York, 1962.
Azevedo, Aluízio de. A Brazilian Tenement. Translated from the Portuguese, O cortiço, by Harry W. Brown. New York, 1926.
Cunha, Euclides da. Rebellion in the Backlands. Translated from

the 16th edition of the Portuguese, Os Sertões, by Samuel Putnam. Chicago, 1944.

Ferreira de Castro, Antonio. Jungle. Translated from the Portuguese, A selva, by Charles Duff. New York, 1935.

Fitts, Dudley, ed. Anthology of Contemporary Latin American Poetry. New York, 1942.

Graça Aranha, José Pereira da. Canaan. Translated from the Portuguese by Mariano Juaquín Lorente. Boston, 1920.

Guimarães Rosa, João. The Devil to Pay in the Backlands. Translated from the Portuguese, Grande sertão: veredas, by James L. Taylor and Harriet de Onís. New York, 1963.

Jurandir, Dalcídio. Marajó. Rio de Janeiro, 1947.

Lins do Rêgo, José. Menino de engenho. Rio de Janeiro, 1932.

—— O moleque Ricardo. 2d ed. Rio de Janeiro, 1936.

Machado de Assis, Joaquim Maria de. Epitaph of a Small Winner. Translated from the Portuguese, Memórias póstumas de Brás Cubas, by Helen Caldwell. New York, 1952.

—— Dom Casmurro. Translated from the Portuguese by William L. Grossman. New York, 1953.

—— Philosopher or Dog? Translated from the Portuguese, Quincas Borba, by Clotilde Wilson. New York, 1954.

Monteiro Lobato, José Bento. Urupês. 2d ed. São Paulo, 1918.

Onís, Harriet de. The Golden Land: An Anthology of Latin American Folklore in Literature. New York, 1948.

Ramos, Graciliano. Infância. Rio de Janeiro, 1945.

—— Anguish. Translated from the Portuguese, Angústia, by L. C. Kaplan. New York, 1946.

Suassuna, Ariano. Auto da compadecida. Rio de Janeiro, 1955.

Taunay, Alfredo d'Escragnolle. Inocência. Translated from the Portuguese by Henriqueta Chamberlain. New York, 1945.

Veríssimo, Érico. Crossroads. Translated from the Portuguese, Caminhos cruzados, by L. C. Kaplan. New York, 1943.

—— The Rest is Silence. Translated from the Portuguese, O resto é silêncio, by L. C. Kaplan. New York, 1946.

—— Consider the Lilies of the Field. Translated from the Portuguese, Olhai os lírios do campo, by Jean N. Karnoff. New York, 1947.

—— Time and the Wind. Translated from the Portuguese, O tempo e o vento, by L. L. Barrett. New York, 1951.

INDEX